Race, Rights, and the
Asian American Experience

Race, Rights, and the Asian American Experience

ANGELO N. ANCHETA

RUTGERS UNIVERSITY PRESS
New Brunswick, New Jersey, and London

Library of Congress Cataloging-in-Publication Data

Ancheta, Angelo N., 1960–
  Race, Rights, and the Asian American experience / Angelo N.
Ancheta.
    p.   cm.
  Includes bibliographical references and index.
  ISBN 0–8135–2463–6 (cloth : alk. paper). — ISBN 0–8135–2464–4
(pbk. : alk. paper)
  1. Asian Americans—Legal status, laws, etc.—United States.
2. Asian Americans—Civil rights—United States.   3. United States—
Race relations.   I. Title.
KF4757.A75A53   1998
342.73'0873—dc21   97–24855
                                                                            CIP

British Cataloging-in-Publication data for this book is available from the British
Library

Manufactured in the United States of America

To Angelo G. Ancheta and
to the memory of
Calixta C. Ancheta

Contents

Tables

Preface

Growing up in San Francisco during the 1960s, I learned early in life about the power of racism. Home was defined by segregation: my parents, like other immigrants from the Philippines, could not rent an apartment in most parts of the city, where the common response was "no Orientals allowed." My father, who first came to this country in the late 1920s, had already faced decades of segregation and knew the limits that it imposed. A United States Navy veteran who had been denied a law enforcement career because of discrimination, he worked as a clerk for the post office, where civil service rules protected workers of color. A former elementary school teacher with two college degrees, my mother also understood the barriers imposed by race and nationality, and she thought it best to abandon her career. She worked as a waitress and later joined my father in the safety of government employment.

Living in a working-class neighborhood and attending a Catholic school, I encountered a steady stream of racial slurs—"chink," "chinaman," "jap," "nip"—from my earliest days in school and in the local parks and playgrounds. The name-calling was never fully accurate—there didn't seem to be enough Filipinos around at the time to require a special epithet—but it was no less assaultive. Raised at a time when the Asian American population was much smaller than it is today, I tried hard to fit in. This meant trying especially hard to be an "American," even though I had never lived anywhere outside of California. My name was too foreign sounding, and it could be a source of shame. I felt compelled to hide the experiences that I gained through encounters with relatives; language and cultural traditions seemed too different from the norm, and could only lead to derision or exclusion.

Fortunately, the overt discrimination began to decline as I grew older. Yet racism often appeared in different and more subtle forms. I recall, for example, going on school trips to visit Chinatown and Japantown and observing my classmates' surprise that I could understand neither Chinese nor Japanese. Over time I also witnessed changes in the population—more people who looked like me began moving into the neighborhood—and in public attitudes about race. I felt less pressure to conform, and I gave up trying to prove that I was more American than anyone else. My sense of racial and ethnic identity became more concrete, and the fears of nonconformity receded. Still, the memories of childhood are deeply etched in my mind, and they remain as clear today as they did thirty years ago.

I have engaged in this exercise in autobiography because anyone writing a book about discrimination and civil rights should be clear about their perspectives on race. My outlook on race was shaped early in life, and race continues to pervade my social reality. Thus, I make no pretense about being neutral or objective about racism. As both a child and an adult I have been subjected to racial discrimination, and as a civil rights lawyer I have spent most of my professional life trying to fight it. This book is as much a reflection of my personal experiences as it is an analysis of contemporary race relations.

In this book I examine racial discrimination through multiple lenses. First, I focus on the experiences of discrimination against the members of one racial group—Asian Americans—within the broader landscape of urban race relations. Second, I focus on the legal system's response to racial discrimination, in particular the doctrines and policies embedded in constitutional law and civil rights legislation. The intersection of these inquiries—how civil rights laws affect Asian Americans and in turn are affected by Asian Americans— is the central theme of this book.

It would be impossible to cover the full array of civil rights issues affecting Asian Americans in the span of a few chapters. I make no attempt to do so. A useful overview is provided by a report produced by the United States Commission on Civil Rights entitled *Civil Rights Issues Facing Asian Americans in the 1990s*. The report includes extensive discussions of the many court cases affecting Asian Americans, and it analyzes several areas, such as employment discrimination, police-community relations, and higher-education admissions, that receive only limited treatment in this book.

My selection of topics has been influenced by my personal work in the area of civil rights. Having been active in Asian American issues in both Northern and Southern California since the late 1970s, I have been a participant in many of the cases and controversies highlighted in this book. Several examples are drawn from areas of law and public policy on which I have worked in the past: litigation involving anti-Asian violence, language rights, and voting rights; advocacy on immigrants' rights; efforts to improve inter-ethnic relations in Los Angeles after the 1992 riots; and the defense of affirmative action in the wake of California's Proposition 209. Although I continue to work as an advocate on these and other issues, I attempt in this book to provide balanced views on controversial issues affecting Asian Americans, such as affirmative action. Nevertheless, my conclusions no doubt reflect my personal biases and perspectives. Because of my affiliation with several organizations that have taken policy positions on key issues affecting Asian Americans and civil rights, I must stress that the positions taken in this book are my own, and do not necessarily reflect the positions of the organizations on which I serve as a member of the board of directors or with which I have been employed.

Some comments on methodology: I am a lawyer by training, and have spent my professional life as a practitioner and a teacher of law. As a lawyer, I have been schooled in doctrinal analysis, which is a unique combination of historical inquiry, linguistic interpretation, and logical argumentation. I employ this method throughout the book, although I take care to avoid the overuse of legal jargon. I draw significantly on progressive legal scholarship dealing with race, which includes a growing body of work known as Critical Race Theory. In recent years, the critical race scholars have produced an innovative literature—employing postmodernist analysis, personal histories, fiction, and other eclectic devices—in which they examine and critique racial ideology. Analyzing societal race relations and paradigms of race, I employ some of the narrative tools of Critical Race Theory, including the use of autobiographical anecdotes. I use more traditional methods in analyzing legal doctrines and recommending changes to those doctrines. I also rely on the writings of sociologists and cognitive psychologists, but I make no attempt to expound or expand on the extensive social science literature dealing with race and discrimination.

As an advocate, I am keenly aware of the limitations of legal theory, especially when advancing the interests of clients in the courts and other forums whose decision makers adhere to tradition and precedent. Many arguments presented in this book reflect a progressive critique of the law, but they also reflect a more conservative problem-solving approach that comes with working within the confines of the legal system. To the extent that my criticisms are compromised by my proposed solutions, I acknowledge that weakness here.

A Note on Terms

I use the phrase "Asian American" throughout this book. A variety of terms, some more inclusive than others, can be used to describe the racial category that I label Asian American. Variations include "Asian Pacific American," "Asian/Pacific Islander," "Asian and Pacific Islander American," and just "Asian." Race is a dynamic concept, and, as I note throughout the book, "Asian American" is a socially constructed category that links people of many ethnicities and origins. In using "Asian American," I do not mean to diminish the experiences of people whose roots are in the islands of the Pacific, who include native Hawaiians, Samoans, Chamorros (Guamanians), Fijians, Tongans, and many others. There are significant differences in the social realities of "Pacific Islanders" compared to "Asians," ranging from physical appearance to immigration history and political interests. Using "Asian Pacific American" glosses over those differences; using a shorter term seems exclusionary. My own preference has been to use "Asian American and Pacific Islander communities" when describing the broadest grouping. I have little doubt that the terminology will continue to evolve over time. In any case, I use the pejorative term "Oriental" only when describing racial categories and attitudes within a historical context.

Race, Rights, and the
Asian American Experience

Introduction

Neither Black nor White

In his 1989 feature film *Do the Right Thing*, filmmaker Spike Lee explores urban race relations by tracing the interplay of a set of characters during a sweltering day in the Bedford-Stuyvesant section of Brooklyn, New York. Lee's film tracks the life of a neighborhood during a twenty-four-hour span, punctuated by interracial tensions that culminate in violence and rioting.

A climactic scene near the end of the film features the movement of an angry mob outraged by the killing of a black youth by white police officers. The crowd's rage is turned on Sal's Famous Pizzeria, a neighborhood restaurant owned and operated by a white family. After Mookie, Sal's only black employee, throws a garbage can through the front window, others in the crowd rush into the restaurant, ransacking and setting fire to it. As flames engulf the pizzeria, the mob turns toward a new target: the grocery store across the street owned by Korean immigrants.

Tensions build as three men lead the others to confront the store's owner, Sonny. Anxious and confused, Sonny swings a broom wildly through the air in a desperate attempt to hold back the crowd, He shouts out:

I not white! I not white! I not white!

I black! I BLACK!

Several people laugh and scoff at Sonny's pleas, He responds, "You, me—same!" One of the men retorts incredulously: "Same? Me black! Open your eyes!" But others in the crowd begin sympathizing with the grocer. They nod their heads in agreement with Sonny and move closer to restrain the men who first challenged him. Sonny extends an open hand in friendship, as another man says "He's all right. He's black." Tensions subside, and the crowd turns and moves on.

Real life is rarely as tidy as cinematic fiction, but the imagery and dialogue from *Do the Right Thing* offer a glimpse into the potential violence that
many Asian immigrants encounter in the nation's inner cities. And since the
film's original release, reality has proved to be far more dramatic than fiction.
The country witnessed the destruction of thousands of Asian American-owned
businesses during the civil unrest in Los Angeles and other cities in the spring
of 1992, following the acquittal of Los Angeles Police Department officers on
trial for the beating of Rodney King.

The scene illustrates the volatility of urban race relations, but it also encapsulates some of the distinctive problems that Asian Americans face as a
racial group. On one level, the idealistic and convenient ending to the mob
scene offers an insight into the parallels between Asian Americans and African Americans. The grocer identified himself as black and many in the crowd
agreed with him because Asian Americans and African Americans share similar histories and experiences with racial subordination in the United States.

On another level, though, the scene portrays a more complex dynamic:
the grocer, caught in the middle of a race riot, invoked an inaccurate but successful appeal to be treated as if black. The crowd initially equated the Korean grocer with the white pizzeria owner because of his store ownership and
his economic stature within the neighborhood. But the grocer took on a new
identity when confronted by the crowd. The entreaty "I black" placed him
squarely on one side of the conflict, resolving any ambiguity about his align-
ment within the neighborhood's racial matrix.

The grocer's transformation is an extreme example but it illuminates a
dilemma that Asian Americans typically encounter in matters involving race.
When discourse is limited to antagonisms between black and white, Asian
Americans often find themselves in a racial limbo, marginalized or unrecog-
nized as full participants. The assertion of other experiences, different from
black or white, can be misunderstood, become trivial or ineffectual, or even
prove to be dangerous. Within a less perilous context, the grocer might have
been expected to declare a different identity—Korean or Asian American. But
placed within a conflict that had been reduced to black versus white, the grocer
assumed the safety of a black identity.

Race Relations in Black and White

"Are you black or are you white?" For Asian Americans the obvious answer
would seem to be "neither." Yet, when questions of race relations arise, a dichotomy between black and white typically predominates. Formed largely

through inequities and conflicts between blacks and whites, discourse on race relations provides minimal space to articulate experiences independent of a black-white framework. The representation of Asian Americans is especially elusive and often shifts, depending on context, between black and white.

Popular works on race suggest that expositions of Asian American experiences are peripheral, more often confined to the footnotes than expounded in the primary analyses. Studs Terkel's *Race* frames race relations through a dialogue about blacks and whites, confined almost entirely to the opinions of blacks and whites. Andrew Hacker's *Two Nations: Black and White, Separate, Hostile, Unequal* contains, as its subtitle implies, extensive discussions of inequality between blacks and whites, but only a minimal analysis of inequality among other racial groups.[1] The controversial books *The Bell Curve* by Charles Murray and Richard Herrnstein, and *The End of Racism*, by Dinesh D'Souza, go to considerable length to expound arguments that blacks as a group are less intelligent than whites and suffer from cultural pathologies that inhibit advancement to the level of whites. When discussed at all, Asian Americans are offered as a "model minority" group, to be contrasted with blacks and likened to whites because of their higher IQ scores and cultural values stressing family, hard work, and educational achievement.

News media portrayals of racial minorities suffer from the same tendency to reduce race relations to a simple black-white equation. Popular television news shows such as ABC's *Nightline* offer recurring programming on race relations, but confine their analyses to black-white relations. Public opinion polls on race and civil rights usually exclude Asian Americans as subjects or as participants, or reduce them to the category of "Other." News coverage of racially charged events is most often framed by black versus white antagonisms. The murder trial of O.J. Simpson, for instance, provoked extensive dialogue on the impact of race and racism on the criminal justice system, but excluded for the most part any perspectives from Asian Americans or Latinos, which is ironic for a trial held in Los Angeles, a city where half of the population is Asian American and Latino.[2]

Public policies that reflect and reinforce race relations also approach race in terms of black and white. Historically, the major landmarks denoting both racial subordination and progress in racial rights have been measured through the experiences of African Americans. Slavery and its abolition, the black codes and the Reconstruction-era constitutional amendments, Jim Crow laws and the desegregation cases culminating in *Brown v. Board of Education*, the struggles of the civil rights movement and the federal legislation of the 1960s—these are the familiar signs that have dominated the landscape of civil rights in the United States. Debates on affirmative action have occasionally shone

the spotlight on Asian Americans, but almost exclusively as unintended victims of affirmative action in higher education. Problems of ongoing racial discrimination and inequality among Asian American communities are largely
ignored.

Not that focusing on black experiences is unjustified. African Americans
have been the largest racial minority group in the United States since the
country's birth, and continue to endure the effects of racial subordination. By
any social or economic measure, African Americans suffer extensive inequality because of race. In describing the African American experience, the statement of the Kerner Commission resonates as strongly today as it did in 1968:
"Our nation is moving toward two societies, one black, one white—separate
but unequal."[3] But to say that our nation is moving toward two separate and
unequal societies, however disconcerting, is fundamentally incomplete. Underlying the Kerner Commission's statement is the assumption that our nation's
cities are divisible along a single racial axis. Cleavages between black and white
persist but American race relations are not an exclusively black-white phenomenon and never have been. The civil unrest in Los Angeles in 1992 is
just one example of the intricacy of contemporary racial dynamics, shedding
light on a host of race-based and class-based conflicts, as well as an array of
racial and ethnic groups—blacks, whites, Asians, Latinos—who were both victims and victimizers.

Black and White by Analogy

Dualism is a convenient lens through which to view the world. Black or white,
male or female, straight or gay—the categories help us frame reality and make
sense of it. In matters of race, a black-white dichotomy has been the dominant model, based primarily on the fact that African Americans, have been
the largest and most conspicuous nonwhite racial group in the United States.
But the legal history of the United States is punctuated by the abridgment of
rights among other racial and ethnic groups such as Asian Americans, and
the country's changing demographics are mandating new perspectives based
on the experiences of immigrants. Still, the black-white model is the regnant
paradigm in both social and legal discussions of race.

How can Asian Americans fit within a black-white racial paradigm? His-
torian Gary Okihiro poses the question this way: "Is yellow black or white?"
Okihiro suggests that Asian Americans have been "near-blacks" in the past
and "near-whites" in the present, but that "[y]ellow is emphatically neither
white nor black."[4] Recognizing the dominance of the black-white paradigm
in the law, Frank Wu adopts a similar view proposing that Asian Americans

have been forced to fit within race relations discourse through analogy to either whites or blacks. He posits that American society and its legal system have conceived of racial groups as whites, blacks, honorary whites, or constructive (legal jargon for "implied") blacks.[5]

For most of the nation's history, Asian Americans have been treated primarily as constructive blacks. Asian Americans for decades endured many of the same disabilities of racial subordination as African Americans—racial violence, segregation, unequal access to public institutions and discrimination in housing, employment, and education. The courts even classified Asian Americans as if they were black. In the mid-nineteenth century, the California Supreme Court held in *People v. Hall* that Chinese immigrants were barred from testifying in court under a statute prohibiting the testimony of blacks, by reasoning that "black" was a generic term encompassing all nonwhites, including Chinese: "[T]he words 'Black person' . . . must be taken as contradistinguished from White, and necessarily excludes all races other than the Caucasian."[6]

Similarly, in *Gong Lum v. Rice*, decided twenty-seven years before *Brown v Board of Education*, the United States Supreme Court upheld the constitutionality of sending Asian American students to segregated schools. Comparing its earlier rulings on the "separate but equal" doctrine, the Court stated: "Most of the cases cited, arose it is true, over the establishment of separate schools as between white pupils and black pupils, but we can not think that the question is any different or that any different result can be reached . . . where the issue is as between white pupils and the pupils of the yellow races."[7] In the eyes of the Supreme Court, yellow equaled black, and neither equaled white.

In more recent years, the inclusion of Asian Americans in civil rights laws and race-conscious remedial programs has relied on the historical parallels between the experiences of Asian Americans and African Americans. The civil rights protections available to Asian Americans are most often contingent upon the rights granted to African Americans. Civil rights laws that apply to Asian Americans, as constructive blacks, can usually trace their origins to a legislative intent to protect African Americans from racial discrimination.

The treatment of Asian Americans as "honorary whites" is more unusual. In the Reconstruction-era South, Asian Americans were initially afforded a status above blacks for a period of time during the nineteenth century; Louisiana, for example, counted Chinese as whites for census purposes before 1870.[8] The status was short-lived: the Chinese were soon reduced to constructive black status under systems of racial segregation. More contemporary race relations controversies appear to have elevated Asian Americans to the status of honorary whites, particularly in the minds of those who oppose race-conscious remedies such as affirmative action. Asian Americans are often omitted from protection in affirmative action programs as a matter of course, lumped with whites even in contexts where Asian Americans still face racial discrimination and remain underrepresented.

The rigidity of the legal system's treatment of race as either black or white is evident in civil rights litigation filed by Asian American plaintiffs in the earlier half of this century. Unlike the fictional grocer in Spike Lee's *Do the Right Thing*, Asian Americans sought to be classified, quite unsuccessfully, as white under the law, in recognition of the social and legal stigmas attached to being categorized as black. Gong Lum, for example, argued that his daughter Martha should not have to attend the school for colored children in Mississippi because "'[c]olored' describes only one race, and that is the negro."[9] Because his daughter was "pure Chinese." Gong Lum argued that she ought to have been classified with whites rather than blacks. The Court rejected this reasoning and held that yellow was black when it came to segregation,

During the late-nineteenth and early-twentieth centuries, Asian Americans sought to be classified as white in attempts to become naturalized citizens.[10] Congress enacted naturalization legislation in 1790 to limit citizenship to "free white persons." After the Civil War, the law was amended to allow persons of "African nativity" or "African descent" to naturalize, but Congress rejected extending naturalization to Asian immigrants. Asian immigrants sought relief through the courts, but had little success arguing that they were white: Burmese, Chinese, Filipino, Hawaiian, Japanese, and Korean plaintiffs were all held to be nonwhite; mixed-race plaintiffs who were half-white and half-Asian were also held to be nonwhite.[11] The United States Supreme Court laid to rest any questions about the racial bar in *Ozawa v. United States*, ruling that Japanese immigrants were not white, and in *United States v. Thind*, ruling that Asian Indian immigrants were not white.[12] Asian immigrants were prohibited by statute from naturalizing through the 1940s, and the racial bar on naturalization was not repealed until 1952.

From today's vantage point, these attempts by Asian immigrants to be classified as white seem absurd and even subordinative, because they symbolically pushed blacks down the social ladder relative to whites and Asians. But when the legal paradigm limits options to black or white and nothing else, curious and unseemly choices inevitably arise. The solution, of course, is to develop and rely on theories that comprehend the complexity of race relations, which includes discerning that the experiences of Asian Americans are not the same as the experiences of African Americans.

Racism in Context: Anti-Asian Violence

To better understand the experiences of Asian Americans, consider how racial subordination operates within a specific context: anti-Asian violence. Racial violence is not a new phenomenon, and the histories of all racial minorities include extensive violence, whether it is the genocide of Native American tribes during the expansion of the United States, the terrorism against blacks in the South, the military conquest and ongoing border violence against Latinos in the Southwest, or the attacks on Asian immigrant laborers in the West. Incidents of anti-Asian violence reveal unique themes of prejudice and discrimination that illustrate the dynamics of racism against Asian Americans.[13]

Chronicling the growth of anti-Asian violence in recent years, a 1986 report by the United States Commission on Civil Rights concluded that "anti-Asian activity in the form of violence, harassment intimidation, and vandalism has been reported across the nation."[14] The National Asian Pacific American Legal Consortium has measured anti-Asian violence during the 1990s and has tracked a wide variety of crimes, including graffiti, vandalism, cross burnings, property damage, arson, hate mail, intimidation, physical assaults, homicides, and police misconduct.[15] Calculating figures is difficult because of underreporting—many immigrants face language barriers or are fearful of the police—and because of major weaknesses in law enforcement's compilation of statistics. The numbers that are available are sobering. Nationally, the number of incidents of anti-Asian violence reported by the National Asian Pacific American Legal Consortium grew from 335 in 1993 to 452 in 1994, 456 in 1995, and 534 in 1996—a 59 percent increase from 1993 to 1996.

The most notorious episode of recent anti-Asian violence was the killing of Vincent Chin in 1982. Chin, a twenty-seven-year-old Chinese American, was celebrating his upcoming wedding at a Detroit bar when he was approached by Ronald Ebens and Michael Nitz, two white automobile factory workers. Ebens and Nitz thought Chin was Japanese and blamed him for the loss of jobs in the automobile industry. After calling Chin a "jap," the two men chased him out of the bar. They eventually caught Chin and proceeded to beat him repeatedly with a baseball bat. Chin died from his injuries a few days later. Ebens and Nitz each pleaded guilty to manslaughter but received only probation and a fine. Ebens was later convicted of federal civil rights violations, but his conviction was overturned on appeal and he was acquitted on retrial. Neither Ebens nor Nitz spent any time in prison for the killing.

A similar incident occurred in 1989 in Raleigh, North Carolina. Jim (Ming Hai) Loo had been playing pool with several friends when he was approached by Robert Piche and his brother Lloyd Piche, who began calling

Loo and his friends "chinks" and "gooks" and blaming them for the death of American soldiers in Vietnam. Once outside, Robert Piche pistol-whipped Loo on the back of the head, causing Loo to fall onto a broken bottle that pierced his brain. Loo died from his injuries two days later. Robert Piche was convicted and sentenced to thirty-seven years in prison; Lloyd Piche was sentenced to six months in prison by a state court, and sentenced to four years in prison for federal civil rights violations.

Another tragic illustration of anti-Asian violence is the multiple killings of Asian American children at the Cleveland Elementary School in Stockton, California, in 1989. Patrick Purdy used an AK-47 assault rifle to spray bullets into a crowded schoolyard, killing five children and wounding over twenty others before turning the gun on himself. Although initially labeled the product of a disturbed mind obsessed with guns and the military, the shootings were later proved to be motivated by racial hatred. A report issued by the California attorney general's office found that Purdy targeted the school because it was heavily populated by Southeast Asian children.[16]

Perpetrators who are affiliated with hate groups have been responsible for many anti-Asian crimes. During the early 1980s, when tensions erupted between Vietnamese immigrant fishermen and native-born fishermen in several coastal states, the Ku Klux Klan engaged in extensive harassment and violence against Vietnamese fishermen along the Gulf Coast of Texas. Federal litigation was required to end a pattern of threats, cross burnings, arsons, and shootings.[17] In 1990, Hung Truong, a fifteen-year-old Vietnamese boy living in Houston, was attacked by two men who were later identified as white supremacist "skinheads." After following Truong and his friends as they walked down the street, the two assailant jumped out of their car, one wielding a club, and shouted "White power." They chased Truong and proceeded to kick and beat him, even as he pleaded for his life. The two men admitted at trial that they attacked Truong because he was Vietnamese.

More common, however, are incidents that do not involve formal hate groups and that occur in day-to-day interactions among people at work in schools, at home, and on the street. Here are some examples, all of which occurred during a ten-month period in California during 1995 and 1996:

- A Chinese American high school student was physically attacked in the parking lot of a fast-food restaurant in the Northern California suburb of Novato by several other students, who shouted "Go back to China where you belong" and "chink, gook, chinaman."
- While walking her dog in a San Francisco park, a Japanese American woman was assaulted by a white woman who grabbed her by the

arm, threw dog feces at her, and cried out "Go home! Go home!"
and "Hiroshima!"

- A Chinese American man was stabbed repeatedly in the parking lot
of a Northern California supermarket by a white male assailant who
later admitted to the police that he wanted to kill a "chinaman"
because they "got all the good jobs."
- A Vietnamese man was killed while he was skating on a high school
tennis court in the Southern California city of Tustin. The assailant
boasted about the killing in a letter to a friend in which he graphi-
cally described the attack and wrote offhandedly, "Oh I killed a jap
a while ago."[18]

Even the virtual world of computer networks has been the site of anti-
Asian intimidation. In September 1996, a threatening electronic message was
sent to about sixty students at the University of California, Irvine—a college
campus whose undergraduate student population is approximately one-half
Asian American—accusing Asians of being responsible for all crimes on campus, ordering them to leave the university, and threatening to hunt them down
and kill them if they did not leave. The e-mail was signed "Asian-hater."[19]

Many incidents of anti-Asian violence arise from conflicts among racial
minorities. During the 1990s, Asian American tenants in San Francisco's public housing projects—primarily Southeast Asian refugees and their families—
were subjected to harassment and violence by African American tenants.
Inadequate institutional policies, including poor overall security and a flawed
racial integration strategy, aggravated cultural differences and tensions among
the tenants, resulting in intimidation and numerous assaults. Many families
feared for their lives and became prisoners in their own homes, while others
moved out of public housing altogether.[20]

Anti-Asian violence is even linked to political rhetoric and public policy
making. During the 1994 campaign for California's Proposition 187, the ballot initiative designed to restrict the rights of undocumented immigrants, racial rhetoric and literature abounded. In Los Angeles, for example, mailboxes
were stuffed with flyers that supported the passage of Proposition 187 and
stated: "WE NEED A *REAL* BORDER. FIRST WE GET THE SPICS, THEN
THE GOOKS, AND AT LAST WE GET THE NIGGERS. *DEPORTATION.*
THEY'RE ALL GOING HOME." Other flyers pointed to the "invasion" of
the "Gooks," stating "they had to go"; references to genocide and "taking back
America" were also common.[21]

Attempting to solve anti-Asian violence is as difficult and troubling an
exercise as reading the graphic reports of the violence itself. The National

Asian Pacific American Legal Consortium has identified several problems on both the national and local level that remain unaddressed by government and policy makers: incomplete reporting and monitoring mechanisms among law enforcement; the weakness or absence of hate crimes laws; inadequate training of law enforcement personnel; insufficient funding for civil rights agencies; and major barriers to reporting, including the absence of bilingual services for limited-English-speaking immigrants.[22]

Even where reporting mechanisms and laws are in place, prosecuting hate crimes is problematic: inadequately trained officers may not collect relevant evidence, and prosecutors may be reluctant to press charges because of the difficulty of proving intent on the part of the perpetrator.[23] The problem is compounded when the victims are recent immigrants who may speak little English and may be reluctant to report the crimes because of their distrust of law enforcement. In some areas of the country, such as New York City, police relations are so poor that police misconduct is itself a major source of anti-Asian violence.[24] At its base, addressing anti-Asian violence means developing explanations and solutions to racial subordination against Asian Americans in general; violence is the most pernicious variation on several general themes.

Racial Themes

Without question, the examples of anti-Asian violence demonstrate that overt racism is still a serious problem for Asian Americans, just as it has been for African Americans and other racial minorities. Some types of anti-Asian violence can thus be explained by treating violence against Asian Americans and other racial minority groups as expressions of white racism. Anti-Asian violence committed by white supremacists targeting anyone who is not white fits within a binary model of race that places all racial minorities in the same category of "nonwhite."

But many incidents of anti-Asian violence suggest that more complex dynamics are at work. Members of one Asian ethnic group are often mistaken for being members of other Asian ethnic groups. Racial and ethnic slurs are interlaced with nativist anti-immigrant rhetoric. Resentment about economic competition, both foreign and domestic, is often implicated. Even hostility rooted in the United States' previous military involvement in Asian countries may be a factor. And a white-nonwhite framework cannot explain racial violence in which members of one nonwhite group victimize members of another nonwhite group. Several basic themes can be gleaned from these and other examples of violence against Asian Americans.

RACIALIZATION

One theme is the importance of *racial* categorizing in anti-Asian violence. The killing of Vincent Chin is an example of how anti-Asian violence is racialized: based on his physical appearance, Chin, a Chinese American, was taken to be a Japanese national by his killers, who had made him the focus of their anger and frustration toward Japanese competition in the automobile industry. A perpetrator who makes the race-based generalization that all Asians look alike puts every Asian American at risk, even if the specific antagonisms are targeted against a smaller subset of people.

The attribution of specific ethnic characteristics to anyone falling within the racial category of "Asian" is common in anti-Asian violence. For example, when Luyen Phan Nguyen, a Vietnamese premedical student, was killed in Coral Springs, Florida, in 1992, he was taunted with slurs at a party and later chased down by a group of men who beat and kicked him repeatedly. Among the epithets directed at Nguyen during the beating were "chink," "vietcong," and "sayonara"—three separate and distinct ethnic slurs.

NATIVISM AND RACISM

Another theme manifested by anti-Asian violence is the centrality of nativism, which John Higham defines as "intense opposition to an internal minority on the ground of its foreign (i.e., 'un-American') connections."[25] Asian Americans are equated with foreigners, or they are at least presumed to be foreign-born. Race and nativism thus intersect to produce a distinctive form of subordination of Asian Americans—what Robert Chang labels "nativistic racism."[26]

In many incidents, Asian American victims are perceived and categorized as foreigners by their assailants: Vincent Chin was transformed into a Japanese national; Jim Loo became a Vietnamese adversary; immigrant merchants were remade as foreign investors and capitalists. Anti-immigrant epithets such as "Go home!" or "Why don't you go back to your own country?" frequently accompany anti-Asian violence, along with specific racial and ethnic slurs. And under the rubric of foreign outsider, Asian Americans fall into an array of unpopular categories: economic competitor, organized criminal, "illegal alien," or just unwelcome immigrant.

Patriotic racism is a peculiar and especially deep-seated form of nativist racism. American military conflicts against the Japanese during World War II, against Koreans and Chinese during the Korean War, and against the Vietnamese during the Vietnam War have generated intense animosity against Asian Americans. During World War II, the federal government's internment of Japanese Americans, most of whom were United States citizens, reflected patriotic racism at its worst, as a formal governmental policy. Intimidation and violence against Asian Americans is still common on December 7 because of the hostility that arises on the anniversary of the bombing of Pearl Harbor by Japan.

RACIAL HIERARCHIES AND INTERRACIAL CONFLICT

A related theme made evident by anti-Asian violence revolves around the intermediate position that Asian Americans appear to occupy on a social and economic ladder that places whites on top and blacks at the bottom. Black-on-Asian hate crimes often contain strong elements of cultural conflict and nativism—blacks, like whites, treat Asians as foreigners. But black-on-Asian crimes also have strains traceable to resentment over the economic achievements of Asian Americans, particularly their entrepreneurial success in the inner cities. The destruction of Korean immigrants' businesses in 1992, many located in the historically black residential area of South-Central Los Angeles, reflected a growing anger against Asian American prosperity.

In this context, the "model minority" stereotype of Asian Americans becomes a two-edged sword, breeding not only incomplete and inaccurate images of Asian American success but resentment and hostility on the part of other racial groups. Racial differentiation often places Asian Americans in a middle position within the racial hierarchy of the United States—neither black nor white, and somewhere between black and white.

The Limits of Black and White

Hate violence is the most extreme form of racial subordination against Asian Americans but it sheds light on important differences between the subordination of Asian Americans and African Americans. A binary model of race based on relations between blacks and whites cannot fully describe the complex racial matrix that exists in the U.S. In terms of representation, a black-white model ignores or marginalizes the experiences of Asian Americans, Latinos, Native Americans, Arab Americans, and other groups who have extensive histories of discrimination against them. A black-white model discounts the role of immigration in race relations and confines discussion on the impact race has had on anti-immigrant policies that affect the nation's growing Asian American and Latino populations. A black-white model also limits any analysis of the relations and tensions between racial and ethnic groups, which are increasingly significant in urban areas where racial "minorities" are now becoming majorities.

In essence a black-white model fails to recognize that the basic nature of discrimination can differ among racial and ethnic groups. Theories of racial inferiority have been applied, often with violent force, against Asian Americans, just as they have been applied against blacks and other racial minority groups. But the causes of anti-Asian subordination can be traced to other factors as well, including nativism, differences in language and culture, perceptions of Asians as economic competitors, international relations, and past military involvement in Asian countries. Recent immigration from Asian countries is elevating culture and language to prominent places on the race relations landscape, challenging even the integrity of the racial category "Asian American." And the promotion in recent years of a "model minority" racial stereotype, based on the high education levels and incomes of some Asian Americans, represents a curious and distorted form of racism, denying the existence of Asian American poverty and inequality. All of these considerations point to the need for an analysis of race that is very different from the dominant black-white paradigm.

Asian Americans and the Civil Rights Laws

Racial discourse finds expression in the civil rights laws—the sections of the federal Constitution and the anti-discrimination statutes designed to address racial discrimination. Hate crimes laws, for instance, create special crimes based on racial violence or augment the punishment for violent crimes when there is finding of racially discriminatory intent. Asian Americans are protected by these laws and other antidiscrimination laws from racial discrimination. But, like other manifestations of race, the antidiscrimination laws define most rights within a black-white framework, and the laws contain significant limitations in accommodating the full array of Asian American experiences. When questions of civil rights move beyond a black-white dichotomy, rights and remedies become problematic and Asian Americans are often left without the full protection of the law.

The laws fail to recognize the intersection of race and nativism found in anti-Asian discrimination. When United States-born Asian Americans suffer discrimination as perceived immigrants, antidiscrimination laws may provide relief, but only if the facts permit a finding of discrimination based on categories of race or national origin, and not on the basis of being perceived as a foreigner. Laws such as the Immigration Reform and Control Act of 1986, which requires employers to verify the immigration status of all newly hired employees, have actually caused more discrimination against Asian Americans because of the common perception that all Asian Americans are immigrants and are therefore more likely to be undocumented.

Governmental ambivalence toward anti-immigrant discrimination is a significant weakness in the system of civil rights enforcement. Most antidiscrimination laws protect immigrants from discrimination based on race or national origin, but they lack specific protections for immigrants as immigrants. Attempts to expand civil rights legislation to protect immigrants have been rebuked in the past. In California, for instance, legislation to protect immigrants from intimidation and hate violence was introduced and passed twice by the state legislature during the mid-1990s, but was vetoed each time by Governor Pete Wilson.

Some laws, such as California's Proposition 187, openly discriminate against undocumented immigrants. Federal laws discriminating against immigrants have gone even further, because the federal laws related to immigration enjoy special constitutional status arising from deference to national sovereignty. Welfare reform legislation enacted in 1996 not only discriminated against undocumented immigrants but against lawful permanent residents—"green card" holders—by stripping many permanent residents of eligibility for entitlement programs such as Food Stamps and Supplemental Security Income, which remained available to citizens. The impact of anti-immigrant policies falls most heavily on Asian Americans and Latinos because of the large numbers of immigrants within their communities and because of the linkage between nativism and race.

Characteristics inherent to immigrants are often ignored in the law. Forms of language-based discrimination dealing with accent and the ability to speak a second language at work are problematic under the civil rights laws, which generally lack explicit protections for language minority groups. Language may serve as a proxy for race, but the nexus between language and race is usually absent in statutes and in judicial interpretations of the law. In addition, the ability to access important government services such as police and fire, emergency health care, and public education is often compromised because of the narrowness of rights related to language and ethnicity.

Within the broader race relations landscape, where Asian Americans are ignored or, increasingly, where they occupy a racial middle ground, civil rights laws are not well equipped to recognize variations in both discrimination and the remedies for discrimination. The "model minority" image often leads to the exclusion of Asian Americans from corrective civil rights programs; Asian Americans are even labeled, along with whites, as victims of affirmative action. The image also leads to antagonisms between Asian Americans and members of other racial groups because of the perceptions of relative inequality and the resentment arising from those perceptions. In the area of interethnic relations, as in other areas, the antidiscrimination laws do not go far enough in recognizing and addressing the problems of Asian Americans.

Organization of the Book

In this book, I attempt to shed further light on the experiences of Asian Americans and to discuss theories of legal rights that broaden the discourse on race and law. Race relations is an expansive subject, and I make no attempt to be comprehensive in my analysis of race or of Asian Americans in particular. I have narrowed the focus of this book to the antidiscrimination laws because they play both an important ideological role in racial discourse and an important practical role in addressing and improving race relations. I focus on Asian Americans not only to provide a representative voice in discussions of race but to use the Asian American experience as a starting point for a broader perspective on race and rights.

In attempting to move beyond a black-white model of racial jurisprudence, I offer three basic arguments. First, I argue that anti-Asian subordination is qualitatively different from anti-black subordination. Rather than being centered on color, which divides racially between the superior and the inferior, anti-Asian subordination is centered on citizenship, which divides racially between American and foreigner. Asian Americans are thus perceived racially as foreign outsiders who lack the rights of true "Americans." Second, I argue that immigration from Asia during the past three decades has shifted racial demography in the United States and has caused ethnicity and other attributes of immigrants to become powerful forces in race relations. Manifestations of ethnicity such as language are now critical factors in the calculus of basic rights. Third, I argue that shifting demographics have created new dynamics in race relations, between racial minorities and whites, and among racial minority groups. Racial hierarchies and intergroup conflict require new theories of race relations that move beyond a simple black versus white paradigm.

The book is an extended essay to support these basic arguments. Chapter 1 provides an overview of the Asian American communities by outlining the history of discrimination against Asian Americans and exploring the demographic trends accompanying the growth of Asian immigrant populations. The history of racial subordination is important because many of the legal doctrines that subjugated Asian Americans in the past retain their validity as legal precedents and continue to have an impact on Asian American communities.

Chapter 2 explores theoretical frameworks for analyzing race and rights. The chapter initially examines psychological and social theories of race and racism. My analysis is eclectic, drawing on theories from psychology, sociology, economics, and historical studies. I later develop a nexus between these theories and legal models of antidiscrimination, providing an overview of basic civil rights jurisprudence and its general deficiencies in addressing racial subordination

Chapters 3 through 7 analyze legal doctrines and policies implicated in the racial and ethnic subordination of Asian Americans. Chapter 3 examines the historical role of law, as well as contemporary anti-immigrant legislation, in reinforcing and reproducing the racialization of Asian Americans as foreigners. Chapter 4 looks at the relationship between race, nativism, and citizenship in discrimination against Asian immigrants. I explore the intersection of the immigration laws and the civil rights laws, and highlight tensions and paradoxes between the two. Chapter 5 examines language as a distinct basis for anti-immigrant subordination against Asian Americans, discussing English-only legislation and how statutes and court-made decisional law have failed to address subordination based on language differences. Chapter 6 investigates ethnic differences in the Asian American population and focuses on the role of law in both shaping and reinforcing Asian American identities. Chapter 7 analyzes interracial dynamics brought on by immigration and the growth of Asian American communities. The chapter looks at the roles that Asian Americans play in racial hierarchies in areas such as school desegregation, affirmative action, and racial violence.

Each chapter concludes with recommendations for changes in both legal doctrine and for general approaches to race relations that accommodate Asian American experiences.

Working Definitions

I discuss theories of race more fully in chapter 2, but for clarity's sake, I offer some working definitions of race and related terms here. I define "race" as a category, based on perceived physical differences, that carries social meanings constructed from historical, economic, political, and legal influences. Because this definition of race is rooted in the perception of others, an individual's race is ascribed through external categorization rather than through identity. That is not to say that one cannot have a racial identity; race and racial identity typically coincide, but as I use the term, race is determined more from without than from within. Social meanings of race are pervasive and can range from individual stereotypes to forms of governmental coercion. These meanings are embedded in our cognition of the world, in our attitudes, in our actions, and in our institutions. Racial cognition and prejudice reinforce and are reinforced by social institutions, including law and the legal system.

"Ethnicity" is a related concept, based largely on attributes that unify members of an ethnic group and provide an identity to which individuals can subscribe. These attributes include, but are not limited to, shared history, language, national origin, or culture. In the context of Asian Americans, I distinguish between racial groups and ethnic groups: "Asian" and "Asian American" describe a racial category; "Chinese," "Japanese," "Filipino," "Vietnamese," "Korean," and other similar terms describe ethnic categories. Ethnicity is neither fixed nor uniform; the experiences of a fourth-generation, U.S.-born Chinese American, for instance, will not be the same as the experiences of a recent immigrant from China. And ethnicity can be transformed through social processes such as immigration. I employ the ethnic group labels primarily to signal differences in immigration history, language, and culture that have found expression in the law.

I also use the term "subordination" to refer to many forms of racial and ethnic discrimination. "Discrimination" carries heavy baggage as a popular expression, and it has different meanings in social science and under the law. I prefer the term "subordination" because it encompasses discrimination and better reflects the power relationships that exist in race relations. Racial subordination, as I use it, is an expression of power based on race in which a dominant person, group, or institution acts to place another person, group, or institution in a lesser or subordinate position relative to the dominant entity. Power and inequality are thus at the root of racial subordination.

One caveat: in analyzing race, there is always the danger of being essentialist by trying to characterize racial subordination as unitary. Notwithstanding the title of this book, there is no uniform Asian American experience that defines the realities of all Asian Americans. Nor is there a single definition that fully captures who Asian Americans are or how they are perceived by others. The experiences of a recent immigrant living in Northern California differ greatly from an upper-middle-class Asian American who grew up in a predominantly white suburb in the Midwest, just as the experiences of a refugee who has resettled in Lowell, Massachusetts, differ immensely from a fourth-generation resident of Hawaii. The intersections of race with ethnicity, gender, class, sexual orientation, and other characteristics variegate and complicate questions of identity and subordination for Asian Americans. But "Asian American" has no less value as a descriptive term. As a racial category,

"Asian" carries a set of social meanings that most people consciously understand. While many of those social meanings may be based on misperceptions, they exist and they are reproduced in everyday interactions, in social and political debate, in economic institutions, and ultimately in the law.

Chapter 1	Legacies of Discrimination

The year 1965 is a landmark in both the history of civil rights and the history of Asian Americans. In 1965, Congress passed the Voting Rights Act, a law designed to protect the most basic political right—the right to vote—and to eliminate racial discrimination in the electoral process. The act is responsible for eliminating state and local barriers to voting, and has encouraged the registration and participation of millions of voters. The passage of the Voting Rights Act came on the tails of Congress's passage of the Civil Rights Act of 1964, the most sweeping civil rights legislation enacted during the twentieth century. The 1964 act prohibits racial discrimination in public accommodations, in federally funded programs and activities, and, most broadly, in public and private employment.

The civil rights movement and the changes in racial attitudes that engendered the civil rights legislation of the 1960s also contributed to the passage of the Immigration Act of 1965. Prior to 1965, Asian immigration had been severely limited by discriminatory laws targeting migrants from Asian and Pacific Island countries. Laws dating back to the nineteenth century had excluded entire classes of Asian immigrants from entering the United States. After 1965, with the removal of a discriminatory system of quotas based on national origin, the immigration laws placed migration from Asia and the Pacific on an equal footing with migration from other parts of the world.

The Immigration Act of 1965 is a watershed in Asian American history. The 1965 act marked both the end of a decades-long era of overt governmental discrimination against Asian Americans and the beginning of an era of renewed immigration and population growth. The 1965 act was the culmination of several reversals in the law that rectified anti-Asian subordination by federal and state government. Laws that sanctioned discrimination against Asian Americans in immigration, naturalization, education, employment, property ownership, and family relations, including marriage, had all begun to fall during the 1940s and 1950s. By 1965, Congress could no longer countenance overt racial discrimination in the immigration laws.

Since the passage of the Immigration Act of 1965, Asian Americans have become the fastest growing racial group in the United States. Fueled primarily by immigration, the Asian American population doubled between 1970 and 1980, and doubled again between 1980 and 1990. Census Bureau figures for 1997 put the Asian and Pacific Islander population in the United States at close to ten million, and projections for the year 2000 put the population at over twelve million.[1] A predominantly U.S.-born population in 1965, the Asian American population is today two-thirds immigrant. Among its members are native-born citizens whose family roots trace back as many as eight or nine generations in the United States; immigrants and the children of immigrants who came after 1965; and refugees from Vietnam and other Southeast Asian countries who entered after the 1970s following the Vietnam War.

The subordination of Asian Americans did not simply end in 1965. The population growth of Asian immigrants has sharpened long-standing racial problems and ushered in new sets of problems. Subordination by government persists in the form of anti-immigrant laws having adverse effects on Asian Americans. Private subordination against Asian Americans—the subordination that arises in the everyday experiences of Asian Americans living and working in society—has changed over time, but many problems have remained constant. While attitudes regarding race have improved, racism and nativism continue to shape Asian American experiences, just as they did when the first waves of immigrant workers from Asia began settling in this country during the nineteenth century.

In this chapter, I examine the history of legal discrimination against Asian Americans. The history of laws that subordinated Asian Americans is often ignored in studies of civil rights. More importantly, though, many of the court decisions involving the rights of Asian Americans have contemporary value because they continue to be used as legal precedents. The focus of this history is governmental discrimination. Government has not been the only source of anti-Asian discrimination, but because the laws are expressions of societal values and ideologies, they embody many of the racial prejudices that continue to subordinate Asian Americans.

Immigration and Discrimination

The history of Asians in the United States is a long one, and can be traced as far back as the 1700s, when Filipino sailors traveling on trading ships settled in the bayous of Louisiana.[2] Significant populations in Hawaii and the West came with the successive waves of laborers who entered the United States in the nineteenth and early twentieth centuries. In the 1840s Chinese immigrants began arriving in Hawaii to work on the plantations and on the West Coast to work in the gold mines and to help build the railroads. Japanese and Filipino workers entered in later years, as did smaller numbers of Korean and Asian Indian immigrants. Economic demands for low-wage labor fueled migration, but economic recessions and overt racism led to intense discrimination against all of these populations in time.[3]

Anti-Asian sentiment arose quickly with the arrival of Chinese laborers. In 1852, a California Assembly committee issued a report critical of Chinese labor, warning of "the concentration within our State limits, of vast numbers of the Asiatic races, and of the inhabitants of the Pacific Islands, and of many others dissimilar from ourselves in customs, language and education."[4] John Bigler, the governor of California, soon called for legislative measures to "check [the] tide of Asiatic immigration"[5] into California through targeted taxation. The nativist Know-Nothing Party, which had organized around anti-Catholic sentiment on the East Coast, organized around the growing anti-Chinese movement on the West Coast during the 1850s. Unions and political parties such as the Workingmen's Party adopted anti-Chinese platforms, and "anti-Coolie" clubs formed in California during the 1860s and 1870s.

When Chinese immigration was limited by federal law in the 1880s, Japanese, Korean, Asian Indian, and Filipino immigrants were recruited for low-wage work in Hawaii and the West Coast, but they too became targets of subordination. In 1905, delegates from over sixty labor organizations met in San Francisco to form the Japanese and Korean Exclusion League, which was later renamed the Asiatic Exclusion League. Organized around the threat of the "yellow peril" and the invasion of the "Asiatic horde," the league's constitution stated: "The preservation of the Caucasian race upon American soil . . . necessitates the adoption of all possible measures to prevent or minimize the immigration of Asiatics to America."[6] The league even blamed anti-Asian violence on immigrants themselves: "In California the insolence and presumption of Japanese, and the immodest and filthy habits of the Hindoos are continually involving them in trouble, beatings. . . . In all these cases, we may say the Oriental is at fault."[7]

Race riots instigated by white workers who resented competition from

Asian workers were common on the West Coast. Anti-Chinese riots led to the deaths of dozens of Chinese laborers in California, Oregon, and other states during the late nineteenth century. Anti-Filipino riots took place in California and Washington during the 1920s and 1930s. In 1930, rioting in Watsonville, California, even arose in response to a local newspaper's coverage of the arrest of a Filipino man who had been seen walking with a white teenage girl, to whom he was engaged to be married. Fueled by angry rhetoric against Filipino workers, the four days of rioting included beatings, shootings, and an attack on a Filipino dance hall by four hundred white men.[8]

Racial segregation was pervasive. Asian immigrants were often refused service in theaters, hotels, restaurants, or they were consigned to areas separate from a whites-only area. Housing segregation was also common. Asians were usually told by landlords and realtors, "No Orientals allowed" or "Only whites allowed in this neighborhood."[9] Residential and commercial enclaves— Chinatowns, Little Tokyos, Little Manilas—developed in many cities because of segregation; they offered immigrants the services of boarding houses, hotels, restaurants, stores, churches, and recreation halls that were unavailable from whites-only institutions.

Restricted by both law and custom from entering the country in large numbers, Asian immigrant women faced severe forms of subordination in the United States. Societal discrimination and patriarchy within ethnic cultures placed Asian immigrant women in marginal economic roles as manual workers, seamstresses, cooks, cleaners, and washers. In the bachelor societies that dominated early immigrant communities, Asian women were often relegated to prostitution, exploiting themselves as cheap laborers and playing a role in the exploitation of migratory men who were unencumbered by families or the costs of raising children.[10]

Anti-Asian sentiment engendered anti-Asian laws. The legal subordination of Asian Americans on the West Coast paralleled the treatment of African Americans in the South following Reconstruction: segregation was sanctioned and discriminatory laws abounded at all levels of government. Anti-Asian laws came in three forms: (1) federal naturalization laws that imposed a racial barrier on Asian immigrants seeking United States citizenship; (2) federal immigration laws limiting migration from Asian and Pacific Island countries; and (3) state and local laws discriminating against Asians, often based on their ineligibility for citizenship. One variation of this discrimination was the wartime treatment of Japanese Americans, who were relocated and interned in concentration camps during World War II. In the vast majority of cases, the courts upheld the constitutionality of anti-Asian legislation.

Racial Bar to Citizenship

In 1790, Congress passed a law to establish a uniform standard for naturalization. The Nationality Act of 1790 stated that "any alien, being a *free white person* who shall have resided within the limits and under the jurisdiction of the United States for a term of two years, may be admitted to become a citizen thereof."[11] Asian Americans did not have a significant presence in the United States at the time, and the law was meant to exclude blacks and members of Native American tribes. In practice, however, the government denied citizenship to Asian immigrants for decades because they were not white.

In 1868, the enactment of the Fourteenth Amendment to the federal Constitution made clear that anyone born in and subject to the jurisdiction of the United States, including former slaves, would be an American citizen. Legislation passed by Congress in 1870 amended the naturalization law to conform with the intent of the Reconstruction amendments and allowed "aliens of African nativity and persons of African descent" to become naturalized citizens.[12] However, Congress considered and rejected attempts to make Chinese immigrants eligible for citizenship under the 1870 law and retained the racial prohibition on naturalization for nonwhite immigrants.[13] Eight years later, a federal court in *In re Ah Yup* upheld the racial bar against Chinese immigrants.[14]

The racial restriction on naturalization even cast doubt on the eligibility of native-born Asian Americans for birthright citizenship under the Fourteenth Amendment. The issue was not resolved until 1898, with the United States Supreme Court's decision in *United States v. Wong Kim Ark*.[15] Wong was born in San Francisco, California, to Chinese immigrants who were permanently residing in the United States. After returning from a trip to China in 1895, he was detained and prevented from entering the country on the grounds that he was not an American citizen. The Supreme Court ruled in his favor, holding that all persons born in the United States, even those born to parents ineligible for naturalization, are citizens of the United States. The Court stated: "The Fourteenth Amendment affirms the ancient and fundamental rule of citizenship by birth within the territory, in the allegiance and under the protection of the country, including all children born of resident aliens. . . ."[16] But at the same time that it affirmed Wong's birthright citizenship, the Court acknowledged the power of Congress to deny citizenship to his parents: "Chinese persons not born in this country have never been recognized as citizens of the United States, nor authorized to become such under the naturalization laws."[17]

The courts isolated Asians as the one racial group that would be ineligible for naturalized citizenship. In a series of cases during the 1920s, the United States Supreme Court ruled that, unless specifically exempted by Congress, Asians did not fall within the category of "free white persons." In *Ozawa v. United States*, the Supreme Court ruled on the question of a Japanese immigrant's eligibility for citizenship.[18] Takao Ozawa, who had been raised and educated in the United States, did not challenge the constitutionality of the racial restriction. Instead, he argued that Japanese were included within the category "free white persons" because of skin color and other attributes. The Court rejected the argument, stating that skin color was not determinative and that "the words 'white person' were meant to indicate only a person of what is popularly known as the Caucasian race."[19] Ozawa, according to the Court, was "clearly of a race which is not Caucasian."[20]

In *United States v. Thind*, the Supreme Court ruled that Asian Indians were barred from naturalization, even though scientific evidence at the time indicated that Indians belonged to the Caucasian race.[21] The popular conception of Caucasian, the Court noted, clearly excluded Indians: "It is a matter of familiar observation and knowledge that the physical group characteristics of the Hindus renders them readily distinguishable from the various persons in this country commonly recognized as white."[22] The Court also indicated that the racial bar applied to other Asians as well: "There is much in the origin and historic development of the statute to suggest that no Asiatic whatever was included."[23]

Congress even went so far as to strip United States citizenship from women who married Asian immigrants. The Cable Act, passed by Congress in 1922, stated that "any woman citizen who marries an alien ineligible to citizenship shall cease to be a citizen of the United States."[24] Legal theories at the time mandated that citizenship between a husband and wife be unitary, with the laws favoring the husband's citizenship over the wife's. Under this reasoning, the government could take American citizenship away from any woman who married an immigrant subject to the racial bar.

Exceptions to the racial bar to naturalization did not come until the 1940s, largely in response to wartime alliances between the United States and particular Asian countries. Chinese immigrants were allowed to naturalize beginning in 1943; Indians and Filipinos were allowed to naturalize beginning in 1946. It was not until 1952, 162 years after passing the Nationality Act of 1790, that Congress removed the racial limitation on naturalized citizenship.[25]

Federal Laws of Exclusion

Racial barriers to naturalization prevented Asian immigrants from gaining full rights of citizenship; racial barriers to immigration prevented Asians from entering the country at all. Responding to claims of both unfair job competition from Asian immigrants and the purported racial inferiority of Asians, Congress passed a series of laws limiting Asian immigration into the United States during the late nineteenth and early twentieth centuries. Beginning with the exclusion of Chinese women under the Page Law of 1875, the laws first sought to curtail the immigration of Chinese, and in time extended the laws to include all Asians. The United States Supreme Court upheld the constitutionality of the immigration laws at every turn.

Anti-Chinese sentiment on the West Coast fueled the passage of restrictive immigration laws in the 1870s and 1880s. The Page Law of 1875 was directed at preventing the entry of prostitutes,[26] but immigration officials effectively limited the entry of nearly all Chinese women by classifying them as prostitutes. In 1882, Congress passed the Chinese Exclusion Act,[27] which excluded Chinese laborers for a period of ten years. The decline in Chinese immigration was precipitous: in 1882, over 39,000 Chinese entered the United States; in 1884, only 279 entered the country; and in 1888, only 10 were admitted.[28] The Scott Act of 1888 expanded the 1882 act by prohibiting the entry of all Chinese laborers, including those who left the United States temporarily with return certificates. Conceding exceptional power over immigration to Congress and the federal government, the Supreme Court upheld the constitutionality of the Scott Act in *Chae Chan Ping v. United States (the Chinese Exclusion Case)*.[29] The Court stated in unambiguous terms that if "the government of the United States, through its legislative department, considers the presence of foreigners of a different race in this country, who will not assimilate with us, to be dangerous to its peace and security, their exclusion is not to be stayed."[30]

Congress passed the Geary Act of 1892 to extend Chinese exclusion for ten more years and to respond to the racist claim that Chinese names and faces were all alike: the act's registration requirements were considered necessary to distinguish between Chinese who were legally in the country prior to exclusion and those who had been smuggled in afterward. Any Chinese immigrant who failed to register with the government within a year became subject to deportation. Among the requirements to obtain a certificate of residency was the testimony of at least one white person, who could act as a credible witness. In *Fong Yue Ting v. United States*,[31] the Supreme Court relied on its earlier decision in the Chinese Exclusion Case and upheld the Geary Act's constitutionality. Congress renewed Chinese exclusion in 1902, and in 1904 Congress passed legislation that extended Chinese exclusion indefinitely. It was not until 1943, when China became an important ally of the United States during World War II, that the Chinese exclusion laws were repealed.

Japanese immigration to the United States began as the Chinese exclusion laws were taking effect. Closely regulated by the Japanese government, migration from Japan focused on sending laborers to Hawaii and California to work on plantations and farms. Although relations between the governments of the United States and Japan were cordial at the time, anti-Japanese sentiment became virulent on the West Coast and calls for restrictions on Japanese immigration resounded throughout the country. The placement of children of Japanese immigrants into San Francisco's "Oriental school," which had been established as a segregated school for the Chinese, raised the ire of the Japanese government and led to diplomatic discussions to address anti-Japanese sentiment in the United States. The result was an agreement negotiated in 1907 and 1908 between the two countries that voluntarily restricted Japanese immigration. Under the Gentlemen's Agreement, as it was commonly known, the Japanese government stopped issuing travel documents to workers destined for the United States. In exchange, the spouses and children of Japanese laborers could migrate to the United States.

Nativist sentiment against Korean and Indian immigrants also grew at the turn of the century, raising new demands for exclusion laws. Congress responded to the calls for Asian exclusion by passing the Immigration Act of 1917,[32] which created a triangular "Asiatic barred zone" whose restrictions paralleled the exclusion of immigrants from China. The zone covered South Asia from Arabia to Indochina, and included India, Burma, Siam, the Malay states, the East Indian islands, Asiatic Russia, the Polynesian islands, and parts of Arabia and Afghanistan.[33]

Seven years later, Congress passed the Immigration Act of 1924,[34] a comprehensive immigration law that established national origin quotas based on the numbers of immigrants living in the United States as of 1890. Because of the demographic makeup of the United States in 1890, the quotas were biased heavily in favor of northern and western Europeans. The act also excluded any "alien ineligible to citizenship," which, because of the racial bar on naturalization, meant all Asians. The primary target of the exclusion was the Japanese, who were still subject to the Gentlemen's Agreement but had never been formally barred by the immigration laws.

Filipinos, who were United States nationals because of the Philippines' colonial status, were not affected by the 1924 act. Because of the need for low-wage labor, Filipino workers were recruited to Hawaii and the West during the 1920s. In time, anti-Filipino sentiment became as vitriolic as other forms of anti-Asian feeling, but exclusion could not be invoked against the inhabitants of an American colony. In time, the movement for Philippine independence combined with American nativism to promote Congress's passage of the Tydings-McDuffie Act in 1934.[35] The act granted commonwealth status to the Philippines and led to independence in 1946. But the Tydings-McDuffie Act also divested Filipinos of their status as nationals, making those in the United States deportable unless they became immigrants. Between 1934 and 1946, Filipinos seeking to immigrate were subject to the immigration laws of 1917 and 1924, and an annual quota of only fifty visas was allocated for the Philippines. Like other Asians, Filipino immigrants were not "free white persons" and were therefore ineligible for naturalized citizenship.[36]

By the 1920s and 1930s, Asian immigration had declined drastically and formed a minuscule percentage of the overall immigration into the United States. The Chinese and Filipino populations actually decreased over time, because of gender imbalances exacerbated by the immigration laws. The repeal of the Chinese exclusion acts in 1943 did little to change migration patterns because complete exclusion was replaced by an annual quota of only 105 visas. The 1952 McCarran-Walter Act revamped much of the immigration system,[37] but retained the quota system of the 1924 act, which severely limited Asian immigration. The 1952 act also created an Asia-Pacific triangle, similar to the Asiatic barred zone in the 1917 act, from which a maximum of only two thousand immigrants could enter the United States each year. Individual quotas for each Asian country typically allowed only one hundred entrants per year. Racial bias within the McCarran-Walter Act was also manifested through restrictions on immigration to anyone who was of at least one-half Asian or Pacific ancestry, regardless of actual country of birth. It was not until reforms were enacted in the Immigration Act of 1965 that race-based exclusions were fully removed from the immigration laws.

State and Local Laws

State and local laws had the most profound effects on the lives of Asian immigrants and their families. Basic rights and liberties—to work, attend school, own property, operate a business, or even marry the person of one's choice—were limited by state and local laws. Some of the laws discriminated through explicit anti-Asian language, but most of the laws relied on the racial prohibition on naturalized citizenship to single out Asian immigrants. Legislative language to deny rights to "aliens ineligible to citizenship" had the clear intent and effect of subordinating Asians.

Chinese immigrants were targeted from the earliest days of their arrival into the United States. In 1852, the California legislature enacted a foreign miners' license tax, which imposed a three dollar monthly tax on every foreign miner who would not—and could not under federal law—become an American citizen. Until it was made void by the federal Civil Rights Act of 1870, the foreign miners' tax generated from one-fourth to one-half of California's total state revenue.[38] In 1855, the California legislature passed a law entitled "An Act to Discourage the Immigration to this State of Persons Who Cannot Become Citizens Thereof," which imposed a landing tax of fifty dollars per person on shipowners transporting passengers ineligible for citizenship. The California legislature became even bolder over time, passing a law entitled "An Act to Prevent Further Immigration of Chinese or Mongolian to This State" one year later, and passing a law entitled "An Act to Protect Free White Labor against Competition with Chinese Coolie Labor" in 1862.

The courts were not immune from discrimination against the Chinese. In 1854, the California Supreme Court overturned the criminal conviction of George Hall, a white man who had been convicted of murdering a Chinese man based on the testimony of one white and three Chinese witnesses. The court ruled in *People v. Hall* that a Chinese witness could not testify against a white defendant in a criminal trial.[39] Relying on a state law which stated that "[n]o Black or Mulatto person, or Indian, shall be allowed to give evidence in favor of, or against any white person," the court extended the discriminatory bar to include Chinese. The court offered three reasons for its decision: Indians and Chinese were of the same racial stock, the word "black" necessarily excluded all races other than Caucasian, and accepting Chinese testimony was just bad public policy. The ruling remained in effect for nearly twenty years.

Local ordinances imposed heavy burdens on immigrant workers and businesses. For example, San Francisco enacted a laundry ordinance in 1873 that imposed a tax schedule of $1.25 on laundries with one horse-drawn vehicle, $4 on laundries with two horse-drawn vehicles, $15 on laundries with over two horse-drawn vehicles, and $15 on laundries with no horse-drawn vehicles at all. The ordinance targeted Chinese laundries, since practically no Chinese laundry operated a horse-drawn vehicle.[40] During the course of the next ten years, the city enacted over a dozen more laundry ordinances that were race-neutral on their face but were intended to discriminate against Chinese immigrants. San Francisco even enacted a "Cubic Air Ordinance," which required that living spaces have at least five hundred cubic feet of space per person; the ordinance was enforced only in Chinatown.

An exceptional court decision occurred in 1886, when the United States

Supreme Court struck down one of San Francisco's ordinances in the landmark case of *Yick Wo v. Hopkins*.[41] Yick Wo, like most Chinese laundry owners in San Francisco in the 1880s, operated a laundry constructed of wood. The city's 1880 laundry ordinance governed the operation of laundries and prohibited wood construction. Yick Wo and two hundred other Chinese laundry owners were denied license renewals under the ordinance, even though they had been operating their laundries for over twenty years. Non-Chinese laundries (including ones with wooden buildings) were granted license renewals. The Supreme Court ruled in favor of the Chinese laundry owners, holding that the ordinance violated the equal protection clause of the Fourteenth Amendment. The Court stated: "No reason . . . exists except hostility to the race and nationality to which the petitioners belong, and which in the eyes of the law is not justified."[42]

Yick Wo was an anomalous decision given the Court's rulings in other cases involving Chinese immigrants, and may have been due to the Court's strong adherence at the time to doctrines protecting business interests and the liberty of contracts. In any case, *Yick Wo* established two important principles that are still invoked in constitutional litigation: (1) noncitizens are protected by the equal protection clause of the Fourteenth Amendment, and (2) a neutrally written law can violate the Constitution if administered in a discriminatory manner.

Educational segregation was another common form of subordination. In 1860, California barred Asians, blacks, and Native Americans from attending the public schools. Twenty-five years later, after the law had been declared unconstitutional, segregated schools were established in California. San Francisco set up "Oriental schools" for Chinese students and other Asian students. A federal court upheld the constitutionality of the segregated schools in 1903.[43] Two decades later, the United States Supreme Court ruled in *Gong Lum v. Rice* that the placement of a Chinese student into a segregated school in Mississippi designed for the "colored races" did not violate the federal Constitution.[44] *Gong Lum* was not overruled until the Supreme Court's decision in *Brown v. Board of Education* in 1954.[45]

The right of Asian immigrants to own property was abridged through "alien land laws." California's Alien Land Law of 1913 targeted Japanese immigrant farmers by prohibiting persons ineligible for citizenship from purchasing land in the state and by limiting lease terms to three years or less. The law was expanded in 1920 to prevent U.S.-born children from gaining title to land and having their parents act as guardians. Both California's law and Washington State's Anti-Alien Land Act were challenged in the early 1920s.[46] The United States Supreme Court ruled in favor of the states, holding that the equal protection clause was not violated in either case. The Court in *Terrace v. Thompson* made clear that Asian immigrants did not enjoy the same rights as citizens: "It is obvious that one who is not a citizen and cannot become one lacks an interest in, and the power to effectually work for the welfare of, the state, and, so lacking, the state may rightfully deny him the right to own and lease real estate within its boundaries."[47] It was not until twenty-five years later that the Supreme Court struck down California's Alien Land Law as unconstitutional.[48]

State laws even interfered with the basic family relationships of Asian Americans. In 1880, California enacted an anti-miscegenation law that prohibited marriages between whites and "Negroes, mulattoes, or Mongolians." The law was extended by the state legislature over fifty years later to include Filipinos, who had been ruled by a California appeals court to be members of the "Malay race."[49] The effects of the anti-miscegenation laws included not only direct interference with personal relationships but the slow destruction of Asian American populations. Because male laborers formed most of the population within the Chinese and Filipino communities, anti-miscegenation laws combined with restrictive immigration laws to limit marriage and births. Anti-miscegenation laws against blacks and Asians were common in western states, and many laws remained on the books until the United States Supreme Court ruled them to be unconstitutional in 1967.[50]

World War II Internment of Japanese Americans

Perhaps the most notorious form of discrimination against an Asian American community during the twentieth century was the relocation and internment of Japanese Americans during World War II. After the bombing of Pearl Harbor plunged the United States into war, antagonisms against Japan blurred with already heated animosity against Japanese Americans. Immediate calls for the removal of Japanese Americans from the West Coast resounded among labor, business, state and local politicians, and the military. Unlike the Japanese Americans in Hawaii, who constituted one-third of Hawaii's population, Japanese Americans on the West Coast formed less than 1 percent of the population and lacked any significant political power to oppose the calls for relocation.

Government intelligence reports of the time indicated that exclusion would be unnecessary, because the vast majority of Japanese Americans were loyal to the United States and did not pose a threat to national security. Nevertheless, on February 19, 1942, President Roosevelt issued Executive Order 9066, which authorized the secretary of war and his commanders to create military areas from which all persons could be excluded in the interest of national defense. Although also applicable to Germans and Italians, the order was targeted against Japanese Americans on the West Coast. A few weeks later, Lt. General John L. DeWitt, the western defense commander, instituted plans to evacuate all persons of Japanese descent from an area bordering the Pacific Ocean. Given only a few days to relocate, Japanese Americans quickly sold or abandoned their homes, and were allowed to carry only a few personal possessions with them. Although the original plan was to relocate communities to other parts of the country, the government interned Japanese Americans in guarded camps in the interior of the United States. Over 110,000 Japanese Americans, the majority of whom were United States citizens, were placed into thirteen isolated concentration camps for the remainder of the war. General DeWitt's oft-cited remark—"a Jap is a Jap"—encapsulated the popular sentiment blurring any distinctions between loyal Americans of Japanese ancestry and wartime adversaries of the Japanese empire.[51]

The internment did not go unchallenged. Four Japanese Americans contested the government's military orders and appealed their cases to the United States Supreme Court: Minoru Yasui, Gordon Hirabayashi, and Fred Korematsu had each been arrested and jailed for violations of different military orders, and challenged their convictions as constitutional violations of due process and equal protection; Mitsuye Endo, who had been held in an assembly center and interned in both California and Utah, filed a writ of habeas corpus arguing that her detention by the federal government was illegal. In June 1943, in *Hirabayashi v. United States,*[52] a unanimous Supreme Court upheld the constitutionality of a governmental curfew order. Relying on the government's argument that Japanese Americans had a "continued attachment" to Japan,[53] the Court held that government possessed extraordinary powers during time of war and could issue an emergency order such as a curfew if necessary to protect the national interest. Noting that Hirabayashi's conviction involved a classification based on race, the Court nevertheless held that military necessity justified the classification. Deciding *Yasui v. United States* on the same day, the Supreme Court employed similar reasoning and reversed a lower court's finding that the curfew order was unconstitutional as applied to United States citizens.[54]

In 1944, in *Korematsu v. United States,*[55] the Supreme Court, in a six-to-three decision, upheld the constitutionality of the military's exclusion order. The Court wrote that "all legal restrictions which curtail the civil rights of a single racial group are immediately suspect" and that "courts must subject them to the most rigid scrutiny."[56] However, the Court also stated: "That is not to say that all such restrictions are unconstitutional. . . . Pressing public necessity must sometimes justify the existence of such restrictions; racial antagonism never can."[57] Despite the important language on the judiciary's strict scrutiny of racial classifications, the Court went on to hold that the exclusion of Japanese Americans from the West Coast was justified by military necessity. The Court yielded to the government's determination that the threat of espionage and sabotage by some was sufficient to justify the exclusion of all Japanese Americans. Discounting the centrality of race, the majority opinion concluded that Korematsu was not excluded because of racial hostility but because the United States was at war with Japan.

Decided on the same day as *Korematsu, Ex Parte Endo* was a victory for Mitsuye Endo but did little to change the legality of the exclusion orders.[58] The Supreme Court skirted the issue of whether the internment was unconstitutional and limited its decision to the issue of whether Endo's detention was valid. The Court held that the government could not continue to detain concededly loyal American citizens. Finding no question of her loyalty to the United States, the Court ordered Endo's release. But, as Justice Frank Murphy noted in a concurring opinion, while Endo was allowed to leave the camps, she was still subject to military orders excluding her from the West Coast. With the war coming to a close, the exclusion orders were soon rescinded by the military, and Japanese Americans were allowed to return to the West Coast.

Four decades later, newly discovered documents showing that the federal government had altered a key government report and had suppressed evidence of Japanese American loyalty in the wartime trials and appeals were used to vacate the original convictions of Gordon Hirabayashi and Fred Korematsu.[59] In both cases, the courts found that the government had committed prosecutorial misconduct. Min Yasui's conviction was also vacated by a federal district court, but without a finding of government misconduct; he passed away during the course of the appeal. Despite the decisions to vacate the original convictions, the United States Supreme Court opinions remain valid as legal precedents. It took the enactment of the Civil Liberties Act of 1988, which issued a formal apology for the internment and granted redress payments to internees, to close the chapter on one of the most ignoble episodes in American legal history.[60]

Post–World War II Racial Reforms

Despite the federal government's discriminatory treatment of Japanese Americans, World War II helped bring in an era of gradual racial reform in the United States. The fight for democracy abroad had a powerful impact on attitudes toward race during the 1940s and 1950s.[61] Although far from ideal,

racial attitudes had begun progressing to a point where formal racial segregation, enforced by government, began losing its ideological power. The same
era that saw the improved treatment of African Americans and new calls for
desegregation also brought support for nondiscrimination against Asian Americans in the law.

The federal courts were among the first institutions to begin chipping away
at state laws discriminating against Asian Americans. In 1948, in *Oyama v.
California*,[62] the United States Supreme Court held that California's Alien
Land Act was unconstitutional. As a child, Fred Oyama had been granted title
to land in California that his father Kajiro was unable to own because of the
state's alien land law. During World War II, while the Oyama family had been
interned, the state government attempted to seize the land because it had been
sold in violation of the Alien Land Act. In a six-to-three decision, the United
States Supreme Court struck down the act as unconstitutional because it violated the rights of Fred Oyama, an American citizen, under the equal protection clause. The Court stated that "the rights of a citizen may not be
subordinated merely because of his father's country of origin."[63] The Court
avoided, though, the issue of whether Kajiro Oyama's rights had been violated as a noncitizen, which would have required the Court to overrule its
earlier decisions upholding the alien land laws.

In 1948, in *Takahashi v. Fish and Game Commission*,[64] the United States
Supreme Court struck down a California statute that prohibited aliens ineligible for citizenship from fishing in the ocean waters off the California coast.
In 1943, the state legislature had amended the California fish and game code
to prohibit Japanese immigrants from obtaining commercial fishing licenses.
In 1945, the legislature amended the law again to include all aliens ineligible
for citizenship. Torao Takahashi had held a fishing license from 1915 to 1942,
before he was interned, and had been denied a license under the amended
law. The Supreme Court invalidated the law as an improper classification based
on alienage. The Court held that the equal protection clause was violated because the state's interest in protecting its "proprietary interest in fish" was insufficient and that the state, unlike the federal government, had only limited
power to make a classification based on alienage.

During the late 1940s and 1950s, legislatures and courts began a slow reversal of the earlier laws that discriminated against Asians. The Oregon Supreme
Court declared the state's alien land law to be unconstitutional in 1949;[65] the
California Supreme Court followed in 1952;[66] the Washington legislature repealed the state's alien land law in 1967.[67] Laws discriminating against all racial minorities, including Asian Americans, were held to be unconstitutional
violations of the equal protection clause. In 1948, in *Perez v. Sharp*,[68] the

California Supreme Court struck down the state's anti-miscegenation law as unconstitutional. The United States Supreme Court also held in 1948 that racially restrictive housing covenants, which had been commonly used to prevent Asian Americans from owning homes, were unconstitutional and could not be enforced by the courts.[69] And the Supreme Court's landmark decision in *Brown v. Board of Education* in 1954 prohibited public school segregation and led to the dismantling of "separate but equal" schools for Asian Americans.

The federal government's reversal of discriminatory immigration and naturalization laws began in the 1940s and culminated with the passage of the Immigration Act of 1965. The Chinese exclusion laws were repealed in 1943, and Chinese immigrants were also allowed to become naturalized citizens. Asian Indian and Filipino immigrants gained the right to naturalize in 1946. Through the advocacy of organizations such as the Japanese American Citizens League, the 1952 McCarran-Walter Act removed the racial bar to naturalization. With the passage of the Immigration Act of 1965, formal barriers based on race and national origin were removed from the immigration laws.

The Immigration Act of 1965 abolished the Asia-Pacific triangle put into place by the 1952 McCarran-Walter Act and removed the discriminatory national origin quotas dating back to the Immigration Act of 1924, which limited visas for most Asian countries to one hundred per year.[70] The 1965 act set an allocation of twenty thousand visas for every country not in the Western Hemisphere, and established a preference system based on reuniting families and meeting the needs of the American economy through the entry of professional and skilled workers.

Anti-Immigrant Discrimination after 1965

Along with the civil rights legislation of the 1960s, the Immigration Act of 1965 marked a shift in the federal government's commitment to formal racial equality. Asian Americans have benefited directly from governmental prohibitions on discrimination in employment, education, housing, public accommodations, business, and immigration. In 1974, for example, the United States Supreme Court ruled in *Lau v. Nichols* that the San Francisco Unified School District violated Title VI of the Civil Rights of 1964 when the district discriminated against limited-English-speaking Chinese students by failing to provide equal educational opportunities through either bilingual or supplemental English instruction.[71]

Governmental subordination of Asian Americans did not magically disappear with the passage of civil rights laws and nondiscriminatory immigration laws. Using 1965 as a watershed year, the history of legal discrimination against Asian Americans can be divided into two distinct eras: a pre-1965 era of explicit discrimination based on race, and a post-1965 era of implicit discrimination based on citizenship and immigration status.

POST–1965 ASIAN IMMIGRATION

The shift toward anti-immigrant laws is in part a reaction to the dramatic changes in the Asian American population that have arisen since 1965. In 1965, Asian Americans numbered approximately 1.4 million, constituting less than 1 percent of the nation's population.[72] The majority of Asian Americans had been born in the United States. When Congress passed the Immigration Act of 1965, few people at the time expected immigration from Asia and the Pacific to form a significant proportion of the new immigration flow to the United States. Testifying before Congress, Attorney General Robert Kennedy estimated that no more than five thousand immigrants from Asia and the Pacific would enter in the first year, and that there would be no significant increases in later years.[73]

The estimates proved to be wrong, and immigration from Asia and the Pacific has grown from 7 percent of all legal immigrants in 1965 to about 40 percent during the 1980s and 1990s. Include with those immigrants who entered under the 1965 act the large number of Southeast Asian refugees who came to the United States following the Vietnam War, and the result is the extraordinary population growth in Asian American communities that we have witnessed over the past three decades.

The Immigration Act of 1965 created two vehicles for immigration to the United States, both of which spurred large numbers of Asian immigrants. Employment-based preference categories led to the entry of many immigrant professionals and technicians, particularly in the health care fields and the sciences. Family reunification led to the entry of large numbers of "immediate relatives"—parents, spouses, and unmarried minor children of United States citizens—who could enter in unlimited numbers. In addition, the family-based preference system authorized the limited entry of selected categories of relatives: spouses and unmarried children of lawful permanent residents; the adult children of citizens; and the brothers and sisters of citizens. The immediate family members of adult children and siblings could also enter as "derivative" beneficiaries. Once immigrant communities developed in the United States, they provided a base for the sponsorship of more immigrants: immigrants who became permanent residents and naturalized citizens could bring in additional family members through the preference system.

Although immigration from all of Asia and the Pacific has increased since

1965, the largest numbers of employment-based and family-based immigrants have come from the Philippines, China, South Korea, and India.[74] Asian immigrants entering through the employment system are usually highly educated and often enter with significant financial resources. Family immigrants are more diverse, having a wider range of education and skill levels because their status is based solely on family relationships. English language ability also varies significantly, with immigrants from India and the Philippines usually possessing greater fluency because English is a language of instruction in those countries.

Since the mid-1970s, humanitarian admissions have been the major source of entry for Vietnamese, Cambodian, Laotian, and other refugees affected by the Vietnam War and the governments of Southeast Asia. The fall of Saigon in April 1975 led to a first wave of over 130,000 Southeast Asian refugees during eight months in 1975.[75] Another wave of 380,000 Southeast Asian refugees arrived in the United States between 1979 and 1981.[76] Additional Southeast Asian immigration has come through special legislation such as the 1987 Indochinese Refugee Resettlement and Protection Act, which allowed the entry of "Amerasian" children whose natural fathers were American servicemen during the Vietnam War.[77]

Undocumented migration, which is difficult to measure because of its inherently secretive nature, also accounts for a significant number of Asian immigrants. Some undocumented Asians enter surreptitiously, through border crossings or port entries. The smuggling of Chinese immigrants, which gained national attention in 1993 with the sinking of the ship the *Golden Venture* near New York City, is one example. However, the vast majority of the Asian undocumented population fall out of legal status by overstaying on temporary visas or by violating the terms of a "nonimmigrant" visa, such as a student visa, by working without authorization. Precluded from lawful employment by the Immigration Reform and Control Act of 1986, undocumented immigrants form the work force for many underground economies that rely on exploitable labor, including agriculture, garment manufacturing, restaurant work, and domestic services.[78]

SHIFTING DEMOGRAPHICS

Taken together, these sources of immigration have led to most of the population growth of the Asian American population since 1965. The number of Asians who entered the United States through legal immigration was 1.6 million during the 1970s and 2.7 million during the 1980s.[79] According to Census Bureau estimates, 86 percent of the Asian and Pacific Islander population growth during the 1990s is due to immigration, leading to projections that the Asian American population will number over 12 million by the year 2000.

If immigration patterns continue, projections for the year 2050 put Asian Americans at close to 10 percent of the national population.[80]

Once predominantly U.S.-born, the Asian American population is now largely immigrant. Nearly two out of every three Asian Americans are foreign-born, and approximately 40 percent of the population are not United States citizens. The growth of the Asian American population has also contributed, along with the growing population of Latinos, to significant shifts in urban demographics. The expansion of new immigrant populations and the long-standing migration of whites from urban cores to smaller cities and suburbs has transformed the racial character of the nation's cities.[81] Most of America's largest cities—including New York, Los Angeles, and Chicago—are now "majority-minority," and many urban areas have concentrations of Asian Americans, Latinos, and African Americans living and working in the same neighborhoods.

Anti-Immigrant Legislation in the 1980s and 1990s

Anti-immigrant legislation enacted during the 1980s and 1990s has been in response to the large number of immigrants entering the United States from Asia and Latin America. The Immigration Act of 1965 removed explicit racial and national origin categories from the laws, but recent legislation has either created programs that have resulted in discrimination against Asian Americans or produced changes in the law that have adversely affected large numbers of Asian immigrants.

In 1986, Congress passed the Immigration Reform and Control Act (IRCA) to address undocumented migration to the United States.[82] The law created an amnesty program to legalize undocumented immigrants who had lived in the United States since before 1982 or who had worked in agriculture for a minimal period. The law also established a system of employment verification and employer sanctions to limit the primary incentive for undocumented migration—jobs. All employers, both private and public, are required to verify the immigration status of newly hired employees, including United States citizens. Failure to verify an employee's status, or to knowingly hire an employee who lacks the authorization to work, subjects an employer to penalties.

Because of employer sanctions, discrimination against Asian Americans and Latinos increased significantly after IRCA went into effect. A report by the federal government's General Accounting Office issued in 1990 found a widespread pattern of discrimination against Asian Americans and Latinos—

including American citizens.[83] Nearly one of five employers surveyed by the GAO admitted that they discriminated on the basis of national origin or citizenship. Despite the GAO report and the recommendation of a federal task force, Congress chose not to repeal employer sanctions.

In the Immigration Act of 1990,[84] Congress made significant changes to the immigration laws dealing with legal immigration. The 1990 act set an overall cap on legal immigration into the United States, retained the basic family reunification system set out in the 1965 act, and expanded the number of employment-based visa categories for highly educated and skilled immigrants. With Asian and Latin American immigration having dominated legal immigration since the 1970s, the law also established a visa lottery system for residents of countries that had not significantly used the family and employment preference systems. But the lottery system has racial and ethnic biases built into it: the beneficiaries of the lottery system are potential immigrants from Europe and Africa; excluded from the lottery are Asian countries such as China, India, South Korea, and the Philippines, and Central American countries such as Mexico and El Salvador.

In 1994, the voters of California passed Proposition 187, a ballot initiative designed to address immigration by denying basic rights and government services to undocumented immigrants.[85] Under Proposition 187, undocumented immigrants are denied access to public school education, to nonemergency health care from state and local government providers, and to government social services. In addition, all individuals—both citizens and noncitizens—are required under the law to prove lawful immigration status in order to obtain a public school education, health care, or social services.

Although enjoined by the courts soon after passage,[86] Proposition 187 had immediate effects on immigrants throughout the state; many immigrants removed their children from schools and avoided seeking health and social services. A number of immigrants died soon after the passage of Proposition 187 because they avoided medical services in fear of the law.[87] Studies on hate violence in Los Angeles and other parts of California also showed a linkage between anti-Latino and anti-Asian violence and the passage of Proposition 187.[88] Anti-immigrant sentiment expanded nationally after the passage of Proposition 187 in California. Similar ballot initiatives were unable to qualify for the ballots of other states, but efforts in Congress led to the passage of measures further limiting the rights of immigrants—both the undocumented and lawful permanent residents.

In 1996, Congress passed the Personal Responsibility and Work Opportunity Reconciliation Act,[89] a comprehensive legislative package intended to overhaul the nation's welfare system. Designed to shift the burden of welfare financing and administration from the federal government to the states, the welfare reform legislation also contains provisions that discriminate against lawful permanent residents living in the United States by removing their eligibility for public entitlements, including Food Stamps and Supplemental Security Income for the elderly, blind, and disabled. The law also gives state governments the option of denying additional benefits, including Medicaid and Temporary Assistance for Needy Families. Although federal legislation enacted the following year would restore benefits to some permanent residents, the impact of the law on low-income Asian immigrants has been enormous, affecting the subsistence income of thousands of poor immigrants throughout the country.[90] Reminiscent of the anti-Asian laws that subordinated "aliens ineligible to citizenship," the welfare reform legislation is race-neutral on its face, but its impact has fallen most heavily on the Asian American and Latino immigrant communities.

Congress's passage of the Illegal Immigration Reform and Immigrant Responsibility Act of 1996 soon after enactment of the welfare reform package marked another severe diminution of the rights of Asian immigrants.[91] While the focus of the immigration reform law is on increasing border patrol resources to address undocumented migration, its scope extends to curtailing the rights of undocumented immigrants to receive federal grants, contracts, loans, or entitlements; limiting the due process rights of applicants for political asylum; and increasing enforcement of the immigration laws by local law enforcement. Although formal restrictions on legal immigration were removed from the final version of the legislation, the immigration reform law sets up economic barriers to family immigration by establishing minimum income requirements for sponsors of legal immigrants. Like the welfare reform legislation, the immigration reform legislation's most adverse effects fall primarily on Asian and Latino immigrants.

Lessons of Legal History

In closing this legal history of Asian Americans, I emphasize two points. First, while the history of Asian Americans is often ignored in general discussions of race, Asian Americans have in fact played an important role in the shaping of civil rights laws in the United States. Despite the setbacks and adversity brought on by federal, state, and local laws, Asian Americans did not allow the laws to go uncontested. Many of these challenges succeeded in affecting legislation and the decisional law of the courts. For example, challenges to the discriminatory laws against Chinese immigrants during the mid-nineteenth century on the West Coast were integral to the passage of Reconstruction-era federal civil rights legislation.[92]

Successful court decisions such as *Yick Wo v. Hopkins*, which established the rights of noncitizens to challenge laws under the equal protection clause, and *United States v. Wong Kim Ark*, which established birthright citizenship under the Fourteenth Amendment, are landmarks in U.S. legal history. Even the infamous case of *Korematsu v. United States*, which upheld the exclusion of Japanese Americans from the West Coast during World War II, established legal standards that were used to strike down laws mandating racial segregation. The passage of legislation such as the Civil Liberties Act of 1988, which granted redress payments to Japanese Americans, demonstrates that Asian Americans today are able to wield significant political influence in the area of civil rights.

Second, the patterns of discrimination that began in the nineteenth century with the first waves of immigrant laborers to the United States have been recurring themes in the statutes and court cases of the twentieth century. It is not a coincidence that the most virulent anti-Asian sentiment has occurred during economic recessions and depressions, when racial scapegoating typically peaks. But even during economic upturns, Asian Americans were consistently treated as foreigners, even, as in the case of the Japanese American internment, when they were United States citizens. Anti-Asian discrimination was explicit during the nineteenth century and for most of the twentieth century; race and nativism have been linked in the subordination of Asian Americans throughout the history of the United States.

Even after the 1960s, with the passage of expansive legislation prohibiting racial discrimination, anti-immigrant sentiment and anti-immigrant legislation have appeared, becoming even more prominent in the 1990s. During this decade, we have witnessed nativist scapegoating that rivals the explicitly racist rhetoric of the late nineteenth and early twentieth centuries. The fact that many of the anti-Asian court decisions from that earlier period—including *The Chinese Exclusion Case* and *Korematsu*—continue to be cited as valid legal precedents demonstrates that Asian Americans must be continually vigilant about abridgments of their rights.[93]

Chapter 2

Discrimination and Antidiscrimination Law

"What are you?" A broad question, but one that I occasionally encounter when meeting someone for the first time. The inquiry is about ethnicity and race, and my usual answer is "Filipino," which typically provokes an assenting nod or a look of mild surprise and an "Oh, really." In response I sometimes ask, "What did you think I was?" The reply varies, depending on where I am and who the person is. When someone knows that I have worked with Asian American community organizations, the response has been "Well, some kind of Asian, but I wasn't exactly sure." When I was the director of an immigrant rights office in Los Angeles that works primarily with Latinos, the response was often, "I thought you were Latino, maybe with some Indian or Asian blood in you." My name can perplex some people, who think that I might be Italian until they see me in person. The most interesting response actually comes from Filipino immigrants, who, noting my height and the high bridge of my nose, often say "You don't look like a Filipino."

A frequent variation of "What are you?" is "Where are you from?" My response, which is often a test of the questioner's meaning, is "Well, I'm originally from San Francisco." A common reply is: "No. I mean where are you *from*? What country?" I provide my stock answers—"I'm Filipino, but I grew up here in the United States," "My parents are immigrants," and so on. I begin awaiting the inevitable remark, intended as a compliment, commenting on my mastery of English: "You speak English very well. No trace of an accent." At this point, I usually move on to another topic, or I begin a discussion on the meaning of being Asian American and try to be optimistic about educating someone who may not know any better. In any case, the dialogue is a reminder that racism comes in many forms, including being complimented on how "American" you are, despite looking like you are not.

How and why does racial discrimination manifest itself against Asian Americans? How should the legal system respond to this discrimination? To answer these basic questions, this chapter discusses both social and legal theories of racial discrimination. The chapter is divided into two parts: the first part covers social theories of discrimination; the second part provides an overview of the antidiscrimination laws, which serves as the entry point for my discussion of the laws affecting Asian Americans.

Biology and Race

To the extent that race is based on physical appearance and physical differences, biology is implicated. Biology is not irrelevant to social classifications. In health policy, for example, biological definitions of race have been linked to predispositions to particular diseases such as sickle-cell anemia in blacks or thalassemia, another disease of the blood, in Asians.[1] As the basis for social relations, however, biological theories of race have fallen into disrepute. Racial classifications based on biological difference are highly inexact because human variability falls along a continuum. Racial categories are biologically underinclusive and overinclusive: genetic characteristics found within any one race can be found among members of another race, and genetic variations within one race exceed the genetic commonalities within the same race. Biological theories of race have been rooted in social Darwinism, eugenics, and other claims of racial superiority, usually reflecting the race of the theorists themselves.

Nevertheless, biological theories of race remain central to an understanding of racial subordination in the United States. The history of subordination against African Americans is replete with references to biologically based definitions of white and black and categories in-between, including "Mulatto" (one-half black), "Quadroon" (one-quarter black), and "Octoroon" (one-eighth black), to describe "mixed-blood" types. The "one drop of blood" rule in many states defined who was not white; having any black ancestor meant classification as black. Asian Americans fell into an array of biological/legal classifications as well, including Mongolian, Malay, and others. In most cases, to be anything but white meant being denied full rights under the law.[2]

Many of the legacies of biological race theory remain a part of the popular and legal vocabulary on race. In the United States Supreme Court's 1987 opinion in *Saint Francis College v. Al-Khazraji*, in which the Court upheld the applicability of federal civil rights legislation to Arab Americans, the Court rejected fixed definitions of race but observed the prevalence of biological racial theories: "There is a common popular understanding that there are three major human races—Caucasoid, Negroid, and Mongoloid."[3] The tripartite system still defines most contemporary racial classification systems. Under the federal government's statistical classification system, race encompasses three major categories, plus a Native American category: (1) white, (2) black, (3) Asian or Pacific Islander, and (4) American Indian, Eskimo, or Aleut.[4]

Biological theorizing is far from dead, however, as demonstrated by Charles Murray and Richard Herrnstein's controversial best-seller *The Bell Curve*, which suggests that differential IQ scores should dictate social ordering among racial groups. Asian Americans play a peculiar role—consistent with the "model minority" image—by being labeled the most cognitively skilled group, placed above whites at the high end of the intellectual bell curve, as opposed to blacks and Latinos, who place at the low end. *The Bell Curve* has been dismissed as both inadequate science and unsound policy by social scientists and policy makers, but it reflects the influence of biology on contemporary debates on race and immigration. Biological race theories still have an effect on public policy making, as shown by the prominence of groups such as the Federation for American Immigration Reform, which has received extensive funding from the Pioneer Fund, an organization committed to the promotion of eugenics research.[5]

Racial Formation

Once biology is dismissed as a fixed determinant of race, the social and political nature of race becomes clear. Race is socially constructed. There are many theories dealing with race and discrimination, ranging from Freudian psychoanalysis to behavioral psychology to Marxist and neo-Marxist theories of political economy to postmodernist cultural studies. To assess the strengths and weaknesses of the law in addressing racial subordination, I use as my starting point the theory of "racial formation" developed by Michael Omi and Howard Winant.[6]

Omi and Winant define racial formation as "the sociohistorical process by which racial categories are created, inhabited, transformed, and destroyed."[7] They pose race as a complex of social meanings that is constantly transformed by political struggles. Racial formation theory suggests that racial attitudes and racial subordination have shifted over time in response to social and political discord. Racial conflict, in essence, transforms the meaning of race.

Racial formation provides a useful framework to describe both the historical treatment of Asian Americans and the evolution of contemporary legal discourse on race. For most of the nation's history, Asians, like other racial minority groups, lacked any significant power and were subjugated based on race. The absence of political power, arising from their relatively small numbers and the formal prohibitions on citizenship, precluded any meaningful racial transformations by Asian Americans or by the government. The gains and accomplishments of blacks, particularly through the civil rights movement, shifted more political power to all racial minorities, including Asian Americans, and led to societal transformations that affected racial attitudes and the law.

A key concept of racial formation theory is *racialization*, which Omi and Winant define as the extension of racial meaning to a relationship, social practice, or group. The racialization of Asian Americans has taken on two primary forms: racialization as non-Americans and racialization as the model minority. The racialization of Asian Americans as foreign-born outsiders—what I label "outsider racialization"—has been a pervasive theme in Asian American history, reflected in the laws of immigration and naturalization and in the internment of Japanese Americans during World War II.

Model minority racialization is a more recent phenomenon. Since the 1960s, Asian Americans have been portrayed as the model minority because of their accomplishments in education and their higher income levels relative to blacks and Latinos, and even relative to whites; the stereotype persists even though Asian Americans still face racial discrimination and many Asian Americans are mired in poverty.

Both forms of racialization have led to the racial subordination of Asian Americans; the model minority stereotype is especially harmful because it subordinates other racial minorities as well through the imposition of illusory "cultural" values that are, by comparison, considered inferior to Asian American values. (I explore outsider racialization more thoroughly in chapters 3 and 4 and the model minority myth in chapter 7.)

Racial formation theory proposes that race is pervasive. Race permeates cognition, attitudes, interactions, economic relations, art, literature, science, politics, and law. Racial subordination is therefore universal—it can occur between two people engaged in a conversation, it can occur in violent behavior between groups and by the government, and it can occur in just about everything in-between. All of us carry some racial baggage based on our experiences, our social interactions, and our exposure to the value systems and ideologies of the society in which we live. How we behave racially may be conscious and explicit, but often it is unconscious and done with the best of intentions.

Unconscious Racism

Charles Lawrence suggests that racism pervades society because it operates primarily on an unconscious level:

> Americans share a common historical and cultural heritage in which racism has played and still plays a dominant role. Because of this shared experience, we also inevitably share many ideas, attitudes, and beliefs that attach significance to an individual's race and induce negative feelings and opinions about nonwhites. To the extent that this cultural belief system has influenced all of us, we are all racists. At the same time, most of us are unaware of our racism. We do not recognize the ways in which our cultural experience has influenced our beliefs about race or the occasions on which those beliefs affect our actions. In other words, a large part of the behavior that produces racial discrimination is influenced by unconscious racial motivation.[8]

Theories of cognitive psychology support the view that racial differentiation begins on an unconscious level.[9] According to cognitive theory, categorizing and stereotyping are normal processes through which people perceive the world and make sense of it. The vast amount of sensory information that individuals must process requires them to simplify complex data and to shape them into something manageable. Stereotyping around race operates much in the same way that stereotyping about any other category operates: individuals have a set of criteria—"schema" is one commonly used term—that they use to understand the world, and they make judgments based on a combination of those criteria and of perceived information.

If a person categorizes another person as Asian because of physical features, they attach certain characteristics to the person. They may attribute a trait such as being foreign-born to the person, because the perceiver's schema categorizes Asians as foreigners. The attribution may be based on previous experience with foreign Asians or on information (perhaps misinformation) gained through some other source, such as parents, school education, or the mass media. Stereotyping, reinforced by experience and learning, might include categorizing all Asians as hardworking and industrious, but unassertive; categorizing Asian men in particular as devious or emasculate; or categorizing Asian women in particular as passive or exotic.

Cognitive theory explains some of the personal examples I described at the beginning of this chapter. On seeing me, another person classifies me by placing me within an established cognitive category, usually "Asian." The person's cognitive schema may link limited English ability, foreignness, or some combination of characteristics with the category "Asian." In other words, the person stereotypes me. The category's limits may be due to any number of factors: a person's only knowing Asians with foreign accents, for example, or only gaining information through a secondhand source such as television, which may provide limited exposure to native-born Asian Americans. And depending on how detailed and accurate the schema, my response (that I am Filipino) or the nature of my response (speaking English with an American accent) may reinforce or be inconsistent with the person's categorization of Asians. In the latter case, the resulting dissonance could lead to expanding the category, or could be ignored as atypical and aberrational.

Cognitive theory posits that categorizing and stereotyping are normal mental processes. This does not mean, however, that all stereotyping is good; much of it actually leads to very destructive behavior. What it does mean is that many forms of discrimination are rooted in unconscious processes. People often categorize, either correctly or incorrectly, without being aware they are doing so. This implies that many causes of discrimination begin without the knowledge or intent of the actor. Since discrimination frequently begins at an unconscious level, racial intent should not always have to be proved to show that racial subordination has occurred.

Prejudice and Aggression

Acts of discrimination can also stem from conscious prejudices that target particular groups or individuals. Milton Kleg suggests that forms of discriminatory aggression fall along a continuum consisting of the following: avoidance, defamation, acts against property, assault, and murder.[10] Avoidance is the most common form of aggression, and can include walking away or not speaking to another person who falls within the group to be avoided, or choosing to live in a neighborhood with few or no residents falling within the group to be avoided. Avoidance can also consist of acts of discrimination, such as not hiring or promoting an individual because of membership in a group.

Defamation involves denigrating a group by oral or written communication, which can range from racial and ethnic jokes to overt labeling and name-calling. A common form of anti-Asian defamation is the use of an accent to mock Asian Americans. For example, during the O.J. Simpson murder trial, United States Senator Alphonse D'Amato employed a derisive Japanese accent on national radio to criticize Judge Lance Ito, a third-generation Japanese American who speaks with a clear American accent.[11]

More destructive acts of aggression, such as property damage, verbal and physical assaults, and killing, while occurring far less frequently than avoidance and defamation, are still commonplace in American society. A prejudice based on the belief that Asian immigrants are taking jobs away from native-born workers could cause an unemployed worker to become angry and resentful, which in turn could lead to aggressive and violent behavior against an Asian American. A related form of aggression is "move-in" violence based on perceptions of the invasion of turf, which can take the form of property damage, threats, or physical violence against Asian Americans who move into areas and neighborhoods that are predominantly non-Asian.

Another typical anti-Asian prejudice is the belief that Asian Americans are foreigners who do not deserve the same rights and privileges as "real" Americans. One example comes from an everyday exchange in 1991, when Japanese American girl scouts who were selling cookies at a Southern California shopping mall were curtly told by a passerby: "I only buy from American girls."[12] Once they are racialized as foreign-born outsiders, Asian Americans can be racially subordinated by any action that distinguishes between citizens and noncitizens, between Americans and foreigners.

Social and Economic Institutions

Mental processes such as stereotyping and developing prejudices are reproduced through social institutions. The reinforcement of anti-Asian stereotypes in the mass media is one example. Asian Americans generally suffer from media invisibility, but when they are portrayed in television and film at all, negative stereotypes abound: organized criminals, gang members, or inscrutable and mysterious "Orientals." Positive and balanced images of Asian Americans have increased over time, but they remain the exception rather than the rule.

Variations in racial subordination are also tied to differences in economic class among Asian American populations. Asian America includes both wealthy entrepreneurs and impoverished refugees, and everything in between. That Asian Americans are found among a variety of economic classes means differential forms of discrimination are applied against them; compare, for example, encountering a "glass ceiling" in being denied a promotion to upper-level management with encountering racial avoidance in being denied access to low-income rental housing. Class also reflects differential abilities to respond to racial discrimination, including gaining access to the legal system. "Differential racialization," as Michael Omi calls it, is a distinct process by which race is made more complex by differences in economic class.[13]

Law and Social Theory

How does the law fit into the matrix of race relations? As part of the historical process of racial formation, the law has played a central role in both upholding and reinforcing racial subordination. In matters of race, law and the
legal system have reflected stereotypes and prejudices that have subordinated
people of color. The "yellow peril" of the late nineteenth and early twentieth
centuries found expression in immigration laws that systematically denied entry
to Asian immigrants for decades. Stereotypes of racial unassimilability provided the basis for the Supreme Court's upholding congressional restrictions
on Asian immigration and denying Asian immigrants the right to become
naturalized citizens. Anti-Japanese prejudices led to alien land laws and the
exclusion and internment of Japanese Americans during World War II. Even
today, scapegoating and the possibility of having "too many Asians" have
brought on renewed calls for restrictionist immigration laws.

Laws are often expressions of societal values, but they are also expressions
of power—personal, institutional, and governmental. For most of the history
of the United States, racial minority groups have been denied political power,
and the expression of their values has been silenced or lost in the din of voices
possessing more power. Law has constructed racial categories, having defined
whiteness—and the power attached to being white—to the exclusion of other
groups, including Asian Americans. And law has either provided the mechanisms for governmental subordination or, in the case of nongovernmental action, purposefully placed outside its coverage most of the racial subordination
that occurs in everyday interactions among individuals and groups.

Yet, there has been genuine progress during the last four decades in American race relations and the legal reforms that have been instituted to address
racial subordination. Societal attitudes toward race have shifted significantly
since the era of formal segregation and race-based immigration exclusions. The
enactment of federal antidiscrimination legislation during the 1960s reflected
the government's commitment to nonsegregation and formal racial equality.
The adoption of nondiscriminatory immigration laws in 1965 demonstrated
a determination to remove anti-Asian bias from the federal laws.

Discrimination and Law

VISIONS OF RACE

The civil rights laws represent the governmental response to racial and ethnic subordination. Federal, state, and local laws guarantee the equal protection of the laws and prohibit discrimination on the basis of race, color, national

origin, and other categories. Antidiscrimination laws reflect a moral consensus condemning formal racial inequality, but as products of both judicial decision making and legislative compromise, the laws also reflect competing visions about the role that race plays—and should play—in American society.

Neoconservatives have embraced a "color-blind" vision of race. Most color-blind perspectives support antidiscrimination laws, but they reject remedial measures that take race into account in apportioning resources such as government contracts or enrollment in higher education. The color-blind vision is reflected in recent Supreme Court decision making around affirmative action, in which conservative majorities of the Court have limited the use of race-conscious remedial schemes to the narrowest of circumstances. The color-blind vision is also reflected in legislation such as Proposition 209, the ballot initiative designed to eliminate governmental affirmative action programs in California.

Color-conscious visions, on the other hand, are rooted in principles that see race-consciousness as a necessary remedy to discrimination and as promoting the benefits of inclusion that accrue to institutions and to society in general from a diverse population. Strong antidiscrimination social policies are needed to help people overcome social and economic disadvantages that are consequences of both past and present discrimination. Race-consciousness is encapsulated in Justice Harry Blackmun's statement in his opinion in *Regents of the University of California v. Bakke*: "To get beyond racism, we must first take account of race."[14]

If political polls are an accurate indicator, the American public is deeply divided over these visions. Exit polls measuring the vote on California's Proposition 209 found strongly polarized voting among the electorate: Proposition 209 passed by a 54 percent to 46 percent margin overall, but white voters voted 63 percent to 37 percent in favor of the proposition, while it was opposed by a margin of 74 percent to 26 percent by African American voters, 76 percent to 24 percent by Latino voters, and 61 percent to 39 percent by Asian American voters.[15]

THE CONSERVATIVE NATURE OF LAW

Racial subordination comes in many forms, only some of which are addressed through the law. Because of its long history upholding racist institutions and policies, the law has been limited in its ability to remedy contemporary racial subordination. Many legal tenets reflect not only antidiscrimination law's doctrinal limits, but the ideological force with which antidiscrimination laws help maintain forms of racial subordination. Antidiscrimination laws actually address a minute portion of the subordination that occurs in the United States,

but they establish the underpinnings for a social reality in which racial subordination can be perceived as exceptional rather than ubiquitous and race-conscious
remedies such as affirmative action can be perceived to be detrimental rather
than beneficial to civil rights.

One example of the conservative nature of antidiscrimination law is the
focus on discriminatory intent in proving violations of the equal protection
clause or of many civil rights statutes.[16] Only under certain statutes and under very limited circumstances does the law recognize discrimination that has
an adverse effect, regardless of the actor's intent.[17] The reasoning behind requiring discriminatory intent is a "perpetrator-victim" paradigm that sees bad
motives—racial bias and prejudice—as the root evil of discrimination. But
there is no inherent reason to require intent in antidiscrimination laws; indeed, contemporary social science demonstrates that discrimination often occurs on an unconscious level. In other areas of law, reckless indifference or
negligence are sufficient to prove liability because legal principles recognize
the need to compensate victims of reckless or negligent acts. An action that
stigmatizes and subordinates someone because of race conveys the same social meaning and has the same impact, whether it is committed intentionally, indifferently, or even unconsciously.[18]

None of this should be surprising, though, because the legal system is an
inherently conservative social institution, reflecting deeply imbedded traditions that maintain relations of power between individuals and groups. The
era of racial reform in the United States has been relatively brief and tempered when measured against the country's much longer and tumultuous history of racial subjugation. Nevertheless, racial rights do matter, for as Kimberlé
Crenshaw notes, rights "have legitimated racial inequality, but they have also
been the means by which oppressed groups have secured both entry as formal
equals into the dominant order and also the survival of their movement in
the face of private and state repression."[19]

Legal Traditions and the Limits of Law

Law has served for most of the history of the United States as the symbolic
and coercive force behind segregation and formal inequality. More recent notions of formal equality—defined primarily as protection under the antidiscrimination laws and equal access to the legal system—set the boundaries of
racial justice. But as a practical matter, even basic access to the system is compromised by economic class differences and by language differences commonly
encountered by recent immigrants to the United States. Within the broader
network of laws, the civil rights laws are further bound by legal traditions that

shape the power of government to regulate behavior and punish actions that are deemed socially unacceptable. Four closely related legal traditions—liberalism, constitutionalism, judicial review, and federalism—are particularly relevant to understanding civil rights jurisprudence.[20]

LIBERALISM

Liberalism refers to the political and legal philosophy that emphasizes personal autonomy and freedom from governmental intrusion. Liberalism maintains that rights and powers find their source in individuals and that state authority is predicated on limited powers granted to government by the people. As a manifestation of political philosophy, legal liberalism limits the scope of law by preventing the government's regulation of most private activity. Legal liberalism finds expression in texts such as the Bill of Rights, which limits the powers of the federal government to intrude on many personal freedoms.[21]

By establishing a barrier between individual autonomy and government action, legal liberalism permits many forms of racial subordination to fall beyond the scope of government regulation. Thus it is outside the government's power to intrude into the private instruction and reinforcement of stereotypes and prejudices that may lead to discriminatory action that is ultimately illegal. Antidiscrimination laws provide no relief for many forms of racial avoidance; no legal remedy exists for everyday acts such as choosing not to talk to someone of another race. Nor do the laws address many forms of racial defamation; most name-calling is permitted by the law.

Liberalism also prevents significant government involvement in remedying economic subordination tied to race. Government regulation of the economy is extensive, but many forms of subordination still occur through economic inequality caused by unregulated or underregulated markets that exist outside the scope of government enforcement. Economic class discrimination also falls outside the scope of antidiscrimination laws dealing with race, national origin, and other protected categories.

Antidiscrimination laws reflect core values within society, but their power is circumscribed by liberal traditions that prevent state intrusion into many activities that may nevertheless be contrary to those values.

CONSTITUTIONALISM

Constitutionalism is an extension of liberal philosophy that limits governmental powers through a written constitution. Two examples of limits on governmental power can be found in the Fifth Amendment to the federal Constitution, which declares that no person can be deprived of life, liberty, or property without due process of law, and in the Fourteenth Amendment, which declares that no state government can deprive any person of life, liberty, or property without due process of law, or deny anyone within its jurisdiction the equal protection of the laws.[22]

Unlike many other national constitutions and international sources of law, the U.S. Constitution does not enumerate a broad array of fundamental rights. For example, there is no "right to education" specified in the text of the federal Constitution, and the Supreme Court has ruled that no fundamental right to education exists under its interpretation of rights implicit in the Constitution.[23] Other than the right to vote found in the Fifteenth Amendment, there is no right specified within the Constitution to be free from racial discrimination. Instead, racial rights fall within the meanings given to broadly written terms such as "due process" and "equal protection of the laws."

The federal Constitution acts primarily as a limitation on governmental action, and thus does not affect most forms of private activity.[24] Federal statutes, however, can reach many types of private behavior, as long as the power to enact the statute is rooted in some authority in the federal Constitution and does not violate any constitutional limit on governmental power.

The Constitution can also restrict the scope of antidiscrimination laws. For instance, the First Amendment to the Constitution prohibits government's abridging the freedom of speech and the freedom of assembly, which offer basic safeguards for individual liberties. The first amendment offers protection from government subordination that can come through restrictions on language usage, such as English-only legislation. But, the First Amendment also provides a shield for many forms of racial subordination that occur through racist speech and expression. In the 1992 case of *R.A.V. v. City of St. Paul*,[25] the Supreme Court struck down a hate crimes ordinance that prohibited racist activities such as cross burning, because those activities could constitute forms of expression protected under the First Amendment.[26]

JUDICIAL REVIEW AND STANDARDS OF REVIEW

The tradition of judicial review provides support for the courts' powers to strike down laws that are inconsistent with the Constitution. In the landmark case of *Marbury v. Madison*,[27] decided in 1803, the Supreme Court held (1) that the federal Constitution is the supreme law of the land and any statute repugnant to the Constitution is void, and (2) that the courts possess the ultimate authority to decide whether a law is repugnant to the Constitution.

A concept related to judicial review is "standard of review," which refers to the level of scrutiny that a court employs in reviewing a statute's constitutionality. In equal protection jurisprudence, the Supreme Court has employed a three-tiered system that looks at the importance of the government's interest and the nature of the law designed to further that interest. From most exacting to least exacting, the standards of review are (1) *strict scrutiny*, in which the court requires that a law be "narrowly tailored" to meet a "compelling" interest; (2) *intermediate scrutiny*, in which the court requires that a law be "substantially related" to an "important" interest; and (3) *rational-basis scrutiny*, in which the court requires only that a law be "rationally related" to a "legitimate" interest.[28]

The differences between "compelling," "important," and "legitimate" and between "narrowly tailored," "substantially related," and "rationally related" are not perfectly clear, but the distinctions are critical in predicting the outcome of a case. A standard of review that is strict in theory is usually fatal in fact,[29] and a standard of review that requires mere rationality almost always survives. There have been, however, notorious exceptions. In *Korematsu v. United States*, the case in which the Supreme Court first articulated a strict scrutiny standard, the Court upheld the constitutionality of race-based exclusion orders that targeted Japanese Americans during World War II.[30]

In general, the Supreme Court has placed "suspect classifications"—race, ancestry, national origin, and, in state legislation, alienage (noncitizenship)—under strict scrutiny.[31] Classifications based on gender and illegitimacy (discriminating against illegitimate children or their parents) are subject to intermediate scrutiny. Other classifications—including economic class, sexual orientation, and, in federal legislation, alienage—are subject to rational-basis scrutiny.

The ordering of classifications has no particular basis in the Constitution, however. John Hart Ely has suggested that classifications are justified by the need to protect "discrete and insular minorities" from discrimination arising through the political process.[32] Racial minority groups have historically been subordinated by legislation enacted by white majorities; courts have employed their powers of judicial review to strike down laws that violate the rights of minority groups. But relying on the judicial process as a balance to majoritarian legislation only goes so far, particularly when the courts are often more conservative than the other branches of government.

Instead, the protection of groups is more likely to reflect changing values regarding the meaning of racial equality. Like societal attitudes toward race in general, judicial attitudes toward equal protection have varied significantly over time. In 1896, when the Supreme Court upheld Jim Crow segregation under *Plessy v. Ferguson*, "separate but equal" forms of treatment provided a sufficient basis for the equal protection of the laws. In 1954, when the Court decided *Brown v. Board of Education*, racial segregation in education became a fundamental violation of equal protection principles.[33]

The Supreme Court's recent rulings on affirmative action reflect a retrenchment in the vision of racial equality, as well as the shifting membership of the Court itself. In 1995, a conservative Supreme Court majority ruled
in *Adarand Constructors, Inc. v. Peña* that federal affirmative action programs
must meet a strict scrutiny standard, overruling two Supreme Court decisions—
one decided just five years earlier—that had applied a lower standard of review to uphold affirmative action programs.[34]

FEDERALISM

Federalism provides the matrix for the broad system of federal, state, and
local laws that govern social behavior, including the prohibition of racial
discrimination. Under the system of federalism, states possess sovereign powers independent of the federal government. State constitutions operate on
the state level to grant separate powers to state executives, legislatures, and
judiciaries.

Federalism limits both federal and state powers. First, the federal government generally cannot intrude in matters that fall within the powers of state
sovereignty. For example, the federal courts cannot review state court interpretations of the meaning of *state* constitutions. (The federal courts do, however, have the power to strike down state laws that violate the *federal*
Constitution.) Second, state governments are preempted from enacting laws
that conflict or intrude into an area governed by federal laws. For example, a
state cannot enact its own immigration law, because of the overriding federal
interest in regulating immigration. The federal court that first halted the implementation of Proposition 187 in California relied primarily on the preemp-
tion principle to support its issuance of an injunction.[35]

The courts have also developed doctrines, based on federalism, that apply differential standards of review to classifications based on alienage
(noncitizenship). Most state classifications that discriminate against noncitizens are subject to the highest standard—strict scrutiny. However, federal classifications based on alienage are subject to the lowest standard—rational-basis
scrutiny. In effect, these different standards mean that the courts will strike
down most state laws discriminating between citizens and noncitizens but will
uphold federal laws committing the same type of discrimination. (I discuss the
inconsistency between race-based and citizenship-based classifications more
thoroughly in chapter 4)

VALUES AND THE CONSTITUTION

The ranking of classifications and standards of review under the equal protection clause implicates a set of basic moral questions regarding discrimina-

tion: If society is committed to remedying racial discrimination, why should classifications that assist racial minorities have to meet such a high standard? If we are committed to both racial and gender equality, why should gender discrimination be treated with less scrutiny than racial discrimination? If racial classifications are treated the same on the federal and state levels, why should the federal government be given more discretion to discriminate against noncitizens than the state governments? And given the stigmas and forms of subordination that attach to being a lesbian, gay man, or bisexual, why does discrimination based on sexual orientation not receive heightened judicial scrutiny?

Sources of Antidiscrimination Law

Subject to the various and often technical legal traditions that affect all laws, the system of antidiscrimination law encompasses an array of federal, state, and local laws, as well as a combination of governmental and private enforcement strategies. Many of the laws overlap: most state constitutions have equal protection sections that have been interpreted by the state courts similarly to the federal court's interpretation of the federal equal protection clause. Moreover, many state and local governments have their own antidiscrimination statutes and civil rights agencies that enforce the law. These multitiered sources of law can be divided into four basic categories: constitutions, statutes, executive regulations, and judicial opinions.

CONSTITUTIONAL LAW

Constitutional provisions limit governmental discrimination primarily through principles of equal protection and due process. The federal Constitution also contains specific provisions outlawing slavery, found in the Thirteenth Amendment, and guaranteeing the right to vote without discrimination based on race, found in the Fifteenth Amendment. State constitutions contain similar rights, and may provide more specific rights depending on the state. For example, the California Supreme Court has ruled that the California Constitution creates a fundamental right to education that is absent from the federal Constitution.[36]

CIVIL RIGHTS STATUTES

Antidiscrimination statutes cover a broader range of activity than constitutional provisions, and can include within their coverage both governmental action and private action. Some antidiscrimination statutes deal with criminal liability. Hate crimes legislation, for instance, creates new crimes based

on racial violence, or punishes violent conduct more severely if there is a finding of racially discriminatory intent. Most antidiscrimination statutes involve
civil liability, which limits the remedies to injunctive relief to compel some
type of action such as hiring or promoting a victim, or to forms of money damages to compensate the victim for a loss resulting from discrimination.

Statutes provide greater specificity than constitutional texts. Statutes state
the categories to be protected under the law—such as race, color, national
origin, religion, sex, disability, and age. There can be overlap among protected
categories. Race and color are usually merged together. Similarly, national origin and ancestry are both interpreted to encompass an immigrant's actual country of origin and the country of origin of one's ancestors. Ethnicity, however,
is usually not specified in antidiscrimination laws, but can be interpreted as
synonymous with national origin. There can also be multiple or intersectional
discrimination combining race and national origin, race and gender, and other
permutations.

Local laws often extend state or federal laws: several cities have antidiscrimination ordinances that address discrimination based on sexual orientation, a category that is absent in most state and federal laws. Coverage of
protected categories can also expand over time. The Voting Rights Act of 1965
was amended in 1975 to include language minorities in addition to racial minorities.[37] As a result, new types of remedies have been required under the
Voting Rights Act, including compelling jurisdictions to provide bilingual ballots and assistance in different languages.

Civil rights statutes typically specify the area of coverage: employment,
housing, education, public accommodations, voting, and commercial transactions. Statutes also indicate the methods to redress discrimination—administrative hearings, litigation—and the remedies available—injunctive relief,
damages, attorney fees. Depending on the scheme contained within a statute, enforcement of a civil rights law may fall on the government, on private
actors who must use the court system or an administrative law system to enforce their rights, or on both government and private actors.

ENFORCEMENT AGENCIES

The federal government and many state and local governments have executive agencies that deal specifically with civil rights enforcement. The United
States Department of Justice has a civil rights division that enforces many of
the criminal and civil statutes involving racial discrimination. Independent
agencies such as the Equal Employment Opportunity Commission are charged
with the enforcement of specific laws, such as Title VII of the Civil Rights
Act of 1964. The enforcement of some laws such as Title VI of the Civil Rights

Act of 1964, is left to multiple agencies because the law applies to discrimination in government assisted programs that are administered by different executive agencies.[38]

Executive and independent agencies can promulgate rules and regulations that have the force of law. In addition, government can rely on executive orders issued by the president or by a state governor that regulate civil rights compliance among government agencies and among government contractors. Many government affirmative action programs are contained in executive orders that require minority recruitment or hiring goals among contractors in order to receive government funding.

JUDICIAL INTERPRETATION

Decisional law based on judicial opinions also defines the scope of antidiscrimination laws. Constitutional texts contain very general language, so judicial opinions interpreting the texts provide the basic source of law. Statutory and regulatory texts are usually more specific, so a judicial interpretation—the "judicial gloss"—can provide clarity on how statutes must be enforced by government agencies or by private actors. Under Title VII of the Civil Rights Act of 1964, the courts have developed two basic theories of liability for racial discrimination litigation: one theory is based on "disparate treatment" and addresses individual discrimination by requiring proof of discriminatory intent; the second theory is based on "disparate impact" and focuses on the discriminatory effects of a policy rather than proof of discriminatory intent.[39]

Judicial interpretations of statutes are not always definitive, however. Many statutes have been designed to modify and even reverse judicial decisions that have restricted the scope of civil rights statutes and litigation. The Civil Rights Act of 1991 overturned seven Supreme Court decisions from 1989 and 1991 that, among other things, placed excessive burdens of proof on plaintiffs in disparate impact cases; limited the scope of section 1981, a Reconstruction-era civil rights law used in employment discrimination litigation; and allowed defendants to escape liability in "mixed motive" cases in which there might have been motives in addition to intentional discrimination.[40]

GOVERNMENT AFFIRMATIVE ACTION

Along with these basic sources of law, there are government efforts to remedy discrimination through voluntary affirmative action. These efforts can include goals and timetables in government hiring, promotions, and contracting; higher education recruitment and admissions programs; and desegregation efforts in public school districts. In addition to the goals of remedying both past and present discrimination, many voluntary affirmative action programs have goals to increase the representation of racial minority groups who have been traditionally underrepresented in many sectors of public life. Diversity admissions programs in many public universities reflect efforts to meet goals of both remediation and inclusion.

The Limits of Antidiscrimination Law

CIVIL RIGHTS ENFORCEMENT

As a practical matter, most forms of racial discrimination go unaddressed because of limitations in the system of civil rights enforcement. Civil rights laws requiring proof of discriminatory intent place a heavy burden on plaintiffs to demonstrate the mental state of discriminators. In many situations, such as applying for a job or seeking housing, it is often impossible to determine whether discrimination has occurred, given the applicant's lack of knowledge about the decision-making process. Without obvious evidence of discrimination—such as an interviewer's saying "I don't know if our clients will want to work with an Oriental"—there is typically insufficient information to raise a claim of discrimination. The use of "testers," individuals of a different race who submit the same application, offers one solution to this problem, but the process is rare because of limited government resources. In general, the demands on government enforcement of the antidiscrimination laws far exceed the resources and funding available to civil rights agencies. And like other forms of litigation, civil rights litigation often takes years to resolve, usually making the transaction costs of raising a discrimination claim higher than the actual relief being sought.

Legal formality operates to limit the potential impact of public policies designed to remedy racial subordination. Procedural requirements—such as the need to exhaust administrative remedies before filing a lawsuit in court—often restrict or postpone the vindication of substantive rights. Formal limits can also be found in the rigid categories designed to protect identified groups. In many cases, formality poses no problem: an individual who can prove that he or she is treated differentially because of race and suffers some detriment because of that treatment has a right and a remedy for the violation of that right.

But many types of inequality simply fall outside the scope of the antidiscrimination laws. The absence of categories dealing with language, immigration status, or citizenship in most antidiscrimination laws reflects political decisions to ignore the rights of immigrants and the nature of discrimination based on nativist racism. In 1994, legislation was introduced in California that would have added immigration status to the list of protected categories under the state's hate crimes laws. The legislation was passed by large votes in both the Assembly and the Senate, but was vetoed by Governor Pete Wilson. Two years later, legislation that would have created the right to be free from "criminal intimidation on the basis of citizenship or legal residency in the United States" was passed by the legislature. The governor vetoed the bill.[41]

The relatively small budgets for federal and civil rights enforcement agencies reflect the enforcement priorities of government; remedying racial subordination clearly falls on the lower end of the hierarchy of governmental law enforcement efforts. The political ideology of governmental leadership is also key. During the Reagan administration, the civil rights division of the Department of Justice was committed to a strategy of undoing the progress that had been made in race-conscious civil rights litigation. When conservative Clarence Thomas headed the Equal Employment Opportunity Commission during the late 1980s, he charted a course that shifted the agency's priorities toward processing individual complaints rather than class actions and other cases that would have broader impact. The result was the creation of an enormous backlog of thousands of cases that took years to resolve.[42]

The limited nature of antidiscrimination laws reflects the weakness of political will to confront racial discrimination directly through measures to make liability for discrimination more severe and to make enforcement of the law more accessible. Even proponents of a "color-blind" society can endorse strong enforcement of antidiscrimination laws. Yet many remedies for discrimination are nothing more than slaps on the wrist, designed to provide some measure of relief to the victim but not to punish the perpetrator.

POLITICS AND LAW

The limits of antidiscrimination law go deeper than the lack of political resolve to improve the enforcement of the laws. The law's treatment of race and inequality, including its treatment of Asian Americans, remains out of step with what social science theories instruct us about the nature of racial discrimination and subordination. Antidiscrimination laws are delimited by philosophical and legal traditions that overlook the pervasiveness of race and proscribe legal intrusion into most social relations involving race. The laws focus on individual discrimination rather than structural subordination brought on by racism's intersection with class. Racism often operates unconsciously, but discriminatory intent is required in all equal protection claims and in most statutory claims of discrimination.

Both constitutional interpretations of equal protection and antidiscrimination legislation frame theories of liability based on fixed categories. Some of these categories—citizenship status in particular—have diminished constitutional status relative to race, which makes nativist racism problematic under the law. And recent judicial interpretations of the law show an extreme aversion to race-consciousness: many rights and remedies are structured to intentionally discount race in an attempt to be color-blind, which seems impossible given what psychological theories tell us about stereotyping and unconscious racism.

Doctrinal principles of federal antidiscrimination law exist within structures of power: Congress, the president, the Supreme Court. Despite the major shifts in racial attitudes reflected by the civil rights legislation of the 1960s, conservative legal traditions and conservative legal decision makers continue to limit the scope of the antidiscrimination laws. Recent efforts by Republican members of Congress and conservative voters to repeal affirmative action programs are attempts to reverse decades of progress in civil rights enforcement. During the past twenty years, conservative majorities on the Supreme Court have shown a strong reluctance to extend racial jurisprudence beyond formal, color-blind conceptions of race relations. As a statement of both policy and of political values, the Court has asserted that remedying societal discrimination is not a compelling governmental interest because it is too remote and amorphous.[43] But if addressing societal discrimination is not a compelling interest, then what is?

Politics and the Wards Cove Case

A specific example of the politics of antidiscrimination law comes from the Civil Rights Act of 1991. One of the cases affected by the 1991 act was *Wards Cove Packing Co. v. Atonio*,[44] a case in which the Supreme Court placed excessive burdens of proof on plaintiffs in disparate impact cases under Title VII. Rather than placing the burden on employers to justify a discriminatory policy because of "business necessity," the Court shifted the burden to employees to prove the *lack* of business necessity. The original plaintiffs in *Wards Cove* were Filipino and Native Alaskan laborers who worked in a cannery operation that one dissenting Supreme Court justice likened to a "plantation economy": workers endured differential work conditions, were placed in segregated housing and eating facilities, and faced racial and ethnic harassment.[45]

Although he vetoed a stronger version of the bill in 1990, President Bush signed the Civil Rights Act of 1991. The 1991 act reversed the legal underpinnings of the *Wards Cove* case, shifting the burden to prove business necessity back to employers. But one obscure exception was included in the 1991 act: section 402 states that "nothing in this Act shall apply to any disparate impact case for which a complaint was filed before March 1, 1975, and for which an initial decision was rendered after October 30, 1983."[46] Only one case fell under this exception: *Wards Cove Packing Co. v. Atonio*. The exception reflected special interest legislation introduced on behalf of Wards Cove Packing and other cannery businesses in Alaska. The exception was thus designed to benefit the company whose very name epitomized the need for the 1991 act. Section 402 was later challenged as unconstitutional by the *Wards Cove* plaintiffs, but it was upheld by a federal appeals court in 1993.[47] Despite repeated advocacy efforts by Asian Americans to enact corrective legislation, the "Justice for Wards Cove Workers Act" never progressed in Congress.

This example illuminates several layers of civil rights politics. On one level is the politics of checks and balances among the branches of the federal government—a conservative Supreme Court decision, a responsive Congress, the president's signing of compromise legislation. On another level is the politics of special interest, including a specific legislative provision that illuminates both the power of business and the relative weakness of Asian American special interest groups. The result of all the politics was the reconstruction of the civil rights laws, in slightly better shape than the point at which the Supreme Court began undercutting the laws. Ultimately, though, it was the workers at the Wards Cove company who fared the worst in these legal and political machinations: they lost in the Supreme Court and when Congress passed a law to correct the decision, the new law did not help them anyway.

In this chapter, I have examined some of the causes of anti-Asian subordination and some of the potential remedies found in the law. The causes are broad and complex, while the remedies are narrow and circumscribed. The problem is not unique to Asian Americans. As a society we still have far to go in bridging the gaps in race relations between cause, effect, and remedy. In the remaining chapters, I examine the limits of existing civil rights laws in addressing the subordination of Asian Americans.

Chapter 3

Looking Like the Enemy

As a law student at UCLA in the early 1980s, I met Fred Korematsu when he and three of his lawyers—Peter Irons, Dale Minami, and Donald Tamaki— were speaking on campus to discuss the litigation to overturn his conviction for violating the Japanese American exclusion orders during World War II. New evidence had been uncovered to show that the federal government had suppressed crucial information in the 1940s before the trial court and ultimately the United States Supreme Court. His case was one of the three *coram nobis* cases, as they had come to be known, which were attempts to reopen his case, along with the cases of Gordon Hirabayashi and Min Yasui. Through a petition for the writ of error coram nobis—a mechanism that allows courts to correct injustices when new evidence suggests errors in the original decision—the legal team was attempting to correct a decades-old wrong at the highest level of government.

Like all of the other students, I was excited and inspired by Fred Korematsu's presence. Nearly forty years had passed since the Supreme Court's original decision in *Korematsu v. United States*, and here was the real thing, not just some name in a law school casebook. His lawyers began with a discussion of the history of the exclusion orders and the internment, and then explained how the recent discovery of government files pointed straight to prosecutorial misconduct: a key government report had been altered and the Justice Department had withheld evidence that would have undermined the need for the exclusion orders. The lawyers all spoke powerfully about the injustices of the exclusion and the internment, and of the need to rectify the wrongs of the past through the *coram nobis* petitions.

When Mr. Korematsu finally rose to speak, the room was completely hushed, with everyone in the crowd hanging on his every word. In a quiet but determined voice, which I discovered in later years was typical of his demeanor, he expressed his anger and disappointment with the government's treatment of Japanese Americans during the war, and how, as an American citizen, he deserved to be treated with the same respect as anyone else. His coram nobis case had opened up some old wounds, he admitted, but it was the only way that the injustices of the past could be corrected. Six months later, the federal district court in San Francisco vacated Fred Korematsu's original conviction for violating the exclusion orders.[1]

The importance of the Supreme Court's original *Korematsu* decision—a decision that remains law—and its impact on contemporary civil rights are perhaps best expressed in Fred Korematsu's own words, in a statement he gave in 1983 during the hearing on the *coram nobis* petition before the federal district court:

> According to the Supreme Court decision regarding my case, being an American citizen was not enough. They say you have to look like one, otherwise they say you can't tell a difference between a loyal and a disloyal American. I thought that this decision was wrong and I still feel that way. As long as my record stands in federal court, any American citizen can be held in prison or concentration camps without a trial or a hearing. That is if they look like the enemy of our country.[2]

The original *Korematsu* case typifies how "looking like the enemy" undermines the protection of basic rights, and how legal doctrine skews considerations of race in laws that discriminate in the "national interest." *Korematsu* is not unique. The casting of Asian Americans as foreigners pervades legal history: "unassimilable masses" of Asians were excluded through restrictive immigration laws; Asian immigrants were denied citizenship through discriminatory naturalization laws; rights were denied to immigrants through alien land laws and other citizenship-based laws. The resurgence of anti-Asian rhetoric in the 1990s that parallels the "yellow peril" rhetoric of the past demonstrates that foreignness is still central to anti-Asian racism.

In this chapter, I explore the role of the law in creating and upholding "outsider racialization," the social construction of Asian Americans as foreign-born outsiders. This chapter focuses on the subordination of Asian Americans when they are perceived and racialized as foreigners and immigrants; I examine the laws that discriminate against immigrants as a targeted class in the next chapter.

Asian Americans as Outsiders

THE RACIALIZATION EQUATION

Asian American = Foreigner. This equation reflects a pervasive theme in the formation of Asian American identities and experiences, and encompasses many of the stereotypes, prejudicial attitudes, and public policies that subordinate Asian Americans. Asian Americans are not the only ones facing this equation; Latinos and Arab Americans are other groups whose locations in the American racial landscape are defined by foreignness. The Asian American perspective is especially important, however, because the Asian American-as-outsider theme has found expression in many of the laws and constitutional cases that define the fundamental powers of government and that demarcate the most basic rights related to race.

The racial experiences of Asian Americans, Latinos, and Arab Americans—groups that Neil Gotanda calls "Other non-Whites"—diverge fundamentally from the experiences of blacks.[3] Subordination falls along a separate axis for these groups. The axis is not white versus black, but American versus foreigner. The color axis and the foreigner axis are both subordinative: they are rooted in racial power relations—between the dominant and the subordinate—and are based on the definitions of "us" versus "them," as set out by those who have the most power to define the terms. But the color dichotomy that operates to cast blacks as inferior to whites differs from the citizenship dichotomy that operates to cast all Asian Americans and "Other non-Whites" as foreign-born outsiders. (This does not mean that Asian Americans have not been thought to be inferior to whites; court cases are replete with statements on Asian inferiority. There are also small but growing numbers of black immigrants from Africa and the Caribbean who face multiple layers of discrimination.)

The construction of Asian Americans and "Other non-Whites" as foreign-born outsiders is a process that I call "outsider racialization." Outsider racialization works in two directions. First, Asian Americans, Latinos, and Arab Americans are racially categorized as foreign-born outsiders, regardless of actual citizenship status. Racialization operates on multiple levels: through psychological cognition and learning, social and political discourse, and institutional structures. Second, ostensibly race-neutral categories such as "immigrant" and "foreigner" are racialized through the same social processes. Just as Asian Americans, Latinos, and Arab Americans are presumed to be foreigners and immigrants, foreigners and immigrants are presumed to be Asian, Latino, or Arab.

Popular discourse has equated negative categories of foreigners or immigrants with racial groups living in the United States: "illegal alien" is equated with Latino; "terrorist" is equated with Arab; "foreign competitor" is equated with Asian. During 1994, when California's Proposition 187 drew attention to undocumented migration, both national and local news coverage of immigration issues focused on the "Mexican" problem; television media repeatedly aired images of Latinos racing across the U.S.-Mexico border, even when the underlying story involved other immigration questions.[4] Unlawful border crossings from Mexico were one source of the overall problem, but the imagery ignored other facets of undocumented migration, including Canadian border crossings and visa overstays from Asia and Europe. The media images only reinforced the equating of Latinos with undocumented immigrants.

Similarly, the near-reflexive accusations that Arab Americans were responsible for the bombing of the Oklahoma City federal building in 1995 exemplify the social construction of Arabs as terrorists in popular discourse.[5] And during the 1996 presidential election campaign, the controversy surrounding illegal campaign donations to the Democratic National Committee from Asia blurred distinctions between Asian business interests and Asian American contributors. United States citizens and lawful permanent residents of Asian descent who participated lawfully in the political process were swept into the debate, despite having no affiliation with Asian interests abroad.[6]

The categories of "illegal alien," "terrorist," and "foreign competitor" are both overinclusive and underinclusive; the reality is that the immigrant and foreigner categories include people from all over the world and that many Asian Americans, Latinos, and Arab Americans do not fall into any of the categories at all. But outsider racialization blurs any distinctions that actually exist.

FORMS OF OUTSIDER RACIALIZATION

The outsider racialization of Asian Americans can be divided into two basic forms: "immigrant" racialization and "foreigner" racialization. Immigrant racialization is the weaker of the two, placing all Asian Americans, regardless of citizenship status, in the category of "immigrant." One example of a civil rights violation resulting from immigrant racialization is the discriminatory treatment of Asian American job applicants during the hiring and employment verification process. Because employers are prohibited by federal law from hiring undocumented immigrant workers, Asian American applicants who are racialized as immigrants are sometimes denied employment through the employers' belief that Asian Americans applicants are—or are more likely to be—undocumented. Asian American applicants who are hired for a job may still face discrimination when the employer requires incorrect or excessive documentation of lawful status; a common request is to ask a United States citizen for a "green card."[7]

The strong version of outsider racialization occurs when Asian Americans are placed in the category of "foreigner." Because of the multiple characteristics that can attach to "foreigner," foreigner racialization is variegated. Racialization as a "foreign visitor" can result in a relatively harmless consequence, such as when Asian Americans are asked whether they speak English. Racialization as a "foreign competitor" can result in economic antagonisms: for example, Asian American businesses are criticized because of the perception that they are causing American workers to lose jobs. It can also result in physical violence, as in the killing of Vincent Chin, who was racialized by his killers as a Japanese competitor in the automobile industry. During times of military conflict, racialization as "foreign enemies" can cause the most intense antagonisms, leading to violence or, as happened to Japanese Americans during World War II, incarceration by the government.

When a furor arose during the 1996 presidential campaign over illegal campaign contributions from foreign business interests in Asia, the media and many politicians confused the issue by questioning the legitimacy of Asian American political activism and campaign contributions. Both President Clinton and Republican candidate Bob Dole proceeded to racialize Asian immigrants as foreigners by calling for campaign finance reforms that would preclude lawful permanent residents from making campaign contributions. In 1997, the Democratic National Committee (DNC) announced unilaterally that it would no longer accept contributions from noncitizens, even though contributions from lawful permanent residents were still permitted under the law at that time.[8] The DNC even went so far as to conduct background checks of Asian American donors. DNC staff inquired into donors' citizenship status and the source of contributed funds; operatives even asked for social security numbers and for permission to run credit checks on the donors.[9]

Because of demographic realities—Asian America is a largely immigrant population—it does not require a great stretch to correlate being Asian with being an immigrant. The presence of a small class of Asian immigrants who conduct business activities in both the United States and Asia can also blur the lines between foreign and domestic investor. But whether one is actually a United States–born citizen or an immigrant alters neither the perceptions nor the prejudices. Through racialization, Asian Americans are subordinated as outsiders who are not truly "American."

Outsiders under Law

Historically, law and the legal system have played a central role in the racialization of Asian Americans as outsiders. In *People v. Hall*, the ignoble decision of the California Supreme Court that Chinese could not testify against whites in court, Chief Justice Hugh C. Murray conveyed the popular sentiment of the day: Chinese immigrants should never possess the same rights as whites. Rubbing salt into the wound inflicted by the court's decision, his opinion states: "The same rule which would admit them to testify, would admit them to all the equal rights of citizenship, and we might soon see them at the polls, in the jury box, upon the bench and in our legislative halls. This is not a speculation, . . . it is an actual and present danger."[10]

The same sentiment can be found in the United States Supreme Court's opinion in *Fong Yue Ting v. United States*, which upheld Congress's power to deport Chinese immigrants for failing to register with the government:

> After some years' experience, . . . the government of the United
> States was brought to the opinion that the presence within our
> territory of large numbers of Chinese laborers, of a distinct race and
> religion, remaining strangers in the land, residing apart by themselves,
> tenaciously adhering to the customs and usages of their own country,
> unfamiliar with our institutions, and apparently incapable of assimi-
> lating with our people, might endanger good order, and be injurious to
> the public interests.[11]

The Court's language is strong: foreignness and the inability to assimilate are treated as almost immutable characteristics that no amount of time can erase. Assimilability takes on especially powerful meanings and becomes the code word for racial exclusion, a pattern that recurs in later Supreme Court decisions.

Immigration statutes such as the Immigration Act of 1917 and the Immigration Act of 1924 were designed to address the unassimilability of Asian immigrants. After the Immigration Act of 1917 created the "Asiatic barred zone," the commissioner of immigration reported that "the provision denying admission to certain natives of barred geographical zones is excellently adopted to meet the difficult problem of Asiatic immigration, which previous to the breaking out of the World War promised to assume dangerous proportions."[12]

In *Terrace v. Thompson*, the Supreme Court employed a twisted logic to make it clear that Asian immigrants did not enjoy the same rights as white citizens to own land. After acknowledging that under federal law European immigrants could become naturalized citizens while Asian immigrants could not, the Court found the contention that Washington State's alien land law discriminated on the basis of race to be groundless: "All persons of whatever color or race who have not declared their intention in good faith to become citizens are prohibited from so owning agricultural lands."[13]

The paradox was that Asian immigrants could not declare their intentions to become citizens even if they wanted to, because of the racial bar. In a logical sleight of hand, the Court acknowledged Congress's use of racial distinctions to determine citizenship, and then ruled that the state's distinction was not based on race but on citizenship. The Court ultimately returned to the more basic theme of unassimilability. Quoting the lower court's opinion, the Supreme Court stated: "It is obvious that one who is not a citizen and cannot become one lacks an interest in, and the power to effectually work for the welfare of, the state, and, so lacking, the state may rightfully deny him the right to own and lease real estate within its boundaries."[14] The Court went on to warn about the dangers of granting too many rights to Asian immigrants: "If one incapable of citizenship may lease or own real estate, it is within the realm of possibility that every foot of land within the state might pass to the ownership or possession of noncitizens."[15] The Court's language implies foreign invasions and potential takeovers by foreign interests.

The same themes are stated explicitly in this passage from *United States v. Thind*, the Supreme Court's decision applying the naturalization bar to Asian Indians:

> It is a matter of familiar observation and knowledge that the group characteristics of the Hindus renders them readily distinguishable from the various groups of persons commonly recognized as white. The children of English, French, German, Italian, Scandinavian, and other European parentage quickly merge into the mass of our population and lose the distinctive hallmarks of their European origin. On the other hand, it cannot be doubted that the children born in this country of Hindu parents would retain indefinitely clear evidence of their ancestry. It is very far from our thought to suggest the slightest question of racial superiority or inferiority. What we suggest is merely racial difference, and it is of such character and extent that the great body of our people instinctively recognize it and reject the thought of assimilation.[16]

First, the Court employs assimilation as a code word for racial exclusion. Justice George Sutherland, the author of the *Thind* opinion, frames the barrier to naturalization as the inability to assimilate, boldly stating that even the U.S.-born children of Asian Indians cannot assimilate in the same manner as Europeans because of their physical appearance. Second, the Court explicitly denies that racial animosity is a consideration in the decision making. Justice

Sutherland goes out of his way to state that there is not even the slightest question of racial superiority or inferiority implied by the Court's opinion, despite the obvious subordination created by a ruling upholding whiteness as the prerequisite for naturalized citizenship.

These two themes—the treatment of Asians as unassimilable foreigners and the masking of racial considerations in legal decision making—form the ideological basis for three of the Supreme Court's most notorious decisions: the Japanese American internment cases.

The "Enemy Race"

The most deplorable episode of foreigner racialization during the twentieth century was the World War II exclusion and internment of Japanese Americans. The forced relocation of over 110,000 Japanese Americans into concentration camps was especially egregious because two-thirds of those who were interned were United States citizens. And those who were lawful permanent residents could not become citizens because of the racial bar on naturalization. The upholding of the curfew and exclusion orders by the United States Supreme Court is especially damning in light of the fact that the Court established an exacting legal standard to review government discrimination based on race, but upheld the military orders anyway.

The racialization of Japanese Americans as foreigners began long before the bombing of Pearl Harbor. Anti-Japanese sentiment had flourished on the West Coast, leading to the alien land laws and other citizenship-based restrictions on basic rights. Popular anti-Japanese rhetoric exploded with the advent of World War II. Henry McLemore, a prominent syndicated columnist, published the following diatribe shortly after the bombing of Pearl Harbor:

> I know this is the melting pot of the world and all men are created equal and there must be no such thing as race or creed hatred, but do these things go when a country is fighting for its life? Not in my book. No country has ever won a war because of the lovely, gracious spirit. . . .
>
> I am for immediate removal of every Japanese on the West Coast to a point deep in the interior. I don't mean a nice part of the interior either. Herd 'em up, pack 'em off and give 'em the inside room in the badlands. Let 'em be pinched, hurt, hungry and dead up against it. . . .
>
> Personally, I hate the Japanese. And that goes for all of them.[17]

The same prejudices can be found in governmental documents attempting to justify the exclusion and internment orders. The *Final Report* of Lt. General John L. DeWitt, the military commander for the western states, contains references to Japanese Americans as "subversive," and "belonging to an enemy race" whose "racial strains are undiluted." Lt. General DeWitt's testimony before a congressional subcommittee in 1943 further demonstrates the military's racialization of Japanese Americans: "I don't want any of them here. They are a dangerous element. . . . It makes no difference whether he is an American citizen, he is still a Japanese. American citizenship does not necessarily determine loyalty."[18]

Anti-Japanese sentiment even spurred a legal attempt to overturn the United States Supreme Court's decision in *United States v. Wong Kim Ark* upholding birthright citizenship under the Fourteenth Amendment.[19] In *Regan v. King*,[20] the plaintiff sought a judicial declaration that persons of Japanese ancestry born in the United States were not citizens of the United States. Although the lawsuit was dismissed, the racism in the plaintiff's arguments was clear: "A Japanese person born in the United States is still a Japanese. The presence of Japanese has resulted and can result only in evil and this evil is intensified by their ability to exercise the privileges of citizenship."[21]

The curfew orders challenged in *Hirabayashi v. United States* and *Yasui v. United States* were upheld as constitutional, based on governmental information implying that Japanese Americans on the West Coast maintained connections with the Japanese empire.[22] But the federal government offered little concrete proof of disloyalty. Instead, the government argued that time pressures precluded any segregation of the loyal from the disloyal, necessitating the application of the curfew order to all persons of Japanese ancestry. As evidence of *potential* group disloyalty, the Court's opinion in *Hirabayashi* refers only to the education of Japanese American children in after-school Japanese language schools, the sending of children for education in Japan, the maintenance of a dual citizenship system by the Japanese government, and the holding of positions of influence within the Japanese American community by permanent resident aliens. The Supreme Court even relied on evidence of discrimination *against* Japanese Americans as a source of potential disloyalty: "There is support for the view that social, economic, and political conditions which have prevailed since the close of the last century, when the Japanese began to come in substantial numbers, have intensified their solidarity and have in large measure prevented their assimilation as an integral part of the white population."[23] While acknowledging the danger of considering ancestry as the basis for government classifications, the Court yielded to the military's decision to issue the curfew order as a rational response to the threat of espionage and sabotage. Military necessity justified the use of a race-based curfew order.

The Supreme Court's opinion in *Korematsu v. United States* says even less than the *Hirabayashi* case about actual disloyalty on the part of Japanese Americans. The Court's majority opinion states that the "exclusion of those of Japanese origin was deemed necessary because of the presence of an unascertained number of disloyal members of the group," and that "[t]here was evidence of disloyalty on the part of some."[24] The Court relied primarily on the findings of potential disloyalty that it discussed in the *Hirabayashi* case. Having acknowledged early in the *Korematsu* opinion that the courts must employ the most rigid scrutiny when reviewing racial classifications, the Supreme Court nevertheless upheld the constitutionality of the exclusion orders because of military necessity.

The most disturbing irony of the *Korematsu* decision lies in the Court's skirting of the basic racial issues after it established an exacting standard for governmental classifications based on race. The closing paragraph of the majority opinion states early on: "Our task would be simple, our duty clear, were this a case involving the imprisonment of a loyal citizen in a concentration camp because of racial prejudice." Disregarding this statement a few sentences later, the Court writes: "To cast this case into outlines of racial prejudice, without reference to the real military dangers which were presented, merely confuses the issue. Korematsu was not excluded from the Military Area because of hostility to him or his race. He *was* excluded because we are at war with the Japanese Empire."[25] The Court's language reveals a predisposition to defer to the military's discretion. The Court made no inquiry into the overinclusiveness of excluding loyal citizens and permanent residents from the West Coast, nor did the Court make an inquiry into the underinclusiveness of a program that targeted people of Japanese ancestry but not people of German or Italian ancestry. By granting lip service to its newly established principle of strict scrutiny, the Court racialized Japanese Americans as enemy aliens.

Justice Frank Murphy, one of three dissenting justices, began his opinion by stating what should have been obvious to the Court majority, that the "exclusion goes 'over the very brink of constitutional power' and falls into the ugly abyss of racism."[26] Noting the extensive evidence of racism contained in Lt. General DeWitt's *Final Report*, his opinion concludes that there was no "reasonable relationship between the group characteristics of Japanese Americans and the dangers of invasion, sabotage, and espionage." The reasons were "largely an accumulation of much of the misinformation, half-truths and insinuations that for years have been directed at Japanese Americans by people with racial and economic prejudices—the same people who have been among the foremost advocates of the evacuation."[27]

The racial injustice of the wartime cases became even more acute with the discovery nearly forty years later that the federal government had misled the courts by (1) suppressing intelligence reports that would have been key evidence of Japanese American loyalty and (2) altering Lt. General DeWitt's final report to make military expediency appear more central to the exclusion than racial animosity. The vacating of the original convictions of Fred Korematsu, Gordon Hirabayashi, and Min Yasui by lower federal courts in the 1980s offered some personal justice to the men who challenged the military orders, but the precedential value of the wartime Supreme Court decisions remains intact. Judge Marilyn Hall Patel, the federal district court judge who vacated Fred Korematsu's conviction, stated in her court opinion:

> *Korematsu* remains on the pages of our legal and political history. As a legal precedent it is now recognized as having very limited application. As historical precedent it stands as a constant caution that in times of war or declared military necessity our institutions must be vigilant in protecting constitutional guarantees. It stands as a caution that in times of distress the shield of military necessity and national security must not be used to protect governmental actions from close scrutiny and accountability. It stands as a caution that in times of international hostility and antagonisms our institutions, legislative, executive, and judicial, must be prepared to exercise their authority to protect all citizens from the petty fears and prejudices that are so easily aroused.[28]

Vietnamese Fishermen and National Security

The government's use of the national interest as a justification for racial discrimination against Asian Americans is not unique to the Japanese American internment. In the late 1980s, when the United States Coast Guard prohibited Vietnamese immigrants from operating fishing boats in the coastal waters of Northern California, the government relied on "national security" to justify its actions.[29] The Coast Guard invoked the Jones Act, a law that was originally designed to protect against foreign incursions into United States territory. The act prohibits noncitizens from owning or operating large boats in coastal waters.

Close to four hundred Vietnamese fishermen were targeted by the Coast Guard; all had entered as refugees, and most were lawful permanent residents who had not yet obtained naturalized citizenship. As noncitizens, they were in technical violation of the law if they operated their boats in coastal waters. Fines were levied against the fishermen, and the Coast Guard threatened to seize boats that were operating illegally. Although the Vietnamese fishermen were the only group targeted under the Jones Act, the Coast Guard denied that race was a motivating factor or even that selective enforcement was at work.

The Vietnamese Fishermen Association of America and several individuals filed a lawsuit in 1989 to enjoin the Coast Guard's enforcement of the law and argued that the Jones Act was unconstitutional, depriving the fishermen of due process and equal protection of the law. Although the plaintiffs obtained a temporary restraining order, the federal district court later denied an application for a preliminary injunction, and an appeal was filed with the federal court of appeals in 1990. In arguments before the Ninth Circuit Court of Appeals, attorneys for the federal government urged the court to uphold enforcement of the Jones Act as a reasonable response to protecting the national security of the United States. Attorneys for the fishermen, on the other hand, argued that the law did not serve a rational purpose and infringed on the fishermen's basic interest in earning a living.[30]

While the litigation was pending, advocates pressured Congress to pass legislation to amend the Jones Act to allow lawful permanent residents and refugees to operate large ships in coastal waters. The lawsuit was dismissed after a bill sponsored by Representative Norman Mineta was passed by Congress and signed into law by President Bush in November 1990.[31] The fishermen gained a victory with the passage of the legislation, but the episode is reminiscent of the discrimination of earlier decades, when Japanese immigrant fishermen were denied licenses by the State of California and when national security was used to justify the internment of Japanese Americans during World War II.

Remnants of War

Foreigner racialization is clearly most dangerous during times of war, when the "national interest" can trump any interest in protecting civil rights. But the racialization of Asian Americans as "enemies" can stretch beyond periods of actual war. Military propaganda that portrays wartime enemies in racial terms becomes part of the racialization process that subordinates Americans of Asian ancestry. Examples include the popular use of the term "japs" during World War II or the vulgar use of the term "gooks" during the Vietnam War. The racial learning that is reinforced through military propaganda can extend long after military activities have ceased. Aggregated military conflicts with Japan during World War II, with China and North Korea during the Korean War, and with North Vietnam during the Vietnam War have bred aggression and hostility against Asians and Asian Americans that persist even today. And when contemporary political rhetoric concerning "trade wars," "drug wars," or the "war on illegal immigration" is used, Asian Americans are among the first to suffer.

The contemporary parallel of military conflict with Japan has become American economic competition with Japanese businesses, especially in the automobile industry. Anti-Japanese rhetoric typically harkens back to World War II incidents such as the bombing of Pearl Harbor by Japan or the bombing of Hiroshima and Nagasaki by the United States. During the 1980s, many Southern California drivers attached bumper stickers to their cars that read "Toyota - Datsun - Honda - and Pearl Harbor." In Flint, Michigan, a display at an automobile exhibit depicted a flying car that was constructed as a caricature of a Japanese face dropping a bomb on Detroit, all against the backdrop of an imperial Japanese flag.[32] In early 1992, when the talk of "trade wars" with Japan escalated, racist rhetoric tied to "Buy American" campaigns escalated as well. In Pasadena, California, a resident put a sign on his front lawn that read "RECESSION: IT'S YOUR FAULT / DON'T BUY JAP PRODUCTS / BUY AMERICAN / WE'RE MAD AS HELL." During the same month, the offices of the Japanese American Citizens League in Los Angeles received a bomb threat in which the caller left an answering machine message that stated, "I'll show you a year of remembrance, you dirty Japs. What we remember is Pearl Harbor."[33] The 1982 killing of Vincent Chin remains the most tragic instance of violence arising from the racialization of Asian Americans as Japanese competitors.

Contemporary anti-Asian violence often reflects a patriotic racism that is the result of foreigner racialization. The 1989 killing of Jim (Ming Hai) Loo in Raleigh, North Carolina, was motivated by animosity linked to the Vietnam War. The two brothers who intimidated and assaulted Loo blamed him and his friends for the deaths of American soldiers in Vietnam. One of the men stated: "I don't like you because you're Vietnamese. Our brothers went over to Vietnam and they never came back. . . . I'm gonna finish you tonight."[34] In 1994, an assailant who had stabbed an Asian American in Sacramento, California, admitted forthrightly to the police that he had attacked his victim "to defend our country."[35]

Borders and the War on Immigration

Foreigner racialization has operated during periods of economic uncertainty, when the scapegoating of immigrants and foreign competitors reaches a peak. The "yellow peril" rhetoric that warned of invasions of Asian immigrant hordes during the early twentieth century is one example. During the 1990s, the same sort of patriotic rhetoric has pervaded political discourse on immigration policy. Supporters of California's Proposition 187 employed quasi-military rhetoric during the 1994 election campaign, placing language in the official voter's guide that endorsed the ballot initiative as "the first giant stride in ultimately ending the illegal alien invasion."[36] Similarly, when they were unable to obtain a political resolution through Congress and the president, several state governments filed lawsuits against the federal government in the mid-1990s to obtain reimbursement for the costs of state services provided to undocumented immigrants. Although the reimbursement lawsuits raised important policy issues, the legal theories employed by the states reinforced wartime analogies: one claim made by the states was that the federal government had violated the Constitution by failing to protect the states from "invasion." The courts summarily dismissed these claims as inapplicable to federal immigration policies.[37]

The "war on illegal immigration" has extended beyond patriotic rhetoric. In practice, the federal government has treated immigrants as if they are foreign invaders. When immigrants from Haiti and China were traveling on the high seas during the late 1980s and early 1990s, their ships were interdicted in international waters. During the same period, when undocumented immigrants from Mexico and Central America crossed over the border in increasing numbers, the government began building blockades.

In 1996, Congress passed the Illegal Immigration Reform and Immigrant Responsibility Act, creating the functional equivalent of a war zone along the U.S.-Mexico border. The act increased the number of border patrol agents by five thousand, to be deployed primarily along the southern border; it mandated the construction of metal fencing in a fourteen-mile border area near San Diego; and it authorized the Justice Department to acquire interdiction equipment, including fixed-wing aircraft, helicopters, night-vision devices, and sensors.[38] The government has further militarized the U.S.-Mexico border by supplementing border patrol agents with the National Guard and other military units.[39]

Borders extend into the interior of the United States as well. The border patrol conducts workplace raids and stops individuals on the street in attempting to arrest and ultimately deport undocumented immigrants. Some industries are more heavily populated by undocumented immigrants—agriculture and garment manufacturing are two—so workplace raids are common in those industries. But there is no profile that can actually encompass the characteristics of an undocumented immigrant, other than lacking proof of lawful immigration status. Physical appearance is not an acceptable correlate, because it can include United States citizens and lawful permanent residents. Language skill is not an indication of unlawful status either, since many lawful permanent residents lack fluency in English.

Inevitably, border patrol enforcement is race-based: Latinos and Asian Americans are the primary targets of the raids and the stops. When the border patrol employs appearance as the basis for its enforcement activities, United States citizens are easily swept in. In 1993, Eddie Cortez, a United States citizen, was mistaken for an undocumented immigrant, stopped on the street, and detained by border patrol agents in Pomona, California, a city near Los Angeles that is a great distance from the U.S.-Mexico border. It turned out that Eddie Cortez was the mayor of the City of Pomona.[40]

The 1996 immigration reform legislation compounds the basic problem by extending the government's authority to work with state and local law enforcement agencies, whose officers can be empowered to investigate, apprehend, and detain individuals suspected of being undocumented immigrants.[41] Empowering local law enforcement to enforce the immigration laws has a facial appeal, but it is bad public policy because local law enforcement officers serve as the primary conduit for the reporting of local crimes. If local police possess the power to inquire into immigration status, including the status of victims or witnesses, immigrants are much less likely to report any crimes at all.

Framing the regulation of immigration as the moral equivalent of war threatens to create the same legal deprivations that arose against Japanese Americans during World War II. The Anti-Terrorism and Effective Death Penalty Act of 1996 (AEDPA) is predicated on a moral war against terrorism, but it deprives immigrants of significant rights.[42] Under AEDPA, the secretary of state can declare any foreign organization a "terrorist organization" based on a determination that the group "threatens the national security of the United States." Decision making is highly secretive, because the government is not required to reveal any evidence in defending its analysis. Immigrants accused of terrorism can be deported on the basis of classified evidence that can be withheld from the immigrant; the immigrant may only be allowed to see a brief declassified summary of the evidence. Arab Americans and others who may be racialized as "terrorists" face the greatest threat from star-chamber procedures that seek to protect national security—paralleling the experiences of Japanese Americans who were interned in the interest of war-time national security.

Racialization in the Immigration Laws

During the 1980s and 1990s, immigration laws have had detrimental effects on Asian American and other predominantly immigrant groups. The removal of explicit racial and national origin categories came with the Immigration Act of 1965, but recent immigration legislation has created programs that have caused race-based discrimination against Asian Americans. Immigrant racialization—the weak form of outsider racialization—is fostered by laws that distinguish between citizens and noncitizens and between classes of noncitizens.

EMPLOYER SANCTIONS

When Congress passed the Immigration Reform and Control Act of 1986 (IRCA), it established a system of employment verification and sanctions that requires employers to check the immigration status of all newly hired employees, including United States citizens.[43] Failure to verify an employee's status, or to knowingly hire an employee who lacks the authorization to work, subjects the employer to civil penalties. In essence, employers have been deputized as immigration agents through the threat of employer sanctions.

After the passage of IRCA, discrimination against Asian Americans and Latinos increased significantly because of the law's employer sanctions provisions. A 1990 report by the federal government's General Accounting Office found a widespread pattern of discrimination against Asian Americans and Latinos attributable to the law's verification requirements.[44] Using a national survey of employers, the GAO study found that nearly 20 percent of all employers committed unlawful discrimination based on national origin or citizenship because of employer sanctions. Percentages were even higher in areas with large immigrant populations, such as New York City, Chicago, Miami, Texas, and California.

Reports from civil rights enforcement agencies across the country revealed regional evidence of discrimination against Asian Americans and Latinos. A survey of over four hundred employers in San Francisco found that one half of the employers in the sample felt that the immigration verification requirements made it riskier to hire people who spoke limited English, that 39 percent of the employers felt it riskier to hire Asians, and that 40 percent felt it riskier to hire Latinos.[45] Despite these and other studies, as well as recommendations from a federal task force on employer sanctions, Congress declined to repeal the verification system under IRCA.

IRCA's system of employment verification has reinforced the immigrant racialization of Asian Americans. The United States Commission on Civil Rights has described the problem as follows: "If employers assume that more individuals in ethnic groups with high proportions of immigrants are likely to be unauthorized workers, then they may be more suspicious of the work authorization of *all* members of the group, and they might be reluctant to hire *any* members of that group at all."[46]

Although federal legislation was introduced in the early 1990s to repeal employer sanctions, it never gained sufficient momentum to gain passage in Congress. Congress moved in the opposite direction by calling for the expansion of employment verification systems under the 1996 immigration reform law. Pilot programs in California, Texas, Florida, Illinois, and New York rely on new—and incomplete—computer databases containing information on immigrants that employers can use to verify status. But any verification system, even one with complete data, only compounds the basic problem of employer sanctions by causing more discrimination against Asian Americans and Latinos.

When it passed IRCA, Congress did acknowledge that an employer verification system could cause discrimination against individuals who would be more likely to be perceived as undocumented immigrants, namely Latinos and Asians. IRCA therefore included provisions that extend coverage of national origin discrimination under Title VII of the Civil Rights Act of 1964 to small employers with between four and fourteen employees.[47] IRCA also created new sections that prohibit discrimination related to citizenship status by employers with four or more employees. Most citizens-only hiring policies are thus illegal under IRCA. (The 1990 Immigration Act added document abuse—discrimination against job applicants who are required to produce incorrect or excessive documentation—to the IRCA sections.)[48]

But the IRCA antidiscrimination provisions are weak, containing a host of exceptions and limitations that are unparalleled in antidiscrimination law. The IRCA provisions are not as extensive as other laws such as Title VII, because they only apply to hiring, recruitment, firing, and retaliation, and not to promotions or to conditions of employment. Like Title VII, the IRCA provisions allow "disparate treatment" claims for cases involving intentional discrimination; the IRCA provisions do not, however, allow "disparate impact" claims, which require no proof of discriminatory intent. The law contains exceptions that allow employers to discriminate between citizens and noncitizens to comply with government contracts, as is done in the defense industry. The law also allows employers to favor a citizen over a noncitizen when two applicants are equally qualified for a position.

Moreover, the IRCA provisions extend coverage only to United States citizens and "protected individuals," a category that includes lawful permanent residents, refugees, and asylees. A major weakness in the law is the requirement that in order to remain a "protected individual" a lawful permanent resident must apply for naturalization within six months of first becoming eligible, which is usually after having resided in the country for five years. Long-time permanent residents, among the people most likely to experience citizenship discrimination, are therefore left unprotected by the law.

IMMIGRATION STATUS AND GOVERNMENT SERVICES

Verification of immigration status has expanded beyond the employer sanctions context. Under California's Proposition 187, all state residents are required under the law to prove lawful immigration status in order to obtain a public school education, health care, or social services. The law would also authorize local law enforcement and verifying officials to inform federal authorities about anyone suspected of lacking proper immigration status. Teachers, health care professionals, and social workers are among those who would become functional immigration agents under the law. Proposition 187 even goes so far as to require the reporting of "suspected" undocumented immigrants. Although enjoined by the courts soon after its passage because of conflicts with federal law and with *Plyler v. Doe*, the Supreme Court decision prohibiting discrimination against undocumented students,[49] Proposition 187 had effects on immigrants throughout the state, including many who removed their children from schools and avoided seeking health services. Despite injunctions issued by the courts, there were numerous reports of inquiries into immigration status by both governmental and nongovernmental offices.

The federal Personal Responsibility and Work Opportunity Reconciliation Act limits the access of undocumented immigrants to almost all nonemergency federal benefits programs.[50] The act also discriminates against many lawful permanent residents by making them ineligible for Food Stamps and Supplemental Security Income, and by granting state governments the option of denying additional benefits, including Medicaid and Temporary Assistance for Needy Families.

To implement the welfare reform law, government agencies must verify immigration and citizenship status, which encourages the same type of discrimination rooted in the employer sanctions provisions of IRCA. Discrimination is even more serious when the verification involves a government benefit program, which may be the only source of income for a low-income citizen or immigrant. A relatively simple problem, such as a lost naturalization certificate, can have dire consequences if verification of citizenship is required to maintain eligibility for benefits.

Racialization and the Antidiscrimination Laws

Regulating immigration to the United States is an exceptionally complex problem. Employer sanctions, border enforcement, and the elimination of government benefits and services to regulate immigration have a rhetorical appeal, and they have been adopted by the federal government as the primary methods for addressing undocumented migration. But the migration of undocumented labor is only part of a larger set of global phenomena that includes the migration of families, the migration of refugees displaced by political strife, and the movement of capital across national boundaries. Enforcing borders, sanctioning employers, and cutting benefits cannot fully deter immigration when there are economic forces at work that either undermine or transcend these policies. Immigration policies cannot stand in isolation of trade and economic policies that promote (or inhibit) economic development in immigrant-sending countries; nor can they effectively regulate immigration without addressing underground economies in the United States that rely on exploited immigrant workers for cheap labor.

At the same time, laws that distinguish between citizens and noncitizens, or between classes of noncitizens, will ultimately have an adverse effect on Asian Americans, Latinos, Arab Americans, and other groups who are racialized as immigrants. Employer sanctions is one public policy that would be best repealed rather than expanded; its costs, including the subordination of racialized groups, are simply too great. But even if employer sanctions policies are maintained, at a minimum the loopholes in the IRCA antidiscrimination laws should be closed so that the law can cover more conditions of employment and more individuals who are adversely affected by verification requirements.

The discrimination against Asian Americans in employment and in other areas suggest that two racialization dynamics must be addressed. First, the meaning of racial discrimination must be expanded to include considerations of foreignness and citizenship status. In other words, racial discrimination against "Other non-Whites" must be recognized as containing elements of anti-foreigner and anti-immigrant animosity. Second, the meaning of citizenship discrimination must be extended to include considerations of race. In other words, anti-immigrant laws and policies that distinguish on the basis of citizenship must be recognized as having racial impacts on groups who have been racialized as foreigners or as immigrants.

Incorporating outsider racialization into antidiscrimination law can be accomplished in two ways: (1) expanding the definition of racial discrimination to recognize that the racial meanings which attach to actions against

Asian Americans and other groups racialized as foreigners contain elements of citizenship discrimination, and (2) expanding antidiscrimination laws to include citizenship and immigration status as protected categories independent of racial discrimination. The courts have not been receptive to the first suggestion: the Supreme Court ruled in 1973, in the context of Title VII of the Civil Rights of 1964, that national origin discrimination was analytically distinct from citizenship discrimination.[51]

On the other hand, recognition of citizenship discrimination independent of race discrimination does exist in the law. The courts have already recognized alienage as a suspect classification in equal protection cases involving state legislation, and the IRCA antidiscrimination provisions recognize citizenship discrimination, albeit in limited circumstances. Using both "citizenship" and "immigration status" as protected categories would add precision to the law by encompassing the different manifestations of both foreigner and immigrant racialization. For example, a United States citizen who suffers discrimination because she is treated as a "green card" holder would be one form of immigration status discrimination; an individual's being treated as if he were undocumented would be another form of discrimination.

Antidiscrimination statutes could be expanded to include citizenship and immigration status discrimination in access to public benefits, education, housing, public accommodations, business transactions, criminal violence, and other areas where discrimination is outlawed. Central to the incorporation of citizenship-based discrimination is the notion of being perceived as a noncitizen. Whether one is a citizen or not, the discrimination is just as invidious. Just like someone's being perceived as the "wrong" race or color, a perception of noncitizenship can lead to acts that subordinate and deny equal worth as a member of American society.

Outsider racialization, as I have defined it, is a broad social process of which law is only one component. The law cannot prevent people from perceiving Asian Americans as immigrants or foreigners, but it can play a role in recognizing that discrimination against Asian Americans is intertwined with foreignness and that there are remedies under the law to address the discrimination.

| Chapter 4 | Race, Immigration, and Citizenship |

In 1994, I delivered a speech in Los Angeles at the Day of Remembrance, an annual event that commemorates the internment of Japanese Americans during World War II. The theme of that year's Day of Remembrance was "Our Immigrant Heritage: A Struggle for Justice." I began my remarks with the following story:

> Sixty-five years ago, a young man named Anselmo left his home in the Philippines to come to the United States and find his fortune. Like many young men of his day, he came to this country to attend college—to become a designer, an artist, perhaps even an architect.
>
> But with the untimely death of his father soon afterward, Anselmo was left heartbroken. He had lived and studied to realize his father's dreams of a better life, and when his father's dreams died, so did many of Anselmo's.
>
> He dropped out of school and began working to support himself. If the laws were written as they are today, he would have become, in our popular phrasing, an "illegal alien."
>
> Like other young men of that era, Anselmo found his way into the tough, low-wage jobs open to Filipinos and other immigrants of color: the restaurants of Washington State, the canneries and packing houses of Alaska, the fisheries of Maine, the farms of central California. He struggled, like the rest of the country, through the Great Depression, and he survived.
>
> He encountered, of course, the overt racism of the time: the segregated housing, the restricted access to stores and restaurants, the threats of violence, and the anti-miscegenation laws that denied one

of the most basic human freedoms—the ability to fall in love with and marry whomever you pleased. Even his personal identity was sacrificed when his supposedly unpronounceable name was changed to oblige a bureaucrat's paperwork.

And yet despite this very hard life, he came to love his adopted country. He defended it as a navyman during World War II. He worked for its government as a postal clerk for over thirty years. He married, bought a home, and raised a family, placing a premium on the democratic values that America, at least in theory, has espoused throughout its history.

The story of Anselmo is not an extraordinary story, but it is a special story, at least for me, because the story of Anselmo is the story of my father. And it is a story that repeats itself countless numbers of times across this state and all across this nation of ours.[1]

For Asian Americans, the immigrant experience is a personal experience. Two out of every three Asian Americans is an immigrant, and the parents or grandparents of most Asian Americans born in the United States were immigrants as well. Public policies that threaten the rights of immigrants or that threaten to restrict immigration—particularly the immigration of family members—are not just political statements, based on economic calculations and aggregated population figures. They are policies that affect people's lives in a personal way. During that speech in Los Angeles, I used the story of my father to preface a critique of anti-immigrant proposals, including the proposal that the United States–born children of undocumented immigrants should not be granted citizenship. The laws were different over sixty-five years ago when the Philippines was still a colony of the United States, but if today's laws applied, my father might have lost lawful status when he dropped out of college and began working. He would have become undocumented, and I would have been one of those people targeted by laws like Proposition 187 or by proposals to deny birthright citizenship to the children of undocumented immigrants.

In this chapter, I examine the immigration laws and the laws affecting immigrants living in the United States. Race and nativism intersect in the laws of immigration, but the laws enjoy a special status that insulates them from judicial review. As a practical matter, this means that Congress and the president can enact almost any proposal based on immigration status or citizenship, regardless of its racial impact. Ideologically, the failure to incorporate obvious racial meanings into immigration laws and anti-immigrant policies means that racism can be masked by any law that is rooted in citizenship, sovereignty, or the national interest.

Nativism and Law

During periods of economic uncertainty, nativism captures much of the public consciousness, and legal change is the ultimate result. As economist Thomas Muller notes, the 1840s, the 1880s, the 1920s, and the 1990s all share common conditions: economic uncertainty and job insecurity; social, ethnic, and cultural disparities between new arrivals and native majorities; and a large and sustained influx of immigrants.[2] Nativist discourse rings with an eerie consistency during these periods. In 1920, when California's Alien Land Law of 1913 was reenacted and strengthened by a ballot initiative, the targets of the campaign were Japanese immigrants. As Justice Frank Murphy noted in his concurring opinion in *Oyama v. California*, the 1948 Supreme Court case that struck down California's alien land law as unconstitutional, the initiative campaign was overtly racist:

> All the propaganda devices then known—newspapers, speeches, films, pamphlets, leaflets, billboards, and the like—were utilized to spread the anti-Japanese poison. The Japanese were depicted as degenerate mongrels and the voters were urged to save "California—the White Man's Paradise" from the "yellow peril," which had somewhat lapsed in the public mind since 1913. Claims were made that the birth rate of the Japanese was so high that the white people would eventually be replaced and dire warnings were made that the low standard of living of the Japanese endangered the economic and social health of the community.[3]

In 1994, when California's Proposition 187—named the "Save Our State" initiative by its supporters—was placed on the ballot, the rhetoric rang out with comparable virulence against Latinos. Images of Latino immigrants racing across the U.S.-Mexico border blanketed television and other media. Harold Ezell, a former regional commissioner for the Immigration and Naturalization Service, argued, "The people are tired of watching their state run wild and become a third world country."[4] Commenting on the need to deny prenatal care to one undocumented immigrant, a supporter of Proposition 187 denounced by implication the high birth rate among immigrants: "She has already had two children here and now she's on her third, and she doesn't even belong here."[5] Another supporter stated bluntly, "I have no intention of being the object of 'conquest,' peaceful or otherwise, by Latinos, Asians, blacks, Arabs, or any other group of individuals who have claimed my country."[6] Like the 1920 alien land law initiative, Proposition 187 passed by an overwhelming majority.

Contemporary nativism even draws support from past nativism. In his

1995 book *Alien Nation*, journalist Peter Brimelow writes approvingly of the California legislature's 1876 report on Chinese immigration, a report which stated that the Chinese "have never adapted themselves to our habits, mode of dress, or our educational system." He describes the passage as "a highly rational and very specific complaint about the difficulty of assimilating immigrants."[7] Brimelow also laments about the racial imbalance caused by recent immigration: "It is simply common sense that Americans have a legitimate interest in their country's racial balance. It is common sense that they have a right to insist that their government stop shifting it. Indeed, it seems to me that they have a right to insist that it be shifted back."[8] He suggests, therefore, that immigration must be restricted, since "the American nation has always had a specific ethnic core. And that core has been white."[9]

Law incorporates nativism in two ways. First, federal immigration laws prevent the entry of "undesirable" immigrants. The Chinese Exclusion Act of 1882, the creation of the "Asiatic barred zone" in 1917, and the Immigration Act of 1924 all reflect waves of nativist sentiment. Second, federal and state anti-immigrant laws subordinate immigrants already living in the United States. The racial bar to naturalization, alien land laws, English-only laws, and citizenship-based restrictions on receiving government services, such as Proposition 187, are typical of laws that have subordinated immigrants.

A troubling irony of Asian American legal history is the prominent and ongoing role that racially discriminatory laws have played in upholding immigration restrictions and anti-immigrant laws. The courts' treatment of the immigration laws as practically immune from judicial review—a doctrine that traces back to the Supreme Court's upholding of the Chinese exclusion laws of the 1880s—is one example. The extension of national sovereignty powers to include federal policies affecting immigrants already living in the United States is another, also drawing support from congressional policies that targeted Asian immigrants.

The Japanese American internment cases instruct us that the placement of national *security* interests above civil rights can subordinate any person, including an American citizen, on the basis of race. The placement of national *sovereignty* interests above civil rights through immigration policies can subordinate even more easily, because the judicial standard for evaluating immigration laws is lower than the standard set out for reviewing racially discriminatory laws in the *Korematsu* case. Cases from the nineteenth century that upheld overt racial discrimination by Congress in the immigration laws form the core of legal precedents that support contemporary restrictions on immigration and immigrants' rights.[10]

Racial Sovereignty and the Plenary Power Doctrine

ASIAN EXCLUSION CASES

The federal government's power over immigration comes as close to absolute as any power found at any level of U.S. government. Established by Supreme Court decisions deferring to the decision-making powers of Congress and the president in matters of immigration, the "plenary power" doctrine reflects the Court's ennoblement of national sovereignty as an overriding governmental interest. The roots of the plenary power doctrine, however, are far from noble. They trace directly to the Court's upholding of the anti-Asian immigration laws of the late nineteenth century, including the Chinese Exclusion Act. Despite the reversal of many racially discriminatory court decisions of the same era—*Plessy v. Ferguson* is the most prominent—the racial exclusion cases have never been overturned or even modified. Instead, they serve as the primary source of law for immigration restrictions and anti-immigrant laws enacted by the federal government.

The federal Constitution does not explicitly mention powers over immigration. The closest reference is the naturalization clause, one of Congress's enumerated powers, which states only that Congress shall have the power "[t]o establish an uniform Rule of Naturalization."[11] It is decisional law—the Supreme Court's rulings on the constitutionality of Congress's early immigration laws—that lays the groundwork for using national sovereignty as the source of federal power over immigration.

In *Chae Chan Ping v. United States (the Chinese Exclusion Case)*,[12] the Court upheld an 1888 law that excluded Chinese immigrants who were returning to the United States from trips abroad. The Court identified the basic issue of congressional power over immigration as an issue of national sovereignty: "That the government of the United States, through the action of the legislative department, can exclude aliens from its territory is a proposition which we do not think open to controversy. Jurisdiction over its own territory to that extent is an incident of every independent nation."[13] According to the Court, among the sovereign powers of government were the power to declare war, to make treaties, repel invasion, regulate foreign commerce, and admit the subjects of other nations to citizenship. The power to regulate immigration was also a basic power of sovereignty. Likening the power to regulate immigration to the power to repel invaders during war, the Court stated: "It matters not in what form such aggression and encroachment come, whether from the foreign nation acting in its national character or from vast hordes of its people crowding in upon us."[14]

Race, according to the Court, was a secondary problem: "The differences of race added greatly to the difficulties of the situation."[15] Nevertheless, racial exclusion was implicit within the powers of sovereignty because regulating Chinese immigration was comparable to repelling a foreign invasion. The Court stated:

> If, therefore, the government of the United States, through its legislative department, considers the presence of foreigners of a different race in this country, who will not assimilate with us, to be dangerous to its peace and security, their exclusion is not to be stayed because at the time there are no actual hostilities with the nation of which the foreigners are subjects.[16]

At the same time that it conceded extraordinary powers to Congress, the Court racialized the appellant and others barred from entry—Chinese immigrants who were returning to their homes in the United States—as foreign enemies.

The Supreme Court extended the federal power to exclude immigrants to the executive branch of government in *Nishimura Ekiu v. United States*.[17] The Court reiterated its earlier holding that sovereignty guided the immigration powers: "It is an accepted maxim of international law, that every sovereign nation has the power, as inherent in sovereignty, and essential to self-preservation to forbid the entrance of foreigners within its dominions or to admit them only in such cases and upon such conditions as it may see fit to prescribe."[18] Just as importantly, the Court held that the judicial branch should yield to the determinations of Congress and the president: "[The power] belongs to the political department of the government, and may be exercised either through treaties made by the President and Senate, or statutes enacted by Congress."[19]

In *Fong Yue Ting v. United States*,[20] the Supreme Court upheld the federal government's deportation power—the power to remove resident immigrants from the country. The petitioners in the case were Chinese immigrants who lacked certificates of residence, including one immigrant who had been unable to produce a credible white witness required under the law to testify to his residency. The Court held that exclusion powers and deportation powers were two sides of the same coin: "The power to exclude aliens and the power to expel them rest upon one foundation, are derived from one source, are supported by the same reasons, and are in truth but parts of one and the same power."[21] Dealing with race in an almost casual manner, the Court stated that "the right of a nation to expel or deport foreigners, who have not been naturalized or taken any steps towards becoming citizens of the country, rests

upon the same grounds, and is as absolute and unqualified as the right to prohibit and prevent their entrance into the country."[22]

Federal powers were not absolute, however. In *The Japanese Immigrant Case*
(*Yamataya v. Fisher*),[23] the Supreme Court provided minimal boundaries for
the immigration powers by holding that constitutional due process protections
applied to individuals who were subject to deportation from the United States.
Nevertheless, the Court ruled that Yamataya—who was alleged to have entered the country illegally—had received due process, even though she had
not been provided with a translator, did not have the assistance of legal coun-
sel, and did not have an opportunity to contest the findings. The Court also
stated explicitly what had been implied in its earlier decisions: "That Congress may exclude aliens of a particular race from the United States . . . and
commit the enforcement of such provisions, conditions, and regulations exclusively to executive officers, without judicial intervention, are principles
firmly established by the decisions of this court."[24]

Over time, the government has granted more procedural due process protections to immigrants in deportation proceedings, but exclusion—the denial
of entry into the country in the first place—is subject to minimal process:
"Whatever the procedure authorized by Congress is, it is due process as far as
an alien denied entry is concerned."[25]

PLENARY POWER

The Asian exclusion cases have never been modified or overturned. Immigration bills that discriminated by race or national origin, such as the Immigration Acts of 1917, 1924, and 1952, were immune from constitutional
challenge because of the plenary power doctrine established in the Asian exclusion cases. The racial bar on naturalization, which existed until 1952, could
never be challenged as unconstitutional; Asian plaintiffs simply sought to be
classified as "white persons" under the law. Over time, racial considerations
were gradually removed from the immigration and naturalization laws by congressional action, not by the courts.

The *Chinese Exclusion Case* and *Fong Yue Ting* continue to be cited in
modern cases to support the plenary power doctrine. In 1972, in *Kleindienst
v. Mandel*,[26] the Supreme Court cited both cases as authority when it rejected
a First Amendment challenge to the denial of a visitor visa to a journalist
who had been scheduled to speak in the United States on the subject of Marx-
ism. The Court did not even attempt to balance First Amendment interests
against the plenary powers of Congress. The Court stated: "The Court without exception has sustained Congress' 'plenary power to make rules for the

admission of aliens and to exclude those who possess those characteristics which Congress has forbidden. [O]ver no conceivable subject is the legislative power of Congress more complete than it is over the admission of aliens."[27]

In 1977, in *Fiallo v. Bell*,[28] the Supreme Court upheld immigration legislation that discriminated on the basis of both gender and illegitimacy by preventing the fathers of illegitimate children from applying for permanent resident visas for their children, even though mothers could do so under the law. Again citing the Asian exclusion cases, the Court ruled that Congress's plenary power over immigration allowed legislation that would be unconstitutional in another context.

By using national sovereignty as the basis for congressional and presidential power over immigration, the Supreme Court established a legal tradition that transcends the federal Constitution itself.[29] Doctrines of judicial review normally give the Supreme Court the final say in matters involving constitutional powers and rights. But the plenary power doctrine requires the courts to defer to the "political" branches of government, even in cases that may impugn basic rights and liberties such as equal protection and freedom of speech. The consequence of the plenary power doctrine is that laws such as the Chinese Exclusion Act or the racial bar on naturalization—laws that are universally condemned by contemporary racial standards—would still be constitutional if enacted today.

Race and National Origin in the Immigration Laws

Racial and national origin preferences still appear in federal immigration legislation. In the Immigration Act of 1990, for instance, Congress included two visa lottery programs designed to favor immigrants of particular national origins.[30] With Asian and Latin American immigration having dominated legal immigration since the 1970s, the 1990 act established a "diversity" lottery system (DV-1) for residents of countries that had not significantly used the family and employment preference systems. The primary beneficiaries of the DV-1 program have been European and African immigrants. In practice, the DV-1 program has excluded any applications from Asian countries such as China, India, South Korea, and the Philippines, and from Central American countries such as Mexico and El Salvador. The 1990 act also established a "transitional" lottery program that operated from 1991 to 1994. Nearly all of the immigrants under this program were from European countries. Ireland received 40 percent of the transitional visas, a reflection of special interest legislation.

Although the lotteries were designed to expand the overall pool of immigrants into the United States, an implicit assumption was that there were already enough Asian and Latino immigrants coming into the country. This assumption is also evident in the fact that in 1990 Congress added diversity visas while choosing not to address the problem of backlogs in the visa system, which most severely affect immigrants from Asia and Latin America. Because the demand for visas greatly exceeds the annual supply, waiting lists for relatives of American citizens and lawful permanent residents with approved visa applications number in the millions, with over one million people waiting in Asian countries alone. Waiting periods for relatives in some Asian countries have exceeded ten to fifteen years.[31] Under the plenary power doctrine, all of these immigration policies are immune from judicial review.

The Supreme Court has not had a recent opportunity to address a challenge to an immigration law that discriminates on the basis of race or national origin. But if the occasion arises to revisit the plenary power doctrine, the Supreme Court would be wise to overrule it, or at least to modify the doctrine so that anachronisms such as the racial exclusion laws can never again go into effect.

It would not tie the hands of Congress or the president to make the immigration and naturalization laws subject to constitutional limits and to judicial review. There is no constitutional right to immigrate to the United States, nor is there a constitutional right to become a naturalized citizen. If Congress chose to pass legislation to end all immigration, that law would be constitutional. But the Constitution embodies particular values—such as equal protection of the laws and freedom of expression and religion—that should not be simply thrown out the window because Congress is legislating in the area of immigration and naturalization. Immigration legislation should be subject to the same review by the courts as other national legislation. And the courts should at least recognize that racially discriminatory immigration laws serve no rational purpose.

Congressional Power over Immigrants

It is one thing to grant Congress and the president the power to regulate the entry of immigrants; sovereign powers are germane to the concept of the nation-state. It is another thing, however, to grant Congress and the president the power to do whatever they please with immigrants who have already entered the United States and are residing in the country. Over time, the courts have incorporated the due process mandates of the Fifth and Fourteenth Amendments into their review of congressional and executive action, including deportation proceedings. Yet, the plenary power doctrine has been used by the courts to extend Congress's regulation of the rights and benefits available to immigrant residents.

In 1976, the Supreme Court upheld the constitutionality of Congress's placing a five-year residency requirement on lawful permanent residents' participation in the federal Medicare program. In *Mathews v. Diaz*,[32] the plaintiffs were a lawful permanent resident and two Cuban refugees who were all over sixty-five years old and had been denied access to the Medicare Part B insurance program, which was financed by both the federal government and the insurance holder. A federal district court ruled that the restriction was unconstitutional because it violated the equal protection and due process rights of the plaintiffs by discriminating against them on the basis of alienage. The Supreme Court disagreed and reversed the lower court, holding that Congress's developing classifications among immigrants and between immigrants and citizens was within its traditional powers over immigration. The Court stated: "In the exercise of its broad power over naturalization and immigration, Congress regularly makes rules that would be unacceptable if applied to citizens. . . . The fact that an Act of Congress treats aliens differently from citizens does not in itself imply that such disparate treatment is 'invidious.'"[33] Once again, the Court cited the plenary power doctrine and *Fong Yue Ting* to support its ruling.

The Court's invocation of the plenary power doctrine in *Mathews v. Diaz* was tempered, however. The Court recognized that, under the Fifth and Fourteenth Amendments, immigrants cannot be deprived of life, liberty, or property without due process of law. The Court also recognized that equal protection was implicated in classifications between citizens and noncitizens and among different classes of noncitizens. Nevertheless, the Court held that because the requirements set out by Congress for Medicare eligibility were not "wholly irrational" they were constitutional. The Court did not grant Congress carte blanche; the legislation was evaluated under the rational-basis test that the courts apply in most due process and equal protection cases.

In a ruling issued on the same day as *Mathews v. Diaz*, the Supreme Court struck down federal civil service rules that limited government employment only to United States citizens. In *Hampton v. Mow Sun Wong*,[34] the plaintiffs, Chinese immigrants in San Francisco who were either terminated from government employment or denied employment because of their noncitizenship, successfully argued that the Civil Service Commission lacked the power—unlike Congress or the president—to impose a citizenship restriction. The Court recognized the impact of the rule on millions of lawful permanent residents: "By broadly denying this class substantial opportunities for employment, the Civil Service Commission rule deprives its members of an aspect of liberty."[35] But soon after the Supreme Court's decision, President Ford issued an executive order mandating a citizens-only government employment policy, which was later upheld by the federal courts, consistent with the plenary power doctrine, as constitutional.[36]

The Supreme Court rulings in *Mathews v. Diaz* and *Hampton v. Mow Sun Wong* are inconsistent when examined together. Justice John Paul Stevens authored both opinions, which makes the inconsistencies even more curious. The Court recognized the subordination that attached to denying permanent residents the opportunity to apply for government employment in the *Wong* case, but, at the same time, the Court gave its imprimatur to the lower courts to uphold the restrictions once the president had authorized them. In *Mathews v. Diaz*, the Court simply yielded to Congress's requirements and classifications with little discussion of the subordination that resulted from differential treatment.

By relying on the plenary power doctrine for support, the Court's reasoning in *Mathews* reflects an analytical weakness—the failure to recognize a distinction between *immigration* policies and *immigrant* policies. The two cannot be completely segregated: denying employment to immigrants can act as a deterrent to immigration, and preventing the immigration of certain individuals (such as classes of family members) can have a detrimental effect on immigrants in the United States. But immigration policies regulating the entry of new immigrants are much different from immigrant policies denying employment or participation in government benefits to immigrants residing in the United States. The liberty and property interests of residents who are denied access to employment or to government benefits are greater than the interests of immigrants who have not even entered the country. The Court at least recognized this in *Hampton v. Mow Sun Wong*, but it created an escape hatch for congressional and presidential action to produce the same anti-immigrant subordination.

The outcomes in the Supreme Court's two cases dealing with federal action against immigrants reflect principles of federalism. Congress, unlike the states, has national powers over immigration. The Court's treatment of state or local legislation is significantly different, demonstrating a recognition of both the limitations of the political process—noncitizens cannot vote—and the subordination of noncitizens as a class. To place the federal cases in perspective, the next section discusses the Supreme Court's rulings on state legislation affecting noncitizens.

Immigrants and Equal Protection

In 1948, in *Takahashi v. Fish and Game Commission*,[37] the United States Supreme Court struck down a California statute that prohibited "persons ineligible to citizenship"—code for Japanese immigrants—from fishing in the ocean waters off the California coast. The Court held that the equal protection clause was violated because the state's interest in protecting its resources was insufficient and that the state, unlike the federal government, had limited power to make a classification based on alienage.

During the 1970s, the Supreme Court extended the reasoning in *Takahashi* and ruled in a series of cases that alienage was a "suspect classification" under the equal protection clause, which demanded strict scrutiny by the courts of state and local legislation discriminating between citizens and noncitizens. In *Graham v. Richardson*,[38] the Supreme Court struck down an Arizona fifteen-year residency requirement and a Pennsylvania restriction on the receipt of state welfare benefits for noncitizens. The Court ruled that noncitizens were a "discrete and insular minority" and that a state's fiscal interest in limiting government resources for citizens was not a sufficiently compelling interest. The Court took special note of the fact that noncitizens pay taxes from which welfare benefits are drawn, just as citizens do. Employing similar reasoning, the Court later struck down a state law that discriminated against lawful permanent residents in the provision of financial assistance for higher education.[39]

In *Sugarman v. Dougall*,[40] the Supreme Court ruled that a state could not bar noncitizens from employment in the state civil service. Given the breadth of civil service positions, ranging from sanitation, typist, and office worker to public policy maker, the Court ruled that an across-the-board employment ban had little, if any, relation to a compelling state interest. The Court did, however, develop a major exception for elective positions and important nonelective executive, legislative, and judicial positions, because those individuals who "participate directly in the formulation, execution, or review of broad public policy perform functions that go to the heart of representative government."[41] In subsequent cases, the Supreme Court struck down state laws that banned permanent resident aliens from practicing law, from becoming licensed civil engineers, and from becoming notaries public.[42] But, because of the exception created in *Sugarman*—an exception that can swallow the rule—the Court has applied a lower level of scrutiny and upheld state laws and regulations that have prevented noncitizens from becoming state troopers, public school teachers, and probation officers.[43]

The *Sugarman* exception makes sense in the abstract—if there is to be any distinction between citizens and noncitizens, it should be in the political arena, where governance ought to be reserved for individuals having the full rights of political membership. But in practice, the Court's rulings upholding citizenship restrictions for state troopers, teachers, and probation officers have been too expansive. Law enforcement positions are arguably related to governance, but the policy-making powers of state troopers and probation officers are very limited. Public school teachers have great influence over the education of children, but it is not a profession for which formal citizenship makes a meaningful difference. As the four dissenting justices in *Ambach v. Norwick* noted, "Is it better to employ a poor citizen teacher than an excellent resident alien teacher? . . . The State will know how to select its teachers responsibly, wholly apart from citizenship, and can do so electively and intelligently."[44]

Even with the exceptions carved out by the Supreme Court, the upholding of alienage as a suspect classification shows that the courts recognize that state classifications based on citizenship are not *immigration* policies but *immigrant* policies which can subordinate lawful permanent residents as a class. The Supreme Court's acknowledgment that alienage classifications can subordinate immigrants is best exemplified in its 1982 ruling in *Plyler v. Doe*, the case in which the Court ruled that states could not discriminate against undocumented immigrant children in the area of public school education.[45]

In *Plyler v. Doe*, a five-to-four decision, the Court struck down a Texas statute that denied local school districts funds for the education of undocumented immigrant children and that allowed school districts to deny free public education to undocumented children. Early in its opinion, the Court rejected the State of Texas's contention that undocumented immigrants were not entitled to the protection of the Fourteenth Amendment: "The Equal Protection Clause was intended to work nothing less than the abolition of all caste-based and invidious class-based legislation."[46] The Court ruled that undocumented immigrants were not a suspect class, since their presence in the country was in violation of federal law. The Court also recognized, based on earlier case law, that education was not a fundamental right. Nevertheless, the importance of public school education and the possibility that the law would promote "the creation and perpetuation of a subclass of illiterates"[47] led the Court majority to reject a mere rational basis test.

The Court instead applied an intermediate level of scrutiny, requiring that the state prove that its law furthered a "substantial goal." The Court then proceeded to strike down the law because the state's interests were not substantial goals that could be furthered by the ban on undocumented children. Although the Court's approach to intermediate scrutiny in *Plyler* was untidy—grafting semi-suspect classification status to the important societal interests in public education—it showed that the courts can recognize when the subordination of immigrants is fundamentally inconsistent with principles of equal protection.

Federalism and Standards of Review

The hodgepodge of standards in the Supreme Court's equal protection cases involving noncitizenship beg for a better ordering. Because of federalism principles and the plenary power doctrine, congressional and presidential action are subject to the most deferential form of judicial scrutiny. State laws, with important exceptions involving political functions, are subject to the most exacting judicial scrutiny. The same policies enacted by one level of government can thus be constitutional in one setting and unconstitutional in another. Federal civil service employment is closed to noncitizens because the president says so, but state civil service employment must be open to noncitizens because states lack a compelling interest in making citizenship distinctions.

Recognizing that Congress and the president have the sole power to regulate immigration, the standard of review for federal *immigration* legislation ought to be a rational-basis test. Immigration legislation would include laws and policies regulating the exclusion, entry, deportation, and naturalization of immigrants. Federal *immigrant* legislation affecting permanent residents and other lawfully residing immigrants ought to be subject to heightened scrutiny. The courts have recognized that state legislation can subordinate immigrants by making distinctions between citizens and noncitizens; the impact of congressional legislation can be just as subordinating. And even under a lower rational-basis standard, the courts should recognize that most distinctions between citizens and lawful permanent residents—the group that is most similar to citizens—lack *any* rational purpose.

The standard of review for federal legislation affecting undocumented immigrants poses a different set of interests. As a class, undocumented immigrants are by definition living in the United States in violation of federal law. The standard of review for any federal legislation involving undocumented immigrants as a class should be a rational-basis test. Subjecting legislation to a rational-basis test does not automatically make it constitutional, however. As the Supreme Court stated in *Romer v. Evans*, the 1996 decision striking down Colorado's anti-homosexuality law, "if the constitutional conception of 'equal protection of the laws' means anything, it must at the very least mean that a bare . . . desire to harm a politically unpopular group cannot constitute a legitimate governmental interest."[48] Thus a law that targeted undocumented

immigrants would be unconstitutional if it had been enacted simply to burden immigrants because they are politically unpopular.

States are already preempted by federal law from enacting *immigration* legislation, although they can enact laws that comply with the federal immigration laws. The basic reasons for making alienage a suspect classification in state
immigrant legislation are still sound: noncitizens historically have been subject to discrimination, they lack political power, and they can be easily subordinated as a class. The "political function" exception is, in theory, a
legitimate basis for limiting some government employment to citizens only,
but it should be limited to those governmental positions that deal with significant public policy making, not to the basic implementation of policies or
to ministerial functions. For state legislation affecting undocumented immigrants, it would add both clarity and consistency to the law to subject state
legislation to an intermediate level of scrutiny if the legislation subordinates
undocumented immigrants through the denial of access to important governmental services. Education affects important societal interests, but so does the
provision of other key government services such as emergency medical care
and preventive programs such as immunizations and prenatal care.

Racialization and Immigration

The experience of Asian Americans suggests that there should not only be
greater congruency between the review of state and federal citizenship-based
legislation, but greater congruency between the review of race-based and
citizenship-based legislation. Racialization operates to link race and citizenship by equating Asian Americans with foreigners and with immigrants. One
consequence of racialization is that both immigration laws and immigrant laws
have racial meanings. Saying that there are too many immigrants coming to
the United States is not a race-neutral statement based on total numbers. "Too
many immigrants" inevitably means that there are too many of certain kinds
of immigrants, and that usually means too many Asians and too many Latinos.
Denying basic government services to immigrants does not fall evenly across
racial groups; because of the demographic realities, the heaviest impacts are
on Asian and Latino immigrants.

Ignoring a linkage between race and citizenship means that the law can
actually provide a haven for racially discriminatory legislation. If there are different judicial standards for evaluating race-based legislation and citizenship-
based legislation—race is examined with strict scrutiny, while alienage is
examined with rational-basis scrutiny—then laws that are couched in the language of citizenship will almost always be constitutional, even if they have

strong racial meanings and impacts. That explicitly discriminatory immigration and naturalization legislation has passed constitutional scrutiny in the past and that those constitutional cases still operate as precedent make the legal standards even more perilous.

One of the main reasons that the Asian exclusion cases continue to be used as precedent in modern constitutional litigation is that they have been de-racialized. It is more difficult to remove racial meanings from a case named "The Chinese Exclusion Case," than from a case named "Fong Yue Ting v. United States," which may explain why *Fong Yue Ting* tends to be cited more often in court cases than *The Chinese Exclusion Case*. But both cases have been stripped of their racial context in the courts' contemporary references and citations. The facts of the cases are never discussed; instead, they are usually the first links in a long chain of court citations—names, volume numbers, and page references—used to support the plenary power doctrine. It seems incongruous with contemporary racial jurisprudence for courts to continue citing cases that upheld racial exclusion laws, but that is the state of the law.

A law such as California's Proposition 187 illuminates the disjuncture between the political racialization and the legal de-racialization of anti-immigrant laws.[49] Racial politics dominated the Proposition 187 campaign. Supporters of the initiative invoked obvious racial images and rhetoric attacking Latinos as the source of undesirable migration. Latino and Asian immigrant rights groups were among the most vocal opponents of the initiative. Exit polls revealed highly polarized voting by race: 63 percent of the white voters voted in favor of the initiative, but 77 percent of the Latino voters, 53 percent of the Asian American voters, and 53 percent of the black voters voted against the initiative.[50]

Yet when they challenged Proposition 187 in federal court, plaintiffs did not—and could not—invoke a legal theory based on racial discrimination. The primary challenges to the law were on federalism grounds: Proposition 187 was, in effect, an attempt by the State of California to regulate immigration into the United States, which would be preempted by federal law because of Congress's exclusive powers over immigration. The equal protection challenge to the law was based on alienage, not race. Proposition 187's provisions restricting the education of undocumented students were in direct violation of the Supreme Court's 1982 decision in *Plyler v. Doe*.

An equal protection challenge to Proposition 187 based on racial discrimination would be extremely difficult, if not impossible, to prove. Because the language of Proposition 187 is race-neutral (it does not on its face discriminate on the basis of race), proof of discriminatory intent would be required to state a claim of racial discrimination in violation of the equal protection clause.

Because the law was enacted by popular vote rather than by a legislature, proof of intent is especially problematic. Even with the overtly racial campaign rhetoric and racially polarized voting, it would be difficult to prove that the intent of the California electorate—as the legislative body—was to discriminate on the basis of race. Without a legal test accommodating either unconscious racism or the racial meanings inherent in the linkage between race and immigration status, an equal protection challenge based on race would undoubtedly fail.

Unequal Citizenship

I have spent most of this chapter discussing the legal standards that the courts apply to immigration and immigrant legislation. The standards of review make a difference, because strict scrutiny and intermediate scrutiny almost always lead to the invalidation of a law, while rational-basis scrutiny almost always leads to the upholding of a law. But how society treats immigrants as immigrants is a larger and more fundamental question than the technical questions about the appropriate standard for courts to follow in reviewing legislation. What rights and responsibilities should noncitizens possess compared to citizens?

Civil rights are often framed by a principle of equality of citizenship. A goal of antidiscrimination law is to guarantee the rights of citizenship to members of groups who have been denied full citizenship in the past: racial and ethnic minorities, women, religious minorities, lesbians and gay men, and the disabled. But, if citizenship is the touchstone that defines civil rights, then noncitizens by definition do not have those same rights.

The Supreme Court has expressed the idea of citizenship in the context of a political community:

> The exclusion of aliens from basic governmental processes is not a
> deficiency in the democratic system but a necessary consequence of
> the community's process of political self-definition. Self-government,
> whether direct or through representatives, begins by defining the
> scope of the community of the governed and thus of the governors as
> well: aliens are by definition outside of this community.[51]

Using a political membership theory of citizenship, noncitizens do not possess the political rights of citizens: noncitizens cannot vote, they cannot serve on juries, they cannot hold certain government jobs. But should political membership define citizenship?[52] Noncitizen residents, including the undocumented, are "persons" under the law, so they have the constitutional and legal rights of citizens. Lawful permanent residents—the term itself implies a lasting relationship with the United States—attend schools, work, and develop deep roots in their local communities. And society imposes many of the same civic responsibilities on noncitizens that are imposed on citizens—the obligation to pay taxes and to be available for service in the United States military are just two. Participation in the life of a community can be just as important as the formalities of membership.

An alternative mediating principle is one based on equality and the prevention of subordination. Kenneth Karst has articulated a principle of "equal citizenship" that is also useful in the context of immigrants' rights:

> Each individual is presumptively entitled to be treated by the
> organized society as a respected, responsible, and participating
> member. Stated negatively, the principle forbids the organized society
> to treat an individual as a member of an inferior or dependent caste or
> as a nonparticipant. The principle thus centers on those aspects of
> equality that are most closely bound to the sense of self and the sense
> of inclusion in a community.[53]

Based on an equality principle, there are few reasons to maintain legal differences between citizens and noncitizens. (A radical egalitarian principle might suggest no differences at all, but that would in effect eliminate the concept of formal citizenship.) Noncitizens should be granted no less respect or worth as a class, nor should they be treated as an inferior caste relative to citizens. Thus, regardless of the actual standard of review, an equality-based argument suggests that most classifications based on citizenship simply do not serve a legitimate governmental purpose.

What rights, then, should attach to citizens but not to noncitizens? The question goes to the basic definition of citizenship—defining what citizenship is can be the same as defining what noncitizenship is not. The political rights that are typically used to define citizenship—the right to vote, the right to hold elected office, the right to serve on a jury, the right to government employment—can be viewed in two ways. First, political rights can be seen as attributes of a first principle defining full membership in American society. Noncitizenship in all its variations—including lawful permanent residency, refugee status, temporary worker or student status, and undocumented status—reflects less than full membership. Second, political rights can be seen as attributes of power between dominant and subordinate classes; citizens have the power to make the rules, and exclusivity is one of the basic goals.

None of the attributes of formal citizenship and noncitizenship are fixed. The plenary power doctrine gives virtual carte blanche to Congress and president in the area of immigration and immigrants' rights. Congress and the president could thus grant many of the rights available to citizens to noncitizens if they chose to. Federalism principles allow state and local governments to grant noncitizens extensive rights. Even the right to vote—considered the most basic right of citizenship—has been made available to noncitizens by state and local government. During the nineteenth century, several states extended the right to vote to noncitizens, partly to expand the number of white male voters.[54] More recently, cities such as Chicago and New York City have allowed noncitizen parents to vote in school board elections. In 1993, the voters of Takoma Park, Maryland, passed a ballot initiative to allow noncitizens to vote in local elections.[55] Thus, membership does not necessarily imply exclusivity.

Nevertheless, the contemporary political trend is not to extend more rights of citizenship to noncitizens; the trend is to deny rights to noncitizens, to scapegoat and subordinate noncitizens. When California's Proposition 187 was enacted into law, voters who cast their ballots in favor of the proposition made a statement about what they thought about undocumented immigrants: undocumented immigrants should not have access to public school education, to nonemergency health care from government providers, or to government social services. The basic statement was "You don't belong here." Yet it is not entirely clear whether those same voters wanted undocumented immigrants to leave the state altogether, particularly when undocumented immigrants are a critical source of labor for the state's largest industry, agriculture, and many other sectors of the economy. Ambivalence toward immigrants is not unusual; it has been a hallmark of American immigrant history.

Congress's passage of a welfare reform bill in 1996 that discriminated against lawful permanent residents by removing their eligibility for public entitlements—Food Stamps and Supplemental Security Income for the elderly, blind, and disabled—made an even stronger statement about how the nation should treat its noncitizens. The immigrant restriction was passed in the political context of a conservative Republican-dominated Congress seeking to end the federal government's commitment to welfare in general; other policy statements about the role of the federal government were being made as well. And even though legislation passed the next year maintained benefits for many immigrants, the subordination of noncitizens suggests that our national values are moving in a disturbing, even tragic, direction. If taking away the subsistence incomes of an especially vulnerable class of lawful permanent residents is not "invidious" discrimination, then what is?

Nativism and Citizenship

Alienage differs from race in one important way: it is not immutable. A lawful permanent resident can become an American citizen through naturalization. (Recall, though, that naturalized citizenship has been a reality for Asian immigrants only since 1952.) There have been proposals in recent years that would shift the nature of the American political community by changing the basic definitions of citizenship. One set of proposals would erect more barriers to naturalized citizenship by changing the requirements for naturalization, including lengthening the residency period for applicants. Another set of proposals would change the nature of birthright citizenship under the Fourteenth Amendment by denying citizenship to the children of undocumented parents. Contemporary nativism has generated these proposals, which reflect attempts to better define "us" and "them" along the lines of formal citizenship. Inevitably, racial meanings are inherent in these proposals—the "them" rhetoric usually refers to racialized immigrants who differ from the core definition of "American."

NATURALIZED CITIZENSHIP

The basic requirements for naturalized citizenship include lawful permanent resident status, a minimum residency period in the United States—five years for most people, three years for spouses of citizens—good moral character, an understanding of English and civics, and allegiance to the United States.[56] There are special provisions for the disabled and for elderly long-time residents that allow certain requirements, such as the English language requirement, to be waived. For example, permanent residents over fifty-five years old who have resided in the United States for over fifteen years can take the civics test in their native languages.

Proposals to restrict naturalization have included increasing the residency period beyond five years, eliminating the English language exceptions for long-time residents, and making the English and civics tests more difficult. None of these proposals seem to be motivated by anything other than erecting additional barriers to naturalization in order to make citizenship less attainable. Entry as a permanent resident already requires overcoming barriers—meeting a basic requirement of a family membership or significant employment skills. Five years of residency is a lengthy period of time, and seems more than sufficient to demonstrate close ties to the United States. Knowledge of English and civics are already required under the law, and there are strong reasons to favor long-time elderly residents because of the difficulties of language acquisition in old age. The value of citizenship is already high, as demonstrated by the hundreds of thousands of applicants who seek naturalized citizenship every year.

BIRTHRIGHT CITIZENSHIP

The Fourteenth Amendment was enacted after the Civil War to guarantee citizenship to newly freed slaves and to overturn the Supreme Court's infamous *Dred Scott* ruling that slaves and their descendants were not citizens under the law.[57] The relevant part of the amendment states: "All persons born or naturalized in the United States, and subject to the jurisdiction thereof, are citizens of the United States and of the State wherein they reside." In 1898, the United States Supreme Court ruled in *United States v. Wong Kim Ark* that all persons born in the United States, even those born to parents who were ineligible for naturalization, were citizens of the United States.[58] The Court stated: "The Fourteenth Amendment affirms the ancient and fundamental rule of citizenship by birth within the territory, in the allegiance and under the protection of the country, including all children born of resident aliens."[59]

Proposals to alter this basic conception of citizenship have centered on enacting legislation or even amending the Constitution to deny birthright citizenship to the children born in the United States to undocumented immigrant parents. These proposals are rooted in attempts to remove incentives to enter the United States illegally. The assumption is that birthright citizenship and the benefits of citizenship, including free education and welfare entitlements, induce immigrants to enter the country. Some proposals have even suggested a distinction based on gender: children born in the United States whose mothers are undocumented would not be citizens, but those whose fathers are undocumented would be citizens. The motivation is apparently to prevent women from entering the country illegally in order to give birth to their children in the United States. There may be people who have this motivation, but tinkering with the Constitution is an excessive solution, particularly when there are more powerful motivations, such as seeking employment or escaping political persecution, that are driving undocumented migration.

Some of the proposals have found theoretical support in the book *Citizenship Without Consent* by Peter Schuck and Rogers Smith. Schuck and Smith propose a citizenship model based on "consent" rather than "ascription," which is predicated on citizenship being ascribed by some objective condition such as being born in the United States. A consensual model would require the mutual consent of the government and the governed before citizenship is granted. Schuck and Smith propose that Congress pass a statute making the citizenship of the children of American citizens and of lawful permanent residents provisional, allowing the children to consent to their citizenship once they become adults, with the government consenting implicitly to their citizenship because of their parents' lawful status. The children of undocumented immigrants, however, would not become citizens, because the government had never consented to their parents' residency in the United States.

A consent-based theory of citizenship has some theoretical appeal, but it poses serious problems. First, it penalizes children, who do not consent to what their parents' actions have been. Second, by denying citizenship to those children, the policy only adds to the growing underclass already residing in the United States with diminished rights. Third, it gives short shrift to the underpinnings of the Fourteenth Amendment and the Supreme Court's ruling in *Wong Kim Ark*. The Fourteenth Amendment was designed to ensure citizenship for "all persons" born in the United States, particularly in response to ambiguities in legal status that attached to being the descendants of an outsider class, namely slaves.

When *Wong Kim Ark* was decided, there was no clear distinction between "legal" and "illegal" immigrants, and given the treatment of Chinese immigrants at the time, their status was certainly less than favorable. As the Supreme Court stated, "Chinese persons not born in this country have never been recognized as citizens of the United States, nor authorized to become such under the naturalization laws."[60] Quoting legislative debate around the Fourteenth Amendment, the Court also noted that Congress accepted the possibility that the children of Chinese immigrants—immigrants who were clearly considered undesirable by members of Congress—could become citizens: "We are entirely ready to accept the provision proposed in this Constitutional Amendment, that the children born here of Mongolian parents shall be declared by the Constitution of the United States to be entitled to civil rights and to equal protection before the law with others."[61] The Court thus recognized that the Fourteenth Amendment was designed to overcome the legal disabilities that could attach to the status of one's parents.

The proposed restrictions on naturalization and birthright citizenship would ultimately limit immigrant empowerment, whether through the denial of the right to vote or the symbolic expansion of the gap between "them" and "us." Proponents of limited naturalization and birthright citizenship seek to make full membership in the political community—formal citizenship status—something more valuable than it already is. Citizenship is valuable. The growing numbers of immigrants who seek to naturalize every year are a measure of that value. But making citizenship more valuable to citizens for value's sake alone is not a sufficient reason to erect the barriers that have been proposed. It is subordination in its purest form.

Chapter 5

Language and Legal Conformity

In 1970, Kinney Kinmon Lau was one of nearly 3,000 Chinese American students attending public school in San Francisco who spoke little or no English. Many of these students were recent immigrants, but most were U.S.-born children who had been educated in schools that had been racially segregated for decades. Despite efforts by parents and community activists urging the San Francisco Unified School District to implement programs to assist the students with English, the school district replied with only minimal effort. The district provided no assistance to nearly 1,800 of the students and less than an hour of daily instruction in a supplemental English class to the remainder.

Kinney Lau and twelve other students became plaintiffs in a class action lawsuit to challenge the school district's inaction as discriminatory and a violation of federal law. The students' claims were initially rejected by a federal district court judge and later by a panel of appeals court judges who were unsympathetic to their requests. In its 1973 opinion to *Lau v. Nichols*, the court of appeals stated bluntly: "The discrimination suffered by these children is not the result of laws passed by the state of California, presently or historically, but is the result of deficiencies created by the children themselves in failing to know and learn the English language."[1]

The United States Supreme Court took the appeal of the *Lau* case later that year, and in a unanimous decision issued in January 1974, the Court ruled that the school district's failure to provide meaningful instruction to the Chinese American students violated Title VI of the Civil Rights of 1964, which bans discrimination in programs receiving federal financial assistance.[2] Writing for the Court, Justice William O. Douglas observed that "there is no equality of treatment merely by providing these students with the same facilities, textbooks, teachers, and curriculum; for students who do not understand English are effectively foreclosed from any meaningful education."[3] Justice Douglas went on to write: "Basic English skills are at the very core of what these public schools teach. Imposition of a requirement that, before a child can effectively participate in the educational program, he must already have acquired those basic skills is to make a mockery of public education."[4]

As a result of *Lau v. Nichols*, school districts throughout the country were required to begin addressing the needs of limited-English-proficient students. Federal agencies began monitoring compliance with *Lau*, and Congress passed the Equal Educational Opportunity Act of 1974, making it a violation of federal law for an educational agency to fail "to take appropriate action to overcome language barriers that impede equal participation by its students in its instructional programs."[5] Kinney Lau and the other students won a final victory when the San Francisco Unified School District entered into a settlement agreement to provide both bilingual instruction and English-as-a-Second-Language (ESL) instruction to the district's limited-English-proficient students.[6]

Speaking in 1994 at a symposium commemorating the twentieth anniversary of the *Lau v. Nichols* decision, Professor Edward Steinman, Kinney Lau's attorney, made the following observation:

> The case was based on a different notion of equality. At that time, the country was focused on problems of racial segregation. A focus on segregation and the treatment of blacks, in essence, provides one notion of inequality: taking people who are the same and treating them differently. That is only half of the coin. The other side of inequality is more subtle, less visible, and equally invidious. It is taking kids who are different and treating them the same.[7]

The second side of inequality that Professor Steinman identifies—treating people who are different as if they are the same—is the subject of this chapter. Despite cases like *Lau v. Nichols*, the laws are far less than effective in addressing racial and ethnic differences. Courts and legislatures have had little trouble recognizing differences in the past; historically, racial and ethnic differences have been the primary bases for subordinating Asian Americans and other racial minorities. But subordination caused by failing to acknowledge and address differences is another matter. Nativism and ideological commitments to racial and ethnic assimilation—the polar opposites of historical ideologies justifying anti-Asian discrimination—pose the greatest challenges to the legal accommodation of difference. In this chapter, I highlight one set of differences, language differences, and the legal responses to those differences.

Language Barriers and Asian Immigrants

Lacking proficiency in English is the greatest social barrier facing Asian im-migrants and refugees in the United States. According to the 1990 census, nearly 56 percent of Asians and Pacific Islanders do not speak English very well, and over one-third live in "linguistically isolated" households, which are defined as households in which no one other than a child speaks just English and no one who is bilingual speaks English very well.[8] Over 40 percent of Chinese, Koreans, and Vietnamese, and the majority of Cambodians, Laotians, and Hmong live in linguistically isolated households. The inability to com-municate in English means, among other things, having difficulty in school, lacking access to most sectors of the labor and business markets, and having limited social interaction with people outside of one's own language group. Limited English proficiency can also mean facing serious barriers in accessing the full array of public services, including emergency police and fire services as well as the health care and judicial systems. As the information age advances with the increasing use of computer technologies and the Internet, the low-income, non-English-speaking population faces the risk of being marginalized and of falling even further behind the English-speaking majority.

Language-based discrimination is a common problem associated with lim-ited English proficiency. One example is a case filed in 1994 by individuals whose life insurance applications were denied by the Northwestern Mutual Life Insurance Company because they were unable to meet the company's English-proficiency requirement. The named plaintiff in the case was a seventy-one-year-old Korean American woman in Northern California whose first language was not English but whose language skills were proficient enough for her to become a naturalized citizen. Her application was denied when an agent had trouble understanding her on a telephone call, even though she had passed both a medical examination and an interview several days earlier. After the filing of a class action lawsuit against Northwestern alleging violations of both federal and state antidiscrimination laws, the company entered into a settle-ment in 1996 in which it agreed to drop its English-proficiency requirements and to expand its marketing and publications to address the needs of non-English-speaking customers.[9]

Providing equal access to Asian immigrants poses a significant challenge for both business and government because of the multiplicity of Asian ethnic groups. There is no "Asian" language that all Asian immigrants and refugees speak. The problem is compounded by the fact that individuals within some Asian ethnic groups speak entirely different languages. For example, Chinese immigrants share a common written language, but their spoken languages in-clude Mandarin, Cantonese, and many others; most Filipino immigrants speak

English, but their primary languages include Tagalog, Ilocano, Cebuano, Visayan, and a host of other languages. English-language acquisition is also a problem for Asian immigrants because of the major differences in syntax, intonation, and vocabulary between English and many Asian languages; elderly immigrants in particular often attain little more than minimal capability in English. The major political constraint on English language acquisition is the low priority given to funding for adult ESL classes. Because of inadequate resources among school districts and community college districts, waiting lists for ESL classes in some cities have numbered in the tens of thousands.[10]

Racialization as a homogeneous population also creates impediments to addressing the language needs of Asian immigrants. When immigrants of Asian ancestry are lumped into a single racial category such as "Asian and Pacific Islander," the needs of a wide variety of language groups may be left unaddressed. Even when there are policies designed to address language differences, Asian immigrants can be shortchanged because of the tendency to view Asian populations in the aggregate. It is not uncommon to find dualistic models of language assistance applied to Asian immigrants as a whole: bilingual education programs and court interpreter programs are often set up to address Latino populations who speak Spanish, but the programs often do not develop sufficient resources to address the *multi*lingual character of the Asian American population.[11]

Asian American experiences illuminate the powerful impact of ethnic and linguistic differences. Like other limited-English or non-English speakers, Asian immigrants can suffer the disabilities of English-only policies that establish barriers to language and communication. But because the Asian American population is heterogeneous, any laws and policies that favor bilingualism must accommodate the wide variety of languages and dialects spoken within Asian America. Diversity takes on its full meaning in attempting to address the multiple language needs of Asian Americans.

Pluralism and Assimilationism

How to best address the needs of a multilingual population is a question that raises basic issues of membership and participation in American society. Few people question the primacy of English as the language of custom and commerce in the United States, and few people discourage the learning of English. The tension arises between accommodating linguistic differences and restricting the use of languages other than English in order to foster civic unity.

This tension is often expressed as a dichotomy between pluralism and assimilationism.[12] Pluralism asserts the value of maintaining ethnic identity.

The maintenance of ethnic group identity comes in the form of oral and written communication in a particular language, as well as other manifestations of ethnicity, such as food, religion, arts, literature, and media. Assimilationism, on the other hand, asserts the value of incorporating ethnic groups into the dominant society. Pluralism and assimilationism are not mutually exclusive: assimilation can be an internal goal of an ethnic group seeking to maintain its identity; members of a predominantly immigrant group may try to shift group identity and be more "American" through language, custom, and politics. But assimilation can also be externally mandated; laws may require conformity through common cultural norms and the exclusive use of English. "Anglo conformity" is one manifestation of assimilationism in the United States, for which the standard that ethnic groups must strive is northern European and English-speaking.[13]

Race, however, has always compounded ethnic assimilation. Assimilationist theories are often based on European immigrant experiences; they suggest ultimate acceptance by the dominant group of an ethnic minority group. The problem with this perspective is that racism has always operated to prevent the assimilation of non-European ethnic groups. As "racial ethnics," Asians were for decades excluded from the United States and from becoming naturalized citizens based on the predicate that they were not assimilable into American society.[14] Nevertheless, assimilationism now predominates in both social and legal discourse. Supreme Court Justice Antonin Scalia's statement in his concurring opinion in *Adarand Constructors, Inc. v. Peña* reflects a neoconservative view of racial assimilation: "In the eyes of government, we are just one race here. It is American."[15]

The legal responses to racial and ethnic differencs reflect the political tensions between pluralism and assimilationism. Many public policies, such as bilingual education and language assistance in voting, have attempted to accommodate ethnic pluralism. Other public policies, such as English-only laws, have attempted to force assimilation through unitary standards of behavior. Like many legislative bodies, the courts have been divided in their treatment of linguistic pluralism and assimilationism. The *Lau* decision reflects one body of cases endorsing legal pluralism, but there is also a large body of decisional law that has rejected pluralism in favor of assimilationism.

Language and Government Responsibility

When the Supreme Court ruled in *Lau v. Nichols* that the failure to provide language assistance to limited-English-proficient students violated Title VI of the Civil Rights Act of 1964, the Court imposed a mandate on school districts to take affirmative steps to address language differences. However, because the Court did not address whether the equal protection clause was violated by the school district's inaction, the *Lau* case left open a set of broader questions, including whether language triggers heightened judicial scrutiny under the equal protection clause and whether the Constitution imposes affirmative duties on government to provide assistance to language minorities. Four years before *Lau v. Nichols*, a federal appeals court ruled in *United States ex rel. Negrón v. New York*,[16] that a criminal defendant's constitutional rights were violated by the failure to provide a court interpreter; the *Negrón* ruling in turn inspired legislation such as the federal Court Interpreters Act of 1978 to guarantee interpreters for criminal defendants.[17]

Outside of the criminal justice arena, the courts have been unwilling to impose duties on government to provide language assistance. The California Supreme Court has ruled that the government's refusal to appoint an interpreter in a civil proceeding did not violate the federal Constitution.[18] In 1978, a federal court of appeals ruled that bilingual education was not mandated by the Constitution or by statute.[19] Several federal appeals courts have ruled that government's failure to provide translated notices for administrative claims and appeals is not unconstitutional; the courts have upheld the provision of notices only in English for unemployment insurance claims, seizures of property, and Social Security claims.[20] One federal appeals court has ruled that there is no constitutional right to take a civil service examination in another language.[21]

For the small number of situations in which the government does have a duty to provide language assistance, civil rights statutes—not judicial interpretations of constitutional rights—have been the primary sources of law. In California, the Dymally-Alatorre Act requires all state agencies that provide information or services to the public to employ bilingual staff and translate materials when the number of non-English speakers is at least 5 percent of the population served by a local office or facility.[22] California's laws extend bilingual services into health care, social services, emergency services, employment, housing, education, licensing, consumer protection, and criminal and civil proceedings.[23] Nationally, the two areas that have had the most significant impact on limited-English-proficient individuals—and have generated the most controversy—are education and voting.

Language Assistance and Education

Linguistic pluralism and assimilationism are perhaps most hotly debated in the area of public education, where competing theories and policies over the education of limited-English-proficient (LEP) students have divided parents, teachers, administrators, school boards, and policy makers. The numbers and needs of LEP students are large and growing. The number of LEP students in the United States is estimated to be at least 3 million; some estimates put the number at over 5 million. In 1996 there were over 1.3 million LEP students in California alone; at close to 80 percent of the total, Latino students were the largest group, followed by Vietnamese (3.6%), Hmong (2.4%), Filipino (1.6%), and Cambodian (1.6%) students.[24] In large urban districts, LEP students often constitute between 15 and 30 percent of the school district. In Los Angeles, one of the nation's largest school districts, close to one-half of the students have been LEP students. Few disagree about the basic goals of promoting academic achievement and fostering the acquisition of English-language skills for these students. The lines have been drawn between supporters and opponents of bilingual education, the teaching method that places LEP students in classes where most of the instruction is conducted in their primary language.

When it issued its ruling in *Lau v. Nichols*, the Supreme Court acknowledged that the failure to address linguistic differences deprived students of equal educational opportunities. The Court did not, however, specify the appropriate methods to achieve the goal of educational equity. Based on the *Lau* decision, section 1703(f) of the Equal Educational Opportunity Act is also cast in broad language, making illegal "the failure of an educational agency to take appropriate action to overcome language barriers that impede equal participation by its students in its instructional programs."[25] Informal guidelines issued by the Department of Health, Education, and Welfare in 1975—known as the "Lau Remedies"—strongly promoted bilingual education, but the guidelines were withdrawn under pressure from the Reagan administration in 1981.[26]

It is clear from *Lau* that "sink or swim" methods of instruction are not sufficient to guarantee educational equity to LEP students. But there are a variety of programs that can be used other than English language "submersion." Variations include structured English immersion, in which classes are taught in English but the teacher is bilingual and can understand the students' primary language; supplemental English instruction in ESL classes; transitional bilingual education programs that teach all subjects initially in the student's primary language, but phase into English-based instruction as the student acquires English skills; and structured home language instruction in which instruction in the primary language is maintained until the primary language is mastered. Proponents of bilingual education argue that teaching academic subjects in the student's primary language provides the best pedagogical method of instruction and offers the smoothest transition to English-only instruction in later grades. Using this approach, students gain better knowledge of all of their subjects, including their primary language, and maintain higher self-esteem when they are placed in regular classes.[27]

Opponents of bilingual education argue that teaching students in their primary language only postpones English-language acquisition and maintains a sense of separatism; structured home language instruction is especially divisive because it promotes making English the student's secondary language.[28] In addition, opponents criticize the added costs of bilingual instruction, particularly when school districts are struggling with diminished resources for all students. Proponents counter that alternatives such as submersion programs only lead to frustration and underachievement among students and ultimately lead to their dropping out of school altogether. The results of many bilingual education programs are mixed: well-implemented and well-financed bilingual programs lead to higher achievement, while poorly implemented and underfunded programs usually lead to lower achievement.[29]

Even when bilingual education is adopted as a school district's LEP theory, many Asian immigrant children are still left without adequate instruction.[30] Because of the multiplicity of Asian languages, school districts often lack a sufficient number of bilingual teachers to provide instruction for all of the different Asian language groups. For example, a district with a large Southeast refugee population may have to address at least five language groups: Vietnamese, Cambodian, Lao, Lao-Mien, and Hmong. It is not unusual to find programs that place Southeast Asian students into a combined "bilingual" education classroom, which cannot be truly bilingual if there is more than one language group in the classroom. The children have been placed in a dressed-up ESL and submersion class. Many classes are taught by temporary instructors or by uncertified teachers with limited experience in either ESL instruction or in bilingual education. During the 1980s, Southeast Asian students in Lowell, Massachusetts, were not only denied adequate bilingual instruction, they were placed into segregated schools with substandard and overcrowded classrooms.[31] Another variation is the tracking of LEP students into classes designed for children with learning disabilities, a process that only exacerbates problems of language acquisition.

Despite the imprecision of *Lau* and the federal laws, the legal standards establishing educational equity for limited-English-speaking students are not the real problem for Asian immigrant children.[32] During the late 1980s, lawsuits in Lowell and in Philadelphia were successful in compelling local school districts to better address the needs of the growing number of Southeast Asian LEP students. The politics of language pose the fundamental problem. The conservative political trend has been to minimize federal and state mandates to allow local school districts the discretion to enact policies that comply with the general principles under *Lau v. Nichols* and little else. The result is fewer financial resources for school districts that might choose to implement bilingual instruction. In California, the state with the largest number of LEP students, the state's ten-year-old comprehensive bilingual education law was allowed to "sunset" in 1987, during a period of strong nativist sentiment. The result has been limited state funding targeted for bilingual education.

Language Assistance and the Voting Rights Act

The Supreme Court's decision in *Lau v. Nichols* was one of the justifications for Congress's amending the Voting Rights Act of 1965 to extend the act's coverage to "language minority groups," defined in the act as "persons who are American Indian, Asian American, Alaskan Natives, or of Spanish heritage."[33] Under its 1975 amendments, Congress recognized that many language-minority groups had been denied equal educational opportunities in the past and that it would be "necessary to eliminate such discrimination by prohibiting English-only elections, and by prescribing other remedial devices."[34] The primary means of addressing language discrimination has been the provision of language assistance in the electoral process, including bilingual ballots.

Under the original 1965 act, literacy tests were recognized as discriminatory barriers to voting; some local jurisdictions established tests that required college-level or even graduate-level English in order to vote. The 1975 amendments added the requirement that written materials and oral assistance for voters be made available in languages other than English under certain circumstances. One of the act's eligibility formulas, known as section 203, requires language assistance in jurisdictions in which (1) a protected group accounted for at least 5 percent of the voting age citizens and (2) the group's illiteracy rate was higher than the national illiteracy rate.[35] Section 203 was amended in 1992 to add another eligibility formula that supplemented the first part of the test, the 5 percent benchmark, with a numerical benchmark. Any jurisdiction containing at least ten thousand voting age citizens of a single language-minority group is also covered by section 203.[36]

Under section 203, several counties in Hawaii, California, and New York are required to provide voting assistance in Asian languages. Most jurisdictions are required to assist only one Asian language group. Los Angeles County is required to provide language assistance to four Asian ethnic groups: Chinese, Filipinos, Japanese, and Vietnamese; the county's large Korean population is not included, however, because their illiteracy rate is below the national rate.[37] The 1992 amendments adding the numerical benchmark of ten thousand were a major development for Asian Americans, who were among the strongest advocates for the amendments; few of the jurisdictions covered by the ten thousand benchmark would have been covered under the 5 percent benchmark.[38]

Governmental compliance with section 203 has varied, depending on the local jurisdiction. In San Francisco, the registrar's office has provided election materials in Chinese for several years, because of prior requirements under the Voting Rights Act and prior litigation against the county.[39] In nearby Alameda County, discrepancies during the November 1994 elections led the federal government to file a lawsuit against the county in 1995 to ensure compliance with section 203; the registrar's office had failed, among other things, to provide signs or notices of the availability of Chinese language assistance, to provide bilingual poll workers, and to make bilingual sample ballots available at polling sites.[40] A consent decree designed to remedy the problems is in effect until the year 2005. Similar problems arose in New York City, where erratic distribution of sample ballots, inadequate assistance from interpreters, and deficiencies in written materials led to Justice Department involvement and the production of formal election procedures by the Board of Elections.[41]

Many of the same criticisms leveled against bilingual education have been made against bilingual ballots: bilingual assistance discourages learning English, employing languages other than English is separatist and divisive, financial costs are excessive. Nativist arguments have focused specifically on the disincentive that bilingual ballots create to immigrants' gaining greater knowledge of English. But the argument is specious: reviewing a ballot once or twice a year in one's primary language should not act as a disincentive to learning English when English skills are far more important for daily use during the remainder of the year. Moreover, the weakness in this particular argument is that it ignores Congress's intent in creating the language assistance amendments in the first place. The amendments were not enacted to benefit voters who were necessarily immigrants. Congress's ban on literacy tests in the original 1965 act recognized that illiteracy was a product of racial discrimination in education against blacks in the South. Because many native-born Latinos and Asian Americans had also been denied equal educational opportunities, the 1975 amendments were designed to remedy educational discrimination suffered by members of these and other language-minority groups.

Many of the voters who now use bilingual ballots are immigrants, but opponents still ignore the important interests and rights that would be compromised through the elimination of language assistance. Bilingual ballots are designed to promote greater participation in the political process, not to encourage separatism. Many elderly immigrants have great difficulty with

English language acquisition, a fact that is recognized under the naturalization law exempting long-term permanent residents from the law's English-language requirements. Even those who possess sufficient English fluency to gain naturalization may still lack the higher level of English comprehension that is necessary to understand ballot language, particularly language explaining complex initiatives and referenda. Without bilingual ballots and other language assistance, these citizens might not be able to participate in the electoral process at all. The justification for bilingual ballots—equal access to the political process—actually suggests expansion, not the elimination, of coverage under the Voting Rights Act.

Government and Official English

The controversies over bilingual education and bilingual ballots reflect the more fundamental debate over linguistic pluralism and the place of languages other than English in public life. The assimilationist response has been to call for the elimination of bilingual instruction and voter assistance, either through legislation that repeals existing laws or through legislation making English the official—and only—language of government.

Calls for the dominance of English are nothing new. Nativist sentiment has triggered proposals supporting the primacy of English throughout American history. Criticizing the German presence in the colonies, Benjamin Franklin invoked rhetoric in 1751 that is strikingly similar to contemporary nativist discourse: "[W]hy should the Palatine Boors be suffered to swarm into our Settlements, and by herding together establish their Language and Manners to the Exclusion of ours? Why should Pennsylvania, founded by the English, become a Colony of Aliens, who will shortly be so numerous as to Germanize us instead of Anglifying them, and will never adopt our Language or Customs, any more than they can acquire our Complexion."[42] Similar sentiment arose during the early decades of the twentieth century, leading several states to enact legislation, later held to be unconstitutional, requiring English to be the sole language of instruction and banning the teaching of German and other foreign languages in public schools.[43]

Custom, not law, has made English the primary language of the United States. However, the laws have not been immune to nativism. The immigration and naturalization laws—the laws that most powerfully reflect American nativism—have established language requirements for admission to lawful permanent residency and to naturalized citizenship. A literacy test for admission to the United States was included in the Immigration Act of 1917 to limit the admission of undesirable European immigrants. The 1917 act excluded "[a]ll aliens over sixteen years of age, physically capable of reading, who can not read the English language, or some other language or dialect."[44] A literacy test is still required under the immigration laws for admission to permanent residency in the United States. The naturalization laws have required knowledge of English since 1906, a year after the Commission on Naturalization admonished that "the proposition is incontrovertible that no man is a desirable citizen of the United States who does not know the English language."[45] The English-language requirement was augmented in 1950 to require not only speaking ability but full literacy in English, a basic requirement that remains intact in the naturalization laws.[46]

Nativist proposals—many in the form of ballot initiatives—have arisen at all levels of government to make English the official language. Through the end of 1996, twenty-two states, nineteen of them since 1984, had adopted English as their sole official language.[47] Some of these laws declaring English the state language are largely symbolic, much like state flowers or state animals. Others contain extensive limitations on the use of languages other than English in government workplaces. Most of the cities and states that have approved official-English laws through ballot initiatives have large Asian and Latino immigrant populations—and predominantly white electorates. In 1989, the voters of Lowell, Massachusetts, approved a referendum declaring English to be the city's official language by a ratio of nearly three to one. In 1986, California voters passed Proposition 63, a constitutional amendment making English the official language of the state, by a vote of 73 percent to 27 percent. Florida's official-English constitutional amendment was passed by the voters by an even larger margin: 84 percent to 16 percent.[48]

Official English and the First Amendment

On their face, official-English laws raise significant constitutional issues. Because official-English laws can prevent communication in other languages by government and its employees, First Amendment rights of free speech are implicated. Arizona's official-English law, Article 28, contains the most extensive limitations on the governmental use of languages other than English, and was challenged as unconstitutional soon after its enactment. Passed as a ballot initiative in 1988 by a margin of one percentage point, Article 28 made English the official language of the State of Arizona and "of the ballot, the public schools and all government functions and actions." Article 28's reach extends to all branches and levels of government in Arizona and to all government officials and employees during the performance of government business. The law prohibits the use of languages other than English by government entities and invalidates any governmental document written in a language other than English. The only exceptions to the blanket rules in Article 28 are to assist students with English-language proficiency, to comply with federal law, to teach a foreign language, to protect public health or safety, and to protect the rights of criminal defendants or victims of crime.

Litigation challenging the constitutionality of Article 28 was initiated by a bilingual state employee who argued that her First Amendment rights were abridged and chilled by the law's extensive prohibitions on the use of non-English languages. Although the First Amendment rights of public employees are limited because of government's interest in regulating its own workers, both a federal district court and a federal court of appeals ruled that Article 28 was overbroad because the plain language of the law restricted the ability of public employees to speak in languages other than English. The courts thus recognized that speaking in another language was a form of pure speech that enjoyed First Amendment protection.

The court of appeals went even further to rule that the law was unconstitutional because it interfered with the ability of the non-English-speaking populace to receive information. In *Yniguez v. Arizonans for Official English*,[49] the court of appeals found that Article 28 "obstructs the free flow of information and adversely affects the rights of many private persons by requiring the incomprehensible to replace the intelligible. . . . The article effectively requires that [government] employees remain mute before members of the non-English-speaking public who seek their assistance."[50] In 1997, the United States Supreme Court vacated the decisions of both the district court and the federal appeals court in *Yniguez* on procedural grounds, leaving the basic question of the constitutionality of English-only legislation under the First Amendment unresolved.[51]

Language and Due Process

Other constitutional rights, including due process and equal protection, are threatened by official-English legislation. During the 1920s, the Supreme Court struck down several state and territorial laws that restricted the use of languages other than English as violations of due process. In *Meyer v. Nebraska*,[52] the Supreme Court struck down a Nebraska statute that mandated English-only instruction in all public and private schools and prohibited foreign-language instruction in grades below the high school level. Ruling that the English-only law unreasonably infringed on liberty interests under the due process clause, the Court stated: "The protection of the Constitution extends to all, to those who speak other languages as well as to those born with English on the tongue. Perhaps it would be be highly advantageous if all had ready understanding of our ordinary speech, but this cannot be coerced with methods which conflict with the Constitution—a desirable end cannot be promoted by prohibited means."[53]

In *Yu Cong Eng v. Trinidad*,[54] the Supreme Court reviewed a law known as the "Chinese Bookkeeping Act," which made it a crime in the Philippines, an American territory at the time, for anyone to keep accounting books in a language other than English, Spanish, or a local dialect. Noting the importance of using a language that the Chinese businesses could understand, the Supreme Court struck down the law on due process and equal protection grounds. The Court stated: "[W]e think the present law, which deprives them of something indispensable to the carrying on of their business, and is obviously intended chiefly to affect them as distinguished from the rest of the community, is a denial to them of the equal protection of the laws."[55] In *Farrington v. Tokushige*,[56] the Supreme Court upheld an injunction against the enforcement of the "Hawaiian Foreign Language School Law," which placed excessive burdens and regulations on the territory's 163 foreign-language schools, of which 9 were providing instruction in Korean, 7 in Chinese, and the remainder in Japanese. The Court found that the liberty interests of language-school owners, parents, and children were infringed in violation of the due process clause.

Meyer and the other English-only cases of the 1920s reflected the Supreme Court's use of the now obsolete "substantive due process" doctrine, which until the mid-1930s prevented any significant government regulation of private economic activity. However, the cases articulate important principles recognizing the value of languages other than English and the detrimental effects that regulation can have on speakers of other languages. A plurality of the Supreme Court acknowledged these principles by citing to both *Meyer* and *Yu Cong Eng* in a 1991 opinion in *Hernandez v. New York*.[57]

In *Hernandez*, the Supreme Court upheld the constitutionality of excluding bilingual jurors, at least in the context of a prosecutor's providing a race-neutral reason for the exclusion. The Court accepted the race neutrality of a prosecutor's doubting whether bilingual jurors could defer to an interpreter's official translation of testimony in Spanish. The impact of the prosecutor's rule was the exclusion of Latinos, but the Court found no racial animus in the prosecutor's decision making. Nevertheless, Justice Anthony Kennedy, writing for a plurality of the Court, noted in *Hernandez* that there could be a close connection between language and race: "It may well be, for certain ethnic groups and in some communities, that proficiency in a particular language, like skin color, should be treated as a surrogate for race under an equal protection analysis."[58]

Official English and Equal Protection

The Supreme Court recognized in *Hernandez v. New York* that official-English laws raise basic issues of equal protection. Nearly two decades earlier, the Court had skirted the equal protection issue in *Lau v. Nichols* by finding only a violation of Title VI of the Civil Rights Act of 1964. Two fundamental questions have thus been left unresolved by the Supreme Court: (1) Do laws such as official-English legislation discriminate against non-English speakers on the basis of national origin, which is already recognized as a suspect classification? (2) Do language-minority groups constitute a separate suspect classification that triggers heightened judicial scrutiny? The Supreme Court made an initial linkage between language and national origin discrimination in *Lau*, but the lower courts remain divided over the basic issues. In the context of the equal protection clause and Title VII employment discrimination litigation, several courts have ruled that language discrimination constitutes national origin discrimination. Some courts, however, have ruled that there is no legal nexus between language and national origin. And no court has ruled that a "language minority" is an independent suspect classification under the equal protection clause.

LANGUAGE AND NATIONAL ORIGIN

The linguistic characteristics of Asian immigrants show how closely intertwined language is with race and national origin. The percentage of Asian Americans who speak an Asian language at home is exceptionally high: among Chinese and Koreans, the figures are over 80 percent; among Vietnamese, Cambodians, Laotians, and Hmong, the figures range between 90 and 95 percent.[59] And the speakers of most Asian languages in the United States are almost entirely composed of native speakers of the language, the vast majority of whom are immigrants. Restrictions on the use of an Asian language necessarily affect a particular class of Asian immigrants.

In *Asian American Business Group v. City of Pomona*,[60] a federal district court recognized this linkage when it struck down a city ordinance that required local businesses displaying "foreign alphabetical characters" to also "devote at least one-half of the sign area to advertising copy in English alphabetical characters." Like several Southern California cities with growing Asian immigrant populations, the City of Pomona enacted its ordinance in 1988 in response to the growing number of business signs in Chinese, Vietnamese, and Korean.

Acknowledging the city's compelling interest in protecting public safety—identifying a location for the police or fire departments—the court nevertheless ruled that the ordinance was unconstitutional. The court began by noting that "a person's primary language is an important part of and flows from his/her national origin."[61] Employing a strict scrutiny standard, the court went on to find that the signage ordinance regulated the choice of language, which is "a form of expression as real as the textual message conveyed. It is an expression of culture."[62] The court held that the ordinance violated the First Amendment because it was not narrow enough to further the city's interest in public safety, since the same objective could have been accomplished by requiring a business to post the number of its street address. The court further ruled that the ordinance violated the equal protection clause: "The subject ordinance expressly discriminates against sign owners who use foreign alphabetical characters in their signs. . . . [T]he use of foreign languages is clearly an expression of national origin. As such, the ordinance overtly discriminates on the basis of national origin."[63]

Other courts have linked language with national origin as a protected category under Title VII of the Civil Rights Act of 1964. Several federal courts of appeals have ruled that discrimination based on accent constitutes national origin discrimination. In *Carino v. University of Oklahoma*,[64] for instance, the court of appeals affirmed a lower court judgment that a Filipino employee who had been demoted from a supervisorial position because of his accent had suffered discrimination based on national origin.

On the other hand, some courts have rejected the connection between language and national origin. In *Soberal-Perez v. Heckler*,[65] a federal court of appeals ruled that the Social Security Administration's failure to provide written notices and oral instructions in Spanish violated neither Title VI nor the equal protection clause. The court of appeals in *Garcia v. Gloor* ruled that an English-only workplace rule did not violate Title VII, because the law did not "support an interpretation that equates the language an employee prefers to use with his national origin."[66] Noting the "choice" that a bilingual employee has in not speaking a language other than English, the court found that "[i]n some circumstances the ability to speak or the speaking of another language other than English might be equated with national origin, but this case concerns only a requirement that persons capable of speaking English do so while on duty." Employing similar reasoning, a court of appeals upheld an English-only workplace rule in *Garcia v. Spun Steak Company*, stating that "[t]he bilingual employee can readily comply with the English-only rule and still enjoy the privilege of speaking on the job."[67] The court's far-reaching opinion did not hold that English-only rules are always permissible, but the court explicitly rejected the EEOC's administrative guidelines on English-only rules, which create a presumption that English-only rules violate the national origin provisions of Title VII.

One of the reasons that the courts have split over the linkage between language and national origin is that there are different classes of people who can be affected by any particular language restriction. One class is composed of limited-English speakers and non-English speakers. A second class is composed of bilingual individuals who have fluency in both English and another language. Within these two classes, there are subclasses of people who speak a particular language: for example, the language group comprising non-English-speaking Korean speakers, or the language group made up of bilingual Spanish speakers. Prohibitions on the use of any language other than English will affect the first class—all non-English speakers—most severely because it precludes any communication among the speakers.

Most courts have recognized the burdens that fall on non-English speakers, but a number of courts have been unwilling to recognize the burdens placed on bilingual speakers who have a "choice" to speak English. The problem with arguing that bilingual speakers have a "choice" in speaking English is that it ignores the stigma that attaches to bilingual employees who are precluded from expressing themselves through a basic trait of identity. As one court has noted, "The mere fact that an employee is bilingual does not eliminate the relationship between his primary language and the culture that is derived from his national origin. Although an individual may learn English and become assimilated into American society, his primary language remains an important link to his ethnic culture and identity."[68] Like forcing someone to sit in the back of a bus, an employer's imposing a blanket English-only rule eliminates any choice in the matter and only subordinates bilingual individuals through restrictions on their use of language.

LANGUAGE AS A PROTECTED CATEGORY

While language and national origin routinely correlate, a clearer path is simply to recognize language groups as protected classes under the equal protection clause and to include language as a distinct basis for discrimination under the antidiscrimination statutes. Congress has already recognized particular classes of language-minority groups under the Voting Rights Act. Congress took note of the extensive historical discrimination on the basis of language in its 1975 amendments to the act: "The Congress finds that voting discrimination against citizens of language minorities is pervasive and national in scope. . . . [T]hey have been denied equal educational opportunities by State and local governments, resulting in severe disabilities and continuing illiteracy in the English langauge."[69]

As a class, non-English speakers suffer many of the disabilities that attach to racial minority status. Non-English speakers are often treated as inferior and unwelcome because of the dominance of English. English-only laws further stigmatize and subordinate non-English speakers by denying them access to government and the political process. Even the court in *Garcia v. Gloor*, a case that upheld an English-only workplace rule, recognized that "to a person who speaks only one tongue or to a person who has difficulty using another language than the one spoken in his home, language might well be an immutable characteristic like skin color, sex, or place of birth."[70]

The courts that have declined to recognize language as the basis for a suspect classification have done so in the context of lawsuits seeking to impose affirmative duties on government to provide assistance to non-English speakers. There is an important distinction, though, between imposing a duty to provide language assistance and restricting any assistance at all through official-English legislation. One requires a benefit, the other requires a burden. An expansive official-English law such as Arizona's Article 28 shows how far the law can go to burden a class of limited- and non-English speakers. By prohibiting almost all use of languages other than English by government employees, English-only laws like Article 28 effectively preclude non-English speakers from participating in major portions of public life.

Accent Discrimination

Language-based subordination occurs not only by distinguishing between English speakers and non-English speakers, but by distinguising between "good" English speakers and "bad" English speakers. A common distinction is based on accent, and Asian Americans are among those most often identified as having "foreign accents" and among those most often subjected to discrimination because of accent. Every English speaker has an accent that may reflect regional origins, whether English is the person's primary language, and even the person's level of education and placement within a social and economic class. But between dominant and subordinate English speakers, the "foreign" accent or the low-status accent can be a source of subordination. As Mari Matsuda notes:

> Speech also positions people socially. In many societies, certain
> dialects and accents are associated with wealth and power. Others are
> low-status, with negative associations. In a society with a speech

hierarchy of this kind, it is quite common that speakers of the low-status speech variety, by necessity, are able to understand speakers of the high-status variety. Speakers of the high-status variety, on the other hand, frequently report that they cannot understand speakers below them on the speech-status scale.[71]

In geographic areas with smaller Asian immigrant populations, the public's lack of familiarity with Asian accents and the social ranking of accents can leave Asian immigrants in subordinate positions relative to native English speakers. Intolerance in public life toward an Asian accent can even lead to political subordination. In 1988, when a Korean American ran for a seat on the city council of Santa Clara, California, the *San Jose Mercury News* issued an editorial opposing the candidate because of his "heavy accent."[72] When United States Senator Alphonse D'Amato employed a derisive Japanese accent on national radio in 1995 to lambaste Judge Lance Ito, who speaks with an obvious American accent, Senator D'Amato displayed a crude form of nativist racism and disparaged an Asian accent considered inferior to an American accent.

Accent discrimination becomes most acute in employment settings, where employers often commit discrimination in denying positions to Asian Americans because they "sound foreign." The General Accounting Office found in 1990 that, because of the employer sanctions provisions of the Immigration Reform and Control Act, a wide range of employers treated foreign-sounding job applicants differently from non-foreign-sounding applicants, including making requests for immigration documents during job interviews and requiring proof of immigration status before hiring.[73]

One example of accent discrimination arose in San Francisco in 1992, when Filipino immigrants who were working as private security guards were removed from their positions in a federal office building at the request of the General Services Administration. The reason given for the removals was "language barriers," even though all of the guards spoke English and none had had trouble in the past communicating with the public. The removal of every Filipino security guard from the building was based on a presumption that their accents hindered communication, an allegation that was based on a single unsubstantiated charge against one unidentified employee. The guards filed a charge of national origin discrimination with the Equal Employment Opportunity Commission, which upheld the charge one year later. A lawsuit was filed in 1993, and the guards were able to win a settlement with their employer and with the federal government.[74]

Courts have recognized that accent discrimination is a form of national origin discrimination, but plaintiffs are often unsuccessful in their attempts to show that their accents do not constitute barriers to effective communication required by their jobs. In *Fragante v. City and County of Honolulu*,[75] the plaintiff, Manuel Fragante, was a highly educated Filipino immigrant who had received all of his formal education in English. A retired military officer, Fragante applied for a clerk's position with the City and County of Honolulu and was ranked first out of 721 applicants on a written civil service examination. Fragante was denied a position after an oral interview, in which one of the interviewers noted that Fragante spoke with a "very pronounced accent which is difficult to understand." Even though the federal district court judge apparently had no trouble understanding Fragante's testimony during his trial, the court concluded that Title VII was not violated because Fragante's accent affected his ability to communicate with the public, which was a job requirement of the civil service position. The court of appeals affirmed the trial court's ruling, finding that the government's hiring decision was based on a reasonable business necessity.

The legal rules set out by the court of appeals in *Fragante* are not hostile to accent discrimination claims; the court ruled that "[a]n adverse employment decision may be predicated upon an individual's accent when—but only when—it interferes with job performance."[76] Nevertheless, the court deferred to the trial court's factual finding that Fragante's accent would interfere with his job performance. The basic problem in accent discrimination cases thus has less to do with recognizing that an accent can lead to discrimination than with recognizing the subjectivity inherent in understanding and valuing an accent. Depending on the listener, whose exposure to a particular accent may range from extensive to none at all, a speaker's accent may seem perfectly understandable or it may seem utterly incomprehensible. In addition, the value placed on an accent may reflect such a low social status that the subordination of any employee with the accent is the likely result.

The trial court judge in *Fragante*, a federal judge who had been transferred from Arizona to hear the case, may have had limited exposure to a Filipino accent and may have felt that the accent presented a barrier to Fragante's communicating with the public. Moreover, the trial judge gave credence to expert testimony that in Hawaii "listeners stop listening to Filipino accents, resulting in a breakdown of communication."[77] Curiously, the court of appeals found no legal error in the trial judge's attention to listener prejudice, which, like customer preference, can be used as a pretext by employers for discrimination.

Because of the subjectivity inherent in understanding and valuing accents, the courts need to develop better standards that address the idiosyncrasies of accent discrimination. One approach might be to look at the "reasonable listener" who will be communicating with an employee. A "reasonable listener" standard would consider how co-workers and listeners within the local community would comprehend the accent. For example, in a geographic area with a large number of Filipino immigrants, the reasonable listener might be expected to interact and become familiar with a Filipino accent. A reasonable listener rule would balance the judge's evaluation of the employee's accent with a community standard, but it would not cater to listener prejudice that might serve as the employer's pretext for discrimination. A reasonable listener rule would still be an objective standard, but it would enable courts to judge communication-based job requirements in a broader context, not just through listening to the plaintiff's accent and to the employer's justification for treating the plaintiff differently because of the plaintiff's accent.

Language and Conformity

Beyond the technical distinctions of legal doctrine, the court cases on English-only and accent discrimination reflect the more fundamental philosophical tensions between pluralism and assimilationism. The federal district court's ruling in the case of *Dimaranan v. Pomona Valley Hospital Medical Center* illustrates a typical assimilationist bent.[78] In *Dimaranan*, the plaintiff was a nurse who challenged a workplace rule that had been instituted to prevent Filipinos in a hospital unit from speaking Tagalog. The court found that the "No Tagalog" rule did not amount to national origin discrimination, because it was necessary to maintain conformity within the workplace. The court stated:

> It is clear that management was not primarily concerned with the use of Tagalog, but rather with the breakdown of cohesion on the M/B unit and the effect of dissension upon the well-being and safety of mothers and their newborns. . . . Management's decision to focus on the use of Tagalog, in an effort to restore crucially important harmony and cohesion, permitted plaintiff to escalate what was merely a management problem into a Title VII case. Language was clearly never the central focus of management, and Tagalog was, so to speak, merely caught in the cross-fire.[79]

The court's opinion reflects both a devaluing of language and ethnic identity and the valuing of cohesion and uniformity within the workplace environment. The court of appeals opinion in *Guadalupe Organization, Inc. v. Tempe Elementary School District* states the assimilationist argument in even starker terms:

> Linguistic and cultural diversity within the nation-state, whatever may be its advantages from time to time, can restrict the scope of the

fundamental compact. Diversity limits unity. Effective action by the nation-state rises to its peak of strength only when it is in response to aspirations unreservedly shared by each constituent culture and language group.[80]

The court's opinion goes on to state that the school district's decision "to provide a predominantly monocultural and monolingual educational system was a rational response to a quintessentially 'legitimate' state interest."[81] In the same way, supporters of official-English legislation propose that the exclusive use of English by government will lead to more harmony and unity among the general public.

The pluralist theme is well-expressed in the opinion of Judge Stephen Reinhardt in his dissent to a court of appeals decision denying a second hearing of *Garcia v. Spun Steak Company*. Judge Reinhardt's dissenting opinion states:

> Language is intimately tied to national origin and cultural identity: its discriminatory suppression cannot be dismissed as an "inconvenience" to the affected employees as *Spun Steak* asserts. Even when an individual learns English and becomes assimilated into American society, his native language remains an important manifestation of his ethnic identity and a means of affirming links to his original culture. English-only rules not only symbolize a rejection of the excluded language and the culture it embodies, but also a denial of that side of an individual's personality.[82]

The divergent opinions among the federal judges should not be surprising. Judicial attitudes parallel the broader political perspectives either favoring the dominance of English or accommodating linguistic diversity in American society.

Language and Power

The subordination of language minorities by dominant groups is at the root of official-English laws and English-only work policies. Like many anti-immigrant policies, English-only laws reflect responses to the growth of nonwhite immigrant populations and to the challenges to dominant power structures engendered by these populations. And like the laws dealing with immigration and immigrants, language-based laws are able to serve as ideological masks for racial discrimination. If, as proposed by those courts that have severed the linkage between language and national origin, language is race-neutral, then language discrimination becomes permissible, even though its effects are as subordinative as race and national origin discrimination. Asian American experiences clearly demonstrate, however, that language cannot be divorced from race.

Asian American experiences with language politics are also instructive. The growth in both population and power among Asian Americans portends political trends tied to nativism and language restrictions. The politics of Monterey Park, California, illustrate what is likely to become a pattern of shifting immigrant and anti-immigrant power struggles in many parts of the country.[83] A middle-class community located near Los Angeles, Monterey Park's Asian American population has grown over the last two decades to become over 50 percent of the city's population. During the mid-1980s, as many Asian immigrants moved to the area and began opening small businesses, members of a predominantly white city council reacted by introducing legislation calling for limitations on immigration and restrictions on the use of languages other than English. English-only laws, signage ordinances, even restrictions on the acquisition of library books in Chinese were among the panoply of policies introduced by city council members.

Asian Americans organized against the nativist policies, and in time more Asian Americans were elected to the city council, while nativist council members were voted out of office. The result was a move away from intolerance and English-only to pluralism and linguistic diversity. The demographics of Monterey Park are unusual, but the shifting political winds are not. Law and ideology only change through political opposition to expressions of nativism such as English-only legislation and workplace rules.

Chapter 6   Race and Identity

In his book *Making and Remaking Asian America through Immigration Policy*, Bill Ong Hing offers insights into the complexities of the Asian American experience by presenting a sampling of comments on Asian American identity. Here are some of those comments:

> I think of myself as Vietnamese. Sometimes I think of myself as Vietnamese American. I never think of myself as Asian American. . . . I check the box Asian American in all my forms (employment, etc.), but that's because they don't have a Vietnamese American box. (Vietnam-born man, age 50, entered as refugee at age 38)

> I think of myself as Asian American. I think of myself as Vietnamese when I'm with other Vietnamese, and I think of myself as American when I'm in Europe. (Vietnam-born woman, age 20, immigrated at age 4)

> I regard myself as American. I grew up in a setting with few other Asians, and I was treated as a regular person by my white friends. So I think of myself as simply American. (American-born woman, Chinese ancestry, age 42)

> I think of myself as Japanese American. The racism that I and my friends have experienced over the years is a constant reminder that I am different and will never be accepted simply as an American. (American-born man, Japanese ancestry, age 66)

> I think of myself as Chinese American. I grew up in Chinatown and went to Chinese school after regular school every day. Both my

parents were immigrants. I've never been out of the Bay Area, and I continue to work, eat, and shop a lot in Chinatown. (American-born man, age 45)

I'm Filipino. I fought in World War II for the United States in the Philippines and not until recently are they going to give me the citizenship I earned. I want to be an American citizen, but I will always be a Filipino. (Philippine-born man, age 75, immigrated at age 63)[1]

The Asian American community comprises many communities. The Asian American experience comprises many experiences. As a population racialized as foreign outsiders, as immigrants, and even as "model minorities," Asian Americans are lumped together as a homogeneous group. Racial categorizing, however, glosses over the extensive diversity within the Asian American population. Economic class, ethnicity, language, immigration status, gender, and sexual orientation are only some of the axes that define identity and difference within Asian America. In this chapter I explore the role of law in both shaping and responding to questions of racial and ethnic identity.

Constructing Asian America

The term "Asian American" is a product of racialization. Unlike outsider racialization, the construction of "Asian American" has been defined through self-identification and internal organizing. Although terms such as "Mongolian," "Asiatic," and "Oriental" have been parts of the racial vocabulary for decades, the term "Asian American" only originated during the late 1960s, as part of a progressive movement that built on the black civil rights movement.[2] Ethnic group identification had in the past been the primary label for describing racial differences—early typologies often referred to a Japanese race or a Filipino race. Framing a new racial identity, progressive leaders on college campuses and in community-based organizations developed a new political label to describe a collective identity and historical experiences with racial subordination. "Asian American" reflected both a nationalist identity—Asian to emphasize race, American to emphasize non-foreignness—as well as an exercise of political power to dispose of the pejorative term "Oriental."[3]

The recent expansion of the label to include variations such as "Asian and Pacific Islander" and "Asian Pacific American" reflects the evolution of the racialization process. Pacific Islanders, by definition, have different origins and different experiences from Asians. Many of the islands of the Pacific, including American Samoa and Guam, are territories of the United States, and their residents enjoy status as United States nationals or as citizens, which allows them to bypass normal immigration restrictions when entering the United States. Civil rights issues involving colonialism and sovereignty affect Pacific Island communities such as Native Hawaiians, and are comparable to problems facing Native American tribes.[4] The push to include "Pacific Islanders," a grouping that, like "Asian" is composed of many subgroups, reflects expanding notions of race and expressions of political power that come with common agendas and increasing numbers.

Both "Asian" and "Pacific Islander" are imprecise terms. Does "Asian" describe a geographical category or a biological/appearance-based category? If it is geographical, where does Asia begin and end? Which islands are the islands of the Pacific? Physical appearance operates along a continuum, but there are noticeable differences among groups. An immigrant from India may not look like an immigrant from Japan, who may not look like someone from the Philippines, who may not look like someone from Tonga. And there is no such thing as a shared "Asian" or "Pacific" language that all Asians and Pacific Islanders can speak and write. These differences are not insignificant, but they can be elided when discussing the most basic questions of anti-Asian racism. What all of these people have in common is outsider racialization: because of appearance, they are all treated as if they are foreign-born outsiders and not really Americans.

Nevertheless, differences do make a difference. Because of the demographic changes engendered by immigration since 1965, the development of a single Asian American racial identity has become problematic. It is possible for racial identity to reflect both ethnicity and race: the terms "African American" and "black" are often used interchangeably (including in this book), but "African American" refers more to ethnicity, implying national origin and cultural attributes, while "black" refers more to race, implying color differences and contrapositioning to "white." But the tendency among many Asian Americans, particularly among recent immigrants, is not to identify along racial lines but along ethnic lines.[5] And while it may be possible to define an "Asian" ethnicity, the variety of languages, cultures, and histories within Asian America suggests that other forms of ethnicity are far more powerful. More appropriate ethnic categories correspond to country of origin and ancestry, as well as common characteristics such as language and culture.[6] Thus someone who identifies as Chinese may be an immigrant from China, but may also be an American-born person whose family history in the United States goes back several generations. Chinese, Japanese, Filipino, Korean, Indian, Vietnamese, Cambodian, Laotian, Hmong, and Thai designate some of the largest Asian ethnic groups in the United States. Hawaiian, Samoan, Tongan, and Gua-manian denote the largest Pacific Islander ethnic categories.

Rather than reflecting some monolithic Asian ethnicity, Asian America reflects "panethnicity," which Yen Le Espiritu describes as "the development of bridging organizations and solidarities among several ethnic and immigrant groups of Asian ancestry."[7] The nationalist "Asian American" identity reflects a commonly held form of identity among American-born individuals of Asian ancestry. But immigration from Asia and the Pacific refuels different forms of identity through the entry of individuals who share common origins, languages, and cultures. Ethnic identity, rather than racial identity, is thus reproduced and reinforced through the flow of new immigrants. Espiritu suggests that coalition building must therefore proceed panethnically by uniting different Asian ethnic groups in political enterprises that parallel racial categorization, such as combating racial violence.[8]

Race remains relevant, however, because it operates as the primary determinant of panethnicity. Externally defined concepts of "Asian"—that is, how non-Asians view Asians—typically ignore the multiplicity of ethnic groups. Racial lumping generates the most common forms of discrimination against Asian Americans, including the ascription of specific ethnic characteristics to all Asian Americans. Here is a simple example, drawn from personal experience. At a supermarket, someone asked me to help find a grocery item for an elderly Chinese woman who spoke no English. Because of my racial appearance, the inquirer attributed ethnic characteristics to me based on two incorrect assumptions: that I was Chinese and, as Chinese, that I could speak Cantonese. A less innocuous example is the "model minority" myth, which ascribes ethnic characteristics—a high valuation of education and an ethic of hard work—to all Asian Americans. Far from complimentary, the extrapolation of "positive" ethnic stereotypes to all Asian Americans glosses over educational and economic inequities among Asian Americans, and engenders resentment toward Asian Americans among other racial minorities. Negative ethnic stereotypes—such as the unwillingness to learn English, unfriendliness, and passivity—breed both racial defamation and racial aggression, including anti-Asian violence.

Dimensions of Difference

The importance of ethnicity within the Asian American population is demonstrated through demographic and economic data, which reveal significant variations among Asian ethnic groups. Other than the collective racial definition itself, there are few social and economic characteristics that apply to

Table 6.1
Population Characteristics of Asians and Pacific Islanders in the U.S., 1990

	Population (% of total A/PI)		Foreign-Born (%)	Linguistically isolated[a] (%)
Total A/PI	7,273,662	(100.0)	63.1	34.4
Chinese	1,645,473	(22.6)	69.3	40.3
Filipino	1,406,770	(19.3)	64.4	13.0
Japanese	847,562	(11.7)	32.4	33.0
Asian Indian	815,447	(11.2)	75.4	17.2
Korean	798,849	(11.0)	72.7	41.4
Vietnamese	614,547	(8.4)	79.9	43.9
Hawaiian	211,014	(2.9)	1.3	8.1
Laotian	149,014	(2.0)	79.4	52.4
Cambodian	147,411	(2.0)	79.1	56.1
Thai	91,275	(1.2)	75.5	31.8
Hmong	90,082	(1.2)	65.2	60.5
Samoan	62,964	(0.9)	22.7	9.3
Guamanian	49,345	(0.7)	11.4	7.1
Tongan	17,606	(0.2)	60.9	21.6
Other A/PI	326,304	(4.5)		

SOURCES: U.S. Departmentof Commerce, Bureau of the Census, We the American Asians, Washington, D.C., 1993, table 3; U.S. Department of Commerce, Bureau of the Census, We the American Pacific Islanders, Washington, D.C., 1993, table 3.
[a] Linguistic isolation refers to persons in households in which no one 14 years or older speaks only English and no one who speaks a language other than English speaks English "very well."

all or even most Asian Americans. Recent immigration is a typical, but not universal, characteristic. With the exception of Japanese Americans, most of the Asian American population is foreign-born. Another common characteristic, tied to immigration, involves English-language ability. With the exception of Filipino and Asian Indian immigrants, there are high rates among all Asian and Pacific Islander groups of linguistic isolation and limited English proficiency. Even among Filipinos and Indians, there are large numbers of individuals who speak little or no English. A third common characteristic of Asian Americans is larger household sizes: most Asian and Pacific Islander groups have an average household size larger than the national average of about three persons per household; some Asian ethnic populations have average household sizes with one to three more members than the national average. A demographic figure such as "median household income" can be misleading, because of the larger household sizes, when applied to Asian Americans—the median household income for Asian Americans is higher than the national figure, but the per capita income is lower.

Although the poverty rate for Asian Americans is higher than the

Table 6.2
Selected Characteristics of Asians and Pacific Islanders in the U.S., 1990

	Per capita median income in 1989 ($)	*In poverty* (%)	*With bachelor's degree* (%)	*In managerial/ professional occupations* (%)
All persons–U.S.	14,143	13.1	20.3	26.4
Total A/PI	13,638	14.1	36.6	30.6
Japanese	19,373	7.0	34.5	37.0
Asian Indian	17,777	9.7	58.1	43.6
Filipino	14,876	6.4	39.3	26.6
Chinese	13,806	14.0	40.7	35.8
Thai	11,970	12.5	32.8	23.6
Hawaiian	11,446	14.3	11.9	20.2
Korean	11,117	13.7	34.5	25.5
Guamanian	10,834	15.3	10.0	17.2
Vietnamese	9,032	25.7	17.4	17.6
Samoan	7,690	25.8	8.0	13.5
Tongan	6,144	23.1	5.8	8.6
Laotian	5,597	34.7	5.4	5.0
Cambodian	5,120	42.6	5.7	9.8
Hmong	2,692	63.6	4.9	12.8

SOURCES: U.S. Departmentof Commerce, Bureau of the Census, *We the American Asians*, Washington, D.C., 1993, table 3; U.S. Department of Commerce, Bureau of the Census, *We the American Pacific Islanders*, Washington, D.C., 1993, table 3.

national average, taken as a whole the Asian American population appears to be doing well relative to the national population: labor force participation, household incomes, and educational attainment are all higher than the national averages. Disaggregating demographic information about Asian Americans along ethnic lines, however, reveals an array of differences in education, occupation, and economic class. Education and income levels are high among certain ethnic groups such as Japanese, Chinese, Filipinos, and Asian Indians, significantly exceeding the national averages. Among other groups, particularly Southeast Asians and Pacific Islanders, poverty rates are high, median incomes are low, and educational attainment is far below the national average.

Labor market and business ownership data reflect patterns of ethnic differentiation. Asian Americans as a whole are more likely to appear in the professional and technical fields. Some groups, such as Japanese, Chinese, and Asian Indians, have a considerably higher proportion of individuals in the professions. On the other hand, large numbers of Asian Americans also appear in the lower-wage service sector, including many Filipinos, Koreans, and Chinese. And the pictures for Pacific Islanders and Southeast Asian populations are significantly different from other Asian groups; these populations are concentrated heavily in the service sector and among operators and laborers, who are the lowest paid workers in the economy.

Contrary to popular perception, Asian and Pacific Islander business ownership and income are roughly proportional to the group's population size,[9] forming approximately 3.5 percent of all businesses and 2.9 percent of all business receipts in the United States in 1992. But, like other social and economic measures, business ownership data show concentrations among Asian ethnic groups. Nearly 60 percent of all Asian and Pacific Islander businesses were concentrated among three ethnic groups: Chinese, Koreans, and Asian Indians. Data from studies of local economies show that ethnic business enclaves have developed in many cities, with ethnic concentrations within particular small business sectors: Chinese restaurants and laundries, Japanese truck farming, Korean grocery stores, Thai restaurants, Vietnamese beauty and nail salons, and Cambodian donut shops.[10]

What accounts for these demographic and economic differences? Immigration history is one explanation. The high incomes among some Asian ethnic groups are not surprising, because many immigrants have entered through the employment-based system, which encourages the entry of highly educated and highly skilled workers. The higher education and income levels of Japanese Americans, the ethnic population with the largest percentage of native-born, are more difficult to explain; often used as examples of "model minority" status, Japanese Americans have median incomes higher even than whites. One reason is the socialized reactions of Japanese Americans to racism and marginalization, including the internment during World War II. By stressing achievement and conformity with "American" norms, many Japanese Americans have exceeded the educational and economic levels of white Americans.

The refugee experience is a major cause of the lower social and economic indicators among Vietnamese, Cambodian, Laotian, and Hmong immigrants. Along with language and cultural differences, wartime traumas, forced uprooting, relocation, and resettlement make the incorporation of Southeast Asian refugee populations into American society especially challenging and complex. In addition, many of the Southeast Asian refugees who entered in the 1980s came from poor, rural backgrounds; many of these individuals lack the education and job skills necessary to advance in the American labor market. Unemployment and welfare dependency have thus evolved into critical problems for many Southeast Asian immigrants and their families.[11]

The economic differences within the Asian American population as a whole and among Asian ethnic populations demonstrate that the "model minority" myth is just that—a myth. Without question, there are many Asian

Americans who have high levels of education and income and reinforce the model minority stereotype, but there are also large numbers of poor and disadvantaged Asian Americans who demonstrate that stereotyping can be dangerous when applied across an entire racial category.

Identity and Group Rights

Ethnic differentiation among the Asian American population raises a set of basic questions: When should race matter? When should ethnicity matter? When should economic class matter? Neoconservative advocates of color-blind individualism argue that race and ethnicity should never matter, and that racial inequalities should (at best) be addressed through public policies addressing economic disadvantage. But completely discounting race and ethnicity is an oversimplified solution, because race and ethnicity continue to be the cause of both group and individual subordination, independent of economic disadvantage. On the other hand, racial lumping, even when designed to remedy group discrimination, often ignores important differences within the Asian American population based on ethnicity, language, immigration history, and economic class. For example, an affirmative action program in higher education admissions that does not include Asian Americans, because they constitute a large percentage of the student body, might exclude disadvantaged and underrepresented Asian ethnic groups such as Vietnamese, Cambodians, Laotians, and Hmong, who are lumped together in the same racial category as well-represented Asian ethnic groups.

To illustrate the intricacies of race and ethnicity within the Asian American population, I next consider three areas in which the laws define and delimit racial identity: census classifications and racial counting, transracial adoptions, and electoral districting. In each of these areas, a black-white racial paradigm has dominated much of the discourse and legal decision making. The Asian American experience adds complexity to these areas because of the expansion of the black-white paradigm to include Asian Americans and because of the multiethnic nature of the Asian American population. I do not attempt to resolve the wide range of issues involved in each of these areas, but I use them to portray some of the difficult questions that arise in the laws dealing with racial identity.

Racial Classifications

Law has always played a central role in the construction of racial and ethnic identities.[12] "One drop of blood" rules—having any ancestor who was black—

defined being black under many state laws. The legal categories of Mulatto, Quadroon, and Octoroon were commonly used to categorize mixed-race individuals to prevent any confusion with the white population. Anti-miscegenation laws defined white purity through bans on marriage, but were less precise in defining nonwhites, since nonwhites could marry among each other but could never marry whites. The racial classifications of nonwhites were broadened under the law in cases such as *People v. Hall* and *Gong Lum v. Rice*, in which Chinese and other Asians were treated as the legal equivalent of blacks. Similarly, *Ozawa v. United States* and *United States v. Thind*, the cases rejecting appeals to classify Asian immigrants as white under the naturalization laws, reinforced definitions of "whiteness" and the racial hierarchies arising from those definitions.

Legal classifications of race and ethnicity exist today, and they continue to evolve in response to political dynamics and changing racial attitudes. Under the federal government's racial and ethnic classification system, I am "Asian or Pacific Islander," or at least I have been since the late 1970s, when the Office of Management and Budget issued the government's primary classification scheme, known as Statistical Policy Directive No. 15.[13] Before the issuance of Directive 15, I belonged to the "Other Races" category. Federal census data collection is more precise: in 1990, I identified myself as Filipino, which placed me under the broader racial category of Asian and Pacific Islander. Under California's classification scheme, I am also Filipino, but I am not necessarily counted as Asian. Under California law, Filipinos are counted separately from Asians.[14] But that has only been the case since the late 1970s, when Filipino American advocates were able to lobby successfully for state legislation that distinguished Filipinos from Asians and Latinos.

Asian Americans first appeared on the federal government's decennial census in 1870, when Chinese were included under the government's "color" question. "Japanese" was added as a category in 1890, and "Filipino" and "Korean" were added in 1930. (Because of small numbers, Koreans were removed from the 1950 and 1960 censuses.) In the 1970 census, Japanese, Chinese, Filipinos, Koreans, and Hawaiians were tallied; all other Asian and Pacific Islander groups were relegated to the "Other" racial category. Racial misclassification through the "Other" category presented serious problems for Asian Americans, reflecting the government's dualistic models of race. For instance, Questionnaire Reference Manuals for the Census Bureau's 1976 and 1977 pretests contained the following guidelines: "If a respondent's answer is 'American,' classify it as 'White'; if it is 'Nonwhite,' classify it as 'Black.'"[15] Thus only whites could be "Americans," while "nonwhites" had to be black.

Undercounting and miscategorizing in the 1960 and 1970 census counts led Asian American activists to become involved in the policies and guide-lines of subsequent censuses.[16] Asian Americans were prominent players in debates preceding both the 1980 census and 1990 census, and advocated suc-cessfully for significant changes to both the census categories and the meth-ods of enumeration. Because of political advocacy by Asian Americans, the number of Asian and Pacific Islander categories increased from five in 1970—Japanese, Chinese, Filipino, Hawaiian, and Korean—to nine in the 1980 cen-sus, adding the Asian Indian, Vietnamese, Guamanian, and Samoan categories. When the Census Bureau attempted to return to write-in categories for the 1990 census, advocates were able to lobby for congressional legislation, in-troduced by Representative Robert Matsui, that required the Census Bureau to retain the Asian and Pacific Islander check-off system. The Census Bureau eventually made the decision to use the check-off system in the 1990 census; the Bureau also designated a specific Asian and Pacific Islander write-in sec-tion with space to include additional Asian ethnic categories.[17]

The main justifications for expanding the number of ethnic categories were (1) the importance of obtaining a full and accurate count of Asian Ameri-can populations, which could be compromised if many individuals self-identified as "Other"; and (2) the need for ethnic data that could be used to provide specific linguistic and cultural services for Asian immigrants. Some of the ad-vocacy was ethnic-based: Asian Indians, for example, were relegated to the category "Other" in the 1970 census, and advocated successfully for their in-clusion as Asians in the 1980 census. Other advocacy was pan-Asian and re-lated to the general method of enumeration: advocates successfully lobbied for the Census Bureau to retain a check-off system in the 1990 census, which was justified by the need to ensure that ethnic-specific data would be ana-lyzed and made available to the public by the Census Bureau.

Employing a check-off system as opposed to a write-in system may seem like a trivial distinction, but the consequences of a group's being miscounted or undercounted on the federal census are enormous. Census data are used to generate statistics that have powerful impacts on public policy. Racial and eth-nic statistics are used to allocate government benefits and resources, to deter-mine electoral representation, and to set standards for government affirmative action programs. Billions of dollars are at stake. The 1990 census reflected a serious undercount that fell most heavily on racial and ethnic minority groups: African Americans were undercounted in the 1990 census by 4.8 percent, Latinos by 5.2 percent, Asians and Pacific Islanders by 3.1 percent, and Na-tive Americans by 5.0 percent, compared to whites, who were undercounted by 1.7 percent.[18] Despite several lawsuits seeking to require the government to use adjusted census figures to address the undercount, the secretary of commerce's adherence to the original census figures was upheld by the United States Supreme Court as constitutional.[19]

Multiracial Identity

During the 1990s, the most important racial counting controversy facing civil rights advocates has been the question of adding a "multiracial" category to the census in the year 2000. Advocates for the multiracial category have argued that existing racial categories are too rigid, precluding the recognition and enumeration of individuals whose parents are of different races.[20] The multiracial category has become a volatile question for African American advocates, because of historical legacies such as the "one drop of blood" rule and customary classifications treating anyone with black ancestry as black. The issue is not easy to resolve, because it raises some of the most fundamental issues of personal identity.

Racial and ethnic intermarriage is a significant social phenomenon among Asian Americans, reflecting both pan-Asian interaction and shifts in marriage patterns after the repeal of discriminatory anti-miscegenation laws. Using 1990 census data, Larry Hajime Shinagawa and Gin Yong Pang have documented high levels of intermarriage among Asian Americans living in California.[21] Shinagawa and Pang found that 29 percent of Asian American men and 36 percent of Asian American women married outside their ethnicity—through interethnic marriages (marrying other Asians outside their ethnic group) and through interracial marriages.[22] Shinagawa and Pang also found intermarriage patterns varied significantly by ethnic group, nativity, and gender. For example, over 50 percent of Japanese American women married non-Japanese men, and of those marriages, over 60 percent were interracial. Over 75 percent of American-born Koreans married non-Koreans; but the pattern was reversed for Korean immigrants, who married primarily within their own ethnicity. Asian interracial marriage rates with whites were higher than with other racial minorities: over 70 percent of interracial marriages for Asian men were with white women, and over 80 percent of interracial marriages for Asian women were with white men.

The debate over the multiracial category raises two sets of issues for Asian Americans. One concerns children who are the products of an Asian interethnic marriage: for example, the children of a Japanese father and a Korean mother. The identity issue is multiethnic rather than multiracial; in other words, a child's racial classification would be Asian, but the child's ethnic classification would be unresolved. The second problem is the basic multiracial issue: one parent is Asian and the other parent is of another race. The census form used in 1990 did not accommodate either situation; the Census Bureau recognized one check-off and only one check-off for the race question.

A multiracial question would attempt to address these issues, but opponents of the multiracial question find it objectionable for two reasons: the lack of specificity in the multiracial category and the lack of safeguards to ensure that civil rights enforcement is not undermined by the category. By itself, a multiracial category adds little to census data other than a recognition that a certain number of individuals self-identify as multiracial, and not as one of the established racial categories. Without additional inquiries, a multiracial question does not determine the different permutations of multiracial identity—white-black, white-Asian, black-Asian, and so on. The likely impact of a multiracial category would be decreases in the number of individuals counted under the existing racial categories, which could undermine a host of civil rights enforcement policies that rely on racial statistics. Federal laws such as the Fair Housing Act, the Equal Credit Opportunity Act, the Home Mortgage Disclosure Act, and a host of economic development and public school desegregation policies could be disrupted by shifts in racial statistics.

In 1997, the federal government attempted to resolve the controversy by recommending changes to Directive 15, the government's data collection guidelines on race. During the summer of 1997, an interagency committee convened by the Office of Management and Budget recommended that a multiracial category should not be adopted. Instead, the committee recommended that Directive 15 should allow respondents to check more than one box to answer the race question.[23] Left unresolved, however, were another set of issues: Should separate counts be tallied for each variation of multiracial identity? Should fractional data be counted, based on parentage and ancestry? How should the ancestry of grandparents and earlier generations be factored into the measurements? And how would multiracial data be used? Because racial data are used for allocating governmental resources, constructing electoral districts, and implementing affirmative action programs, should a multiracial person be counted among those eligible for protection under the antidiscrimination laws and for the benefits of race-conscious remedial programs? Like all census questions, the multiracial question is an inquiry about identity and self-designation. But it is not identity that determines whether one suffers discrimination; it is being perceived by someone else as a member of a particular racial or ethnic group that leads to acts of discrimination.

One proposed solution is simply to eliminate racial inquiries, because fixed racial categories appear to be breaking down over time. Racial categories are becoming more fluid, but eliminating all racial counting is an extreme and absolutist solution. Racial differences still matter in American society, and as long as they do, racial counting should be maintained. Ruth Colker has suggested reconciling the competing interests, recognizing both identity and community perceptions, by proposing three questions: "What is your self-identity?" "What is your community identity?" and "What are the countries of origin of your parents?"[24] These questions provide more detail, but the second question is still problematic—a crude variation is "Can you pass?"—because it means trying to read the minds of people who might discriminate against you.

The counting of multiracial persons must be judged not only by its impact on identity but by its impact on racial subordination. The addition of a multiracial category may undermine existing racial categories, but it may also illuminate new and different forms of discrimination, including being ostracized and treated as a nonmember by two racial groups. When public policies are racially binary—anyone who identifies as a multiracial person is still not white under the law—the impact on existing categories is minimal. When racial variations do matter, multiracial individuals can fall within a variety of racial classes (black-white, Asian-white, black-Asian, and others) composed of people whose ancestries reflect combinations of historical subordination. In any case, since not being treated as white continues to make a difference in American society, multiracial individuals should be counted among those who may suffer racial discrimination and subordination as a class.

The fuzziness along the edges of racial boundaries raises vital issues of identity, but it does not undermine the most basic racial and ethnic counting issues involving Asian Americans. Asian immigration continues to refuel ethnic identity, through the entry of individuals and families who come from countries whose populations have much greater ethnic homogeneity than the population of the United States. The need for ethnic- and language-specific data for health care and social services remains vital, making the use of check-off systems and ethnic classifications as important as in prior censuses. At the very least, the collection of ethnic data offers a counterweight to the continuing racialization of Asian Americans as a homogeneous group.

Transracial Adoptions

Transracial adoptions pose a vexing set of questions involving racial identity. Should couples of one race be prevented from adopting a child of another race? How should racial identity be considered in raising a child? What ethnic and cultural traditions, if any, should be incorporated into a child's upbringing? The nexus linking race, identity, and legal rights is rarely as momentous as when the laws set the boundaries on one of the most basic of human relationships—the relationship between a parent and a child.[25]

The pairing of adopted children and parents of the same race, known as "race matching," has become a major issue because of the imbalances between the number of couples seeking adoption and the number of children available for adoption. Requiring race matching consigns many nonwhite children to foster care because the number of children greatly exceeds the number of same-race couples seeking to adopt. Race matching is based on assumptions about racial and cultural identity and on the ability of adoptive parents to provide an environment in which racial identity is fostered. The realities of American race relations force color-conscious parenting. No matter how a nonwhite child is raised, the child will still encounter racial prejudice and discrimination growing up. Tensions inevitably arise between parental control over the child's upbringing and the interests of the child in coping with racial difference and discrimination. Transracial adoptions thus raise difficult questions about identity and parental responsibility: Could (and should) children be raised as if they were of the same race as their adoptive parents? What obligations fall on parents to ensure that children are able to identify with people of the same race or ethnicity? What is a child's "native" culture?

Asian American experiences complicate the picture because of the array of ethnicities and languages within the Asian American population. Children of Asian ancestry put up for adoption come from two sources: Asian American children born in the United States, and children born in Asian countries who are adopted by parents in the United States. Intercountry adoptions constitute a significant number of transracial adoptions and have become common for American couples seeking newborn and younger children. Asian countries such as South Korea, China, and the Philippines provide large numbers of adoptees for couples in the United States. Child rearing takes on added dimensions when considering Asian immigrant children. Consistent with race matching, should there be ethnicity matching? Should an adopted child from Korea receive instruction in Korean culture and the Korean language in order to help develop a stronger ethnic identity? What elements of ethnic culture should be stressed? Or should the child be raised with a "second generation" Asian American identity to help cope with racial discrimination and to attempt to bridge the personal identity of the child with the parents' identity?

Narratives from transracial adoptees reveal an array of responses about personal identity. Many Asian American adoptees with white parents report few problems being raised among whites and few instances of overt discrimination against them. Others report confusion over personal identity and great difficulty identifying with their parents' race; some even report discrimination from members of their own family. Still others report a stable and comfortable home life but a striking, often shocking, disparity when exposed to racism outside of their home. The following response, taken from a Michigan State University student's statement on the Internet, is typical: "I didn't know what Korean culture was; it wasn't an option. So I did my best to be American. But I was constantly told I wasn't fulfilling it because I wasn't a perfect American because I was Asian. I didn't look American. I wasn't blonde. I wasn't tall."[26] Regardless of personal identity, all transracial adoptees must address the realities of discrimination in American society.

The debate over transracial adoptions in the United States reflects competing visions of race consciousness. Embracing a color-blind vision of race, many advocates for transracial adoptions suggest that race should never be a consideration in adoptions. Literature from the conservative Institute for Justice, for instance, states that its litigation strategy "will seek to prevent the government from using race to keep minority children in the throes of the state and out of loving homes."[27] On the other extreme, many color-conscious advocates propose that transracial adoptions should never be allowed. Since 1972, the National Association of Black Social Workers has taken the position that black children should only be placed with black families in order to preserve black identity and culture. Through the federal Indian Child Welfare Act, tribal interests in preserving Native American identity supersede the interests of potential adoptive parents.[28]

Splitting the difference between the two extremes, Congress enacted the Multiethnic Placement Act of 1994.[29] The Act prohibits a child placement agency receiving federal financial assistance from categorically denying placements or delaying placements for adoption on the basis of race, color, or national origin. The act also allows agencies to consider the cultural, ethnic, or racial background of the child and the capacity of the prospective parent to meet the needs of a child with a particular background. State laws vary: some laws are consistent with the federal law and allow the consideration of race and ethnicity among several factors to be weighed when matching parents and children; other laws prohibit any consideration of race or ethnicity.

The Supreme Court has not decided the constitutionality of laws or decisions either prohibiting or requiring race matching.[30] Because of the Court's recent conservative rulings on race-conscious public policies, it is likely that the Court would strike down a legal requirement of race matching as a violation of the equal protection clause. However, the Court would probably uphold under strict scrutiny a policy that allowed race to be considered flexibly among other factors used to match parents and children.

The basic question posed by transracial adoptions is the question posed by any adoption: What action is in the best interests of the child? Absolutist positions are too drastic—requiring race matching in all cases may lock a child in foster care for years, while a color-blind approach simply ignores the realities of racial discrimination. Race cannot be the only factor considered in an adoption placement, but the importance of racial identity in a society pervaded by racial subordination cannot be underestimated. Race-consciousness is inescapable in the rearing of any child in the United States.

Identity and Electoral Politics

Electoral districting, the drawing of geographical boundaries to create constituency districts for elected and appointed officials, is often based on the recognition that racial minority groups vote as blocs. Both the equal protection clause and the Voting Rights Act prohibit forms of racial gerrymandering that divide minority populations between electoral districts in order to dilute political power achieved through minority bloc voting. Race-conscious electoral districting presupposes, therefore, that racial identity can be equated with political identity.

The law of race-based districting has been in a state of flux since 1993, when the Supreme Court began entertaining equal protection challenges to the creation of "majority-minority" districts.[31] In 1986, the Supreme Court developed standards to determine when an election system or the drawing of district lines could violate section 2 of the Voting Rights Act. In *Thornburg v. Gingles*, the Court established a three-part test that grounds vote dilution in evidence of racially polarized voting behavior:

> First, the minority group must be able to demonstrate that it is
> sufficiently large and geographically compact to constitute a majority
> in a single member district. . . . Second, the minority group must be
> able to show that it is politically cohesive. . . . Third, the minority
> must be able to demonstrate that the white majority votes sufficiently
> as a bloc to enable it . . . usually to defeat the minority's preferred
> candidate.[32]

A violation of section 2 can thus exist when a large and cohesive minority population has been unable to elect candidates because white voters consistently vote against minority candidates. When vote dilution of a minority community occurs because of an electoral system, such as an at-large system in which officials are elected citywide, the typical remedy is to create districts in which at least one district contains a majority-minority population. Similarly, if the challenge is to a districting plan, the remedy is to redraw district lines to accommodate a majority-minority population.

Thornburg v. Gingles is still law, but more recent Supreme Court rulings have cast increasing doubt on the use of race in electoral districting. The Supreme Court ruled in *Shaw v. Reno* and *Miller v. Johnson* that race-conscious districting could violate the equal protection clause if districts were drawn in a highly irregular shape to accommodate racial minorities or if districts were drawn with race as the predominant factor.[33] Race can still be considered in electoral districting but only when used in tandem with other factors such as maintaining geographic compactness, preserving county and precinct lines, and keeping communities of interest together. Considering *Thornburg v. Gingles* with the Court's more recent cases leads to the conclusion that race-conscious districting will most likely fail to meet strict scrutiny unless there is evidence to show that race-conscious districting is necessary to prevent a violation of the Voting Rights Act, which is an exceptionally high standard to meet.

Asian American involvement in voting rights litigation has been limited for a number of reasons. First, the population of Asian American voters within a given jurisdiction is usually too small to form a numerical majority within a district. Even in areas such as California or New York where there are major concentrations of Asian Americans, the number of voting age citizens forms a much smaller percentage of the population because of the large number of Asian immigrants. Second, Asian American populations in many areas of the country tend to be geographically dispersed, which makes the creation of compact districts more difficult. Third, the Asian American population is heterogeneous, composed of multiple ethnic groups who may have different party affiliations and political attitudes.[34]

The very existence of an "Asian American vote" is not entirely clear. The body of empirical studies on Asian American voting behavior is growing, but it is still very incomplete. Voter registration studies have shown a mixture of patterns, often linking party affiliation with ethnicity and generation.[35] For instance, Vietnamese Americans show a strong tendency to register as Republicans because of socialization that opposes any connection of political activity to communism. Other Asian ethnicities tend to register with the Democratic Party, but at lower rates than blacks or Latinos. Second and third generation Asian Americans register more often with the Democratic Party, while first-generation immigrants who have become naturalized citizens split more evenly between the major parties.[36]

Voting behavior studies have shown Asian American support for Asian American candidates, usually along ethnic lines, and for positions on ballot measures that have strong effects on Asian American populations. For instance, exit polls conducted by the Asian American Legal Defense and Education Fund during the 1980s and 1990s have found strong communities of interest in New York City's Chinatown population.[37] Exit polls conducted by

the Asian Law Caucus in Northern California during 1994 found strong pan-
Asian support and even stronger ethnic-specific support for local Asian Ameri-
can candidates.[38] Studies conducted by the Asian Law Caucus and the Asian
Pacific American Legal Center of Southern California found high levels of
Asian American opposition to Proposition 187 in the 1994 elections and to
Proposition 209 in the 1996 elections.[39]

The tendency to racialize voting behavior because of the Voting Rights
Act and *Thornburg v. Gingles* has led Asian American advocates to pursue strategies that link Asian ethnic populations.[40] The Coalition of Asian Pacific
Americans for Fair Reapportionment (CAPAFR) was formed in California following the 1990 census to prevent the fragmentation of Asian American populations between electoral districts. CAPAFR developed sets of plans to create
state Assembly districts in Northern California and Southern California that
maintained Asian American population concentrations. One state Assembly
district proposed by CAPAFR for central Los Angeles would have linked concentrations of Japanese, Korean, Filipino, and Chinese American populations.
Another district in the San Gabriel Valley would have joined predominantly
Chinese and Japanese American populations. A third concentration was
formed in the southern part of Los Angeles County known as the South Bay,
which contains large Japanese American, Filipino, and Pacific Islander populations. None of these districts was majority-Asian, but the CAPAFR strategy was to prevent the division of Asian American populations in order to
have the capacity to influence elections by acting as a swing voting bloc.[41]
As one of the attorneys working with CAPAFR, I presented these plans in
arguments before the California Supreme Court, which had been charged with
creating the final plan after the legislature and the governor had reached a
stalemate. The supreme court's plan ultimately accommodated the San Gabriel
Valley and South Bay concentrations, but divided most of the other Asian
American populations between districts.[42]

The CAPAFR strategy was based on maintaining pan-Asian blocs to
maximize the number of Asian Americans within each district. But the empirical base for pan-Asian voting was based more on voting potential, rather
than on actual voting history. Most of the population concentrations were predominantly immigrant, with large numbers of noncitizens who might in the
future be eligible for naturalized citizenship. Nor was there a well-developed
pattern of pan-Asian voting in some of the areas. Informal polling in the down-
town Los Angeles area, for instance, had shown that ethnic bloc voting had
occurred in prior elections, but pan-Asian voting behavior had not been fully
established. Drawing on analogies to African American and Latino voters, who

had stronger histories of bloc voting, CAPAFR actually racialized the Asian ethnic populations as a political unit, using combined racial statistics in attempting to concentrate populations within electoral districts.

Nevertheless, the importance of providing some degree of advocacy on redistricting, which occurs only once every ten years, made the pan-Asian strategy compelling, even if, at the time, the empirical base was lacking. Pan-Asian voting patterns do appear to be developing in response to conservative policies attacking immigration and affirmative action, which directly affect Asian Americans.[43] Whether the Asian American population will "grow into" a political bloc around broader issues and candidates is a question whose answer continues to evolve along with the Asian American population itself.

Many Asian American candidates have had success in gaining votes from predominantly non-Asian populations. The election in 1996 of Governor Gary Locke in the State of Washington is one example.[44] But in other parts of the country, Asian American elected officials are virtually nonexistent. In Southern California, for example, no Asian American has ever sat on the Los Angeles County Board of Supervisors, even though over 10 percent of the county's population is Asian American. Studies from different parts of the country have shown strong evidence of white bloc voting against Asian American candidates.[45] There is still a need for race-consciousness in electoral districting and in correcting discriminatory electoral systems. As the Asian American voting population grows, the development of pan-Asian and ethnic-specific coalitions will require new political strategies that adapt to the multiplicity of Asian American identities. Pan-Asian voting blocs cannot be presumed to exist in areas with high Asian American populations, but neither can they be dismissed out of hand. Whether Asian American voting blocs, ethnic or pan-Asian, actually develop will always depend on local circumstances.

Intersection and Identity

In analyzing Asian American experiences, race and ethnicity are the most obvious manifestations of identity. But focusing on race often excludes the analysis of other facets of identity—gender, sexual orientation, language, disability, age, religious belief, immigration history, and others—that also intersect with race, ethnicity, and class to determine an individual's life experiences and the subordination to which that individual may be subjected. Some characteristics, such as gender or disability, may be externally apparent, making the individual subject to overt subordination. Others, sexual orientation and immigration status, may be more private, perhaps even secretive because of the social stigmas or legal consequences attached to those attributes. These characteristics can be the sources of multiple forms of subordination. Patriarchy and homophobia, for instance, can cause internal subordination within ethnic cultures, which compounds problems of externally imposed subordination.

Consider the intersection of race and gender. Women of color are often relegated to the margins of both racial and feminist theories, ignoring the fact that race and gender combine in the subordination of women of color.[46] Being an "Asian woman" is more than just being Asian and a woman. The category possesses a distinct set of attributes that is more than the sum of race and gender as individual categories. Patriarchy within Asian ethnic cultures may construct one form of subordination. Racism and sexism within a society dominated by white men creates additional forms of subordination.

Depictions of the mysterious Oriental woman—passive, subservient, even sexually alluring and concupiscent—constitute a unique and powerful ideological image that combines race and gender. Despite the social and economic advancement of Asian American women, the image is still pervasive in American society, whether it comes in the form of the Asian mail-order bride or the unassuming business professional. The image leads to stereotypes, prejudices, and discrimination at many levels of social interaction, ranging from denials of corporate promotions to the domination of Asian women in relationships involving domestic violence.[47]

Intersectional discrimination can have even more complex permutations. Consider the situation of an Asian immigrant woman who is undocumented, speaks little English, and works as a laborer for cash and at less than the minimum wage. This profile fits the typical laborer found in many garment sweatshops in California and the East Coast.[48] The case of the Thai garment workers who were enslaved in a Southern California homeshop in the mid-1990s is perhaps the most publicized and extreme example of garment worker abuse. Forms of subordination occur at several levels and in various combinations: the typical garment worker is a member of a racial minority group; she is a woman; she is poor and underpaid; she is deportable; she has limited English-speaking ability. While she has rights under the law to protect her from racial discrimination,[49] should she encounter discrimination it may actually be the least of her problems. Her immigration status may preclude her from raising any claim involving the government. Her low income may preclude her from gaining the assistance of an advocate. Her limited English skills may preclude her from raising any claim at all. The basic point is that race does not act in a vacuum as the source of subordination.

The limits of law in addressing intersectional discrimination are evident in the Supreme Court's equal protection jurisprudence, which has established different standards of review for different facets of group identity. Race and national origin are subject to the highest level of judicial scrutiny, gender is subject to intermediate scrutiny, and economic class and sexual orientation are each subject to low-level scrutiny. Immigration status is subject to varying levels of scrutiny, depending on whether the actor is the federal government or state government. Intersectional discrimination illuminates the inherent inconsistency in having separate standards for race and gender, for example. Would a "mixed-motive" law be subject to strict scrutiny because of race, or to intermediate scrutiny because of gender? There is no reason to have a lower standard of review for gender when the synergy of race and gender may produce subordination that is more severe than either one by itself.

In the area of statutory interpretation, the courts have only recently begun recognizing the nature of intersectional discrimination. In 1994, in *Lam v. University of Hawaii*,[50] a federal court of appeals acknowledged that the intersection of race and gender creates unique forms of employment discrimination against Asian American women. Maivan Lam, a woman of Vietnamese and French ancestry, had sued the University of Hawaii on charges of race, national origin, and sex discrimination after she had been denied a position as the director of a program at the Richardson School of Law. The position that Lam sought was eventually filled by a white woman. Overruling a summary judgment ruling based on the judge's decision to look at race and gender in isolation of each other, the court of appeals stated:

> [T]he attempt to bisect a person's identity at the intersection of race and gender often distorts or ignores the particular nature of their experiences. Like other subclasses under Title VII, Asian women are subject to a set of stereotypes and assumptions shared neither by Asian men nor by white women. In consequence they may be targeted for discrimination "even in the absence of discrimination against Asian men or white women." . . . [I]t is necessary to determine whether the employer discriminates on the basis of the *combination* of factors, not just whether it discriminates against people of the same race or of the same sex.[51]

The *Lam* decision reflects a new and positive trend in the law to recognize that race intersects with many facets of identity to create the predicates for subordination.

Identity is, by definition, a personal matter. Despite the array of legal classifications and their often inflexible strictures, the law rarely forces any person to identify as a member of a particular group. Identities shift and evolve, expand and contract, regardless of what the law says. But the law can—and should—change to address the richness of multiple identities. Asian American experiences demonstrate that race is only one of many dimensions defining personal identity.

Chapter 7	Law and Racial Hierarchy

San Francisco's Lowell High School is one of the leading academic high schools in the United States. Selected through a competitive admissions process, the students at Lowell are high achievers. Almost all go on to attend institutions of higher learning, including some of the nation's most prestigious colleges and universities. Generations of San Franciscans who have graduated from Lowell High School have gone on to excel in business, the sciences, the arts, and the professions.

As a public school within the San Francisco Unified School District, Lowell High School has been subject to a consent decree that grew out of litigation initiated in 1978 to desegregate the city's public schools.[1] The court-approved settlement signed in 1983 mandated that at least four out of nine specified racial/ethnic groups must be enrolled at each school within the district. The consent decree also required that no school could have an enrollment of more than 45 percent of any single racial/ethnic group (40 percent at "alternative" schools, including Lowell High School). The nine groups identified in the consent decree were "Spanish-Surname, Other White, Black, Chinese, Japanese, Korean, Filipino, American Indian, and Other Non-White."[2]

After the signing of the consent decree, the demographics of the school district shifted significantly. In 1983, African American students constituted the largest racial/ethnic group within the district; within a few years both Chinese American and Latino students had surpassed their numbers.[3] In 1997, students of Asian ancestry made up one-half of the students in the district; one out of every three high school students was Chinese American. The student bodies continue to evolve because of "white flight" to suburban areas and the growth of Asian and Latino populations through immigration.

In 1994, the parents of Chinese American students filed a lawsuit challenging the legality of the desegregation consent decree. In order to gain admission to Lowell High School, Chinese American applicants were required to score several points higher than all other racial/ethnic groups, including whites, on an admissions index that combined students' grade point averages and standardized test scores. Because of the large number of Chinese American students seeking admission to Lowell, differentiated admissions scores provided one way of limiting enrollment to maintain the 40 percent ceiling under the consent decree. The Chinese American Democratic Club, a supporter of the lawsuit, issued a statement criticizing the burdens placed on Chinese students:

> Because of the racial ceilings, if a Chinese American student hopes to
> attend the competitive academic Lowell High School, he must
> achieve a near-perfect score on the exam and grade evaluation. If the
> applicant is White—he can receive a score in the 85th percentile and
> still gain entrance to Lowell. These policies have resulted in discrimi-
> nation against Chinese American students.[4]

Rather than seeking to modify the consent decree and adjust the ceilings to deal with the changing demographics, the Chinese American parents' legal papers requested that the desegregation plan be dismantled altogether. Pitting themselves against both the school district and the civil rights groups who filed the desegregation case, the parents argued that admissions to Lowell High School should be based on "merit," with no limits on enrollment based on race or ethnicity.

The head of the local National Association for the Advancement of Colored People (NAACP), one of the original plaintiffs in the desegregation litigation, responded with the following statement: "The Chinese are the largest group at most of the best schools in the city. They can't have it all. If anything, I'd say lower the caps, don't raise them—otherwise we're headed back to segregated schools, only all Chinese instead of all white."[5] Even after the school board changed the Lowell High School admissions program in 1996 to eliminate the differentiated index scores, the parents' lawsuit still moved forward in an attempt to remove the ceilings on admissions.[6]

Although dismissed by the trial court in 1997, the Lowell High School litigation encapsulates the complexities of contemporary race relations. As immigration has transformed urban demographics from a binary racial dynamic to a more complex multiracial and multiethnic dynamic, new types of discordance and racial conflict have arisen. School desegregation is just one arena in which population changes have engendered new social and legal relationships, forming the basis for both competition and cooperation. The conflict between the Chinese American parents and the civil rights advocates in the Lowell High School case is more exceptional than typical, but it illuminates significant gaps in legal theories based on a black-white racial paradigm.

This chapter assesses the legal responses to the changing demographics and the new forms of discrimination arising through Asian American population growth. The racialization of Asian Americans as both foreigners and as the "model minority" has led to an array of problems, including the exclusion of Asian Americans from race-conscious affirmative action programs and intergroup conflict that leads to anti-Asian violence. After examining demographic data and the changing character of race relations, I focus on three areas of law to illustrate some of the unfolding dynamics: voting rights, affirmative action, and racial violence.

The New Demographics

Although the highest concentrations of Asian Americans are in Hawaii and California, Asian immigrants and refugees form large and growing populations throughout the country. Refugee resettlement has spurred the growth of Southeast Asian communities in predominantly white areas in Minnesota and Wisconsin. The immigration of professional Asian immigrants and their families has spurred suburban population growth in Illinois, Texas, and New Jersey. Secondary migration—migration after entering the United States—has led to the development of Hmong communities in the small towns and rural areas of California's agricultural Central Valley. Cities on the West Coast have blossomed into multiracial and multiethnic centers with no racial group forming a clear majority of the population.

It is no longer possible to speak of urban America in terms of black and white. The growth of Latino and Asian American populations through immigration has changed the basic composition of our nation's cities. In California, Asian Americans often form 10 to 20 percent of city populations. One out of every three residents of San Francisco is Asian American. Reflecting post-1965 patterns of immigration, most of the cities that have large Asian concentrations also have large Latino populations, some exceeding the size of longer-established African American populations. In some of the nation's largest cities—New York, Los Angeles, Chicago, Houston—whites no longer form a majority of the population (see table 7.1).

The City of Long Beach in Southern California is representative of the

Table 7.1
Selected Characteristics of Cities with Largest Asian or Pacific Islander
Populations, 1990

	Asian or Pacific Islander population	Percentage of Total Population		
		ASIAN OR PACIFIC ISLANDER	BLACK	HISPANIC[a]
New York, NY	512,719	7.0	28.7	24.4
Los Angeles, CA	341,807	9.8	14.0	39.9
Honolulu, HI	257,552	70.5	1.3	4.6
San Francisco, CA	210,876	29.1	10.9	13.9
San Jose, CA	152,815	19.5	4.7	26.6
San Diego, CA	130,945	11.8	9.4	20.7
Chicago, IL	104,118	3.7	39.1	19.6
Houston, TX	67,113	4.1	28.1	27.6
Seattle, WA	60,819	11.8	10.1	3.6
Long Beach, CA	58,266	13.6	13.7	23.6

SOURCE: U.S. Department of Commerce, Bureau of the Census, *County and City Data Book* (Washington, D.C., 1994), table 3.
[a] Persons of Hispanic origin may be of any race.

multiracial and multiethnic mix that is developing in many urban centers in the United States. A city of more than 400,000 people, located just south of Los Angeles, Long Beach is an industrial center with a significant portion of its economy devoted to the nearby harbor, which serves as a major transportation hub for the Pacific Rim region. According to 1990 census figures, 13.6 percent of the city's population is Asian or Pacific Islander, 13.7 percent is African American, and 23.6 percent is Latino.[7] Long Beach is home to the largest Cambodian population in the nation, most of whom entered as refugees during the 1980s. There are also large Filipino and Pacific Islander populations in the area, along with an array of other Asian ethnic groups.

Many Cambodian families in Long Beach live in poverty, sometimes mired in welfare dependency, but a significant number have entered the entrepreneurial ranks. A commercial enclave, often called "Little Phnom Penh," runs along several blocks in a working-class area of the city; stores owned by Vietnamese, Chinese, blacks, Latinos, and whites sprinkle the area as well. The residential area surrounding Little Phnom Penh is racially diverse, serving as the home for lower-income whites, blacks, Asians, and Latinos. Like many urban areas, it has its share of interethnic tensions and youth violence. In April and May of 1992, during the civil unrest that shook many of the nation's cities, it was the Cambodian store ownership that was most heavily hit by rioting. Many store owners simply chose to close down and leave the area, while some stayed and rebuilt successful businesses.[8] A number of owners whose businesses have thrived still reside in the neighborhood, but many have moved from the urban core to surrounding suburban areas. The commercial area continues to grow as the population increases.

The patterns are never the same, but there are close parallels in other California cities and in cities throughout the country that have large Asian refugee and immigrant populations. Economic development, school desegregation, electoral districting, language politics, human relations—the panoply of urban public policies—are all made more complex because of the racial and ethnic diversity of urban populations that are expanding through immigration and refugee resettlement.

Another important demographic trend—a trend that reveals the heterogeneity within Asian America—is the growth of Asian American populations in suburban areas. Some of the highest percentages of Asian American populations can be found in suburbs. In Southern California's predominantly middle-class San Gabriel Valley, Asian Americans, most of whom are immigrants from China, Hong Kong, and Taiwan, constitute the largest single racial group. Nearly 60 percent of the population of Monterey Park is Asian American. In Northern California, suburbs such as Daly City, Union City, and Milpitas have large Filipino immigrant populations that with other Asian ethnic groups constitute near-majorities.

Immigration policies provide one explanation for the trend. Since 1965, the immigration preference system has favored the entry of highly skilled and highly educated immigrants and their families, some of whom enter with significant financial resources. By design, these immigrants enter the middle class because they are recruited and employed by companies that offer middle-class wages. In cities such as Los Angeles, immigrant entrepreneurs also form a segment of the suburban populations; although their businesses are often located in the urban core, many reside miles away in middle-class areas.[9]

Unlike urban centers, however, many suburbs to which Asian Americans have been moving are areas that in the past have been predominantly white. New race and class dynamics are at work. First, the economic class advantages that many Asian Americans possess allow them to move to suburban areas in the first place; unlike many blacks and Latinos with lower incomes, these Asian Americans possess the economic means to make entry into the suburbs a real option. Second, the benefits of legal commitments to ending discrimination have been accruing to Asian immigrants as they enter the country. New immigrants have not been burdened with the long history of overt anti-Asian racism. Third, there may in fact be a greater tolerance among suburban whites for Asian Americans—at least initially—than for blacks and Latinos. The "model minority" stereotype may work to an advantage for Asian

Americans moving into neighborhoods populated by large numbers of white families.

But racism is still inescapable, even in the most affluent neighborhoods. Increased Asian immigration to Monterey Park during the 1980s was met with political hostility, which included the enactment of subordinative legislation such as an official English ordinance, English language signage requirements, and restrictions on the purchasing of library books in Chinese.[10] In Jersey City, New Jersey, a group known as the "dotbusters"—a crude reference to the *bindi* worn on the forehead by many Asian Indian women—engaged in a pattern of vandalism and assaults against the area's Asian Indian population during the late 1980s.[11] The City of Garden Grove, in Orange County, California, settled a lawsuit in 1995 with a group of Vietnamese American youth whose civil rights were violated by police officers who had stopped and photographed them as suspected gang members—simply because of their racial appearance and clothing.[12]

Between Black and White

In light of the demographic realities, a black-white paradigm is inadequate in dealing with the spectrum of racial and ethnic issues, including many forms of discrimination against Asian Americans. The failure to expand racial policies to include Asian Americans can lead to inequitable outcomes, including the denial of basic rights and remedies. In Los Angeles, for example, Asian Americans were excluded from a 1980 consent decree that required the Los Angeles Police Department to set specific goals to increase the number of women, blacks, and Latinos on the force to reflect the city's population. The city only began its Asian American recruitment campaign in 1995, when the percentage of officers of Asian or Pacific Islander ancestry was less than one-half of the group's percentage of the city population.[13]

Nonrecognition is just one problem that can arise through the application of a binary racial paradigm to Asian Americans. Treating racial and ethnic minority groups as equivalent and interchangeable can also lead to unjust results. For instance, a school desegregation plan that treats students of color as all alike can flout the rights of limited-English-proficient students, who may be placed in schools and classrooms where their language needs are ignored or mishandled. Even in an area involving language rights, the tendency to treat problems dualistically—for instance, using Spanish as the model for bilingual education—means that diverse Asian American groups may be given short shrift. Another deficiency in a binary racial paradigm arises in interminority conflict. When Asian Americans are victims—or act as victimizers—in interracial and interethnic disputes, the problems cannot be summarily dismissed as aberrational or attributable to white racism. Real conflicts exist.

The place of Asian Americans within a racially stratified society takes on an added twist because of the "model minority" stereotype. Although there are historical roots for the model minority image—Asian immigrant workers were often portrayed in the 1800s and early 1900s as better and harder-working laborers than blacks—the model minority image has taken on powerful dimensions in recent years. Since the late 1960s, Asian Americans have been characterized in the popular media as the model minority because of their accomplishments in education and their higher income levels relative to blacks, Latinos, and even whites.

The stereotype has some basis in reality. High intermarriage rates with whites, the movement into predominantly white suburbs, and disproportionate representation in higher education indicate that many kinds of overt discrimination are no longer operating to prevent the advancement of Asian Americans. The advantages of economic class have allowed the entry of many Asian Americans into sectors of life where African Americans and Latinos remain underrepresented. Discrimination is still a chronic problem for Asian Americans, but differential racialization—manifested in the model minority image—has evolved to place Asian Americans in an intermediate racial position, between black and white in a racial hierarchy.

Antidiscrimination laws treat many racial problems generically. Discrimination committed by an Asian American employer against a black employee, for instance, is covered by Title VII and other employment discrimination laws dealing with race. But interracial tensions in a racially stratified society are not so easily resolved through legal measures. Addressing competition among racial groups for scarce resources, such as jobs or seats in higher education, is unclear when the civil rights laws are designed to protect minority groups equally. And the invocation of antidiscrimination laws may be inappropriate in some instances. The laws punishing racial violence deal with black-on-Asian hate crimes, but the reduction of interracial tensions is not necessarily served through a strict adherence to the proscriptions of hate crimes laws. Tensions can be exacerbated when interracial conflict is placed at the center of more complex and deep-seated social problems involving race, poverty, and social disadvantage.

Voting Rights and Multiracial Jurisdictions

As I noted in chapter 6, Asian Americans have only recently begun serious efforts in voting rights advocacy, including redistricting and gaining language assistance for limited-English-speaking voters. The existence of a monolithic "Asian American vote" is debatable, but there are clear patterns of voting behavior that indicate common interests and responses to issues such as immigration and affirmative action, which have direct effects on Asian Americans.

In geographic areas in which Asian American populations are large enough to qualify for bilingual ballots or to form significant voting blocs, the demographic mix usually includes whites, blacks, and Latinos as well.[14] Voting rights litigation and electoral districting involving Asian Americans thus occur in multiracial and multiethnic settings, which raise a host of issues involving political cooperation and conflict.

A basic problem of nonrecognition can be traced to the history of the Voting Rights Act itself. Enacted in 1965 to address the egregious abridgments of franchise rights against blacks in the Deep South, the Voting Rights Act was originally written to prohibit discrimination on the basis of race. Although Asian Americans would most likely have qualified as a racial minority group under the original legislation, Asian Americans were not explicitly mentioned as a protected category until 1975, when the act was amended to include language-minority groups.[15] Nonrecognition can also occur in voting rights litigation in which Asian American voters are not among the plaintiffs challenging the legality of an electoral system. In a number of cases involving combined classes of African Americans and Latinos, Asian Americans were not included in the litigation even though they formed significant portions of city populations. In *Badillo v. City of Stockton*, for instance, Asian Americans were omitted, despite the fact that Asian Americans constituted over 20 percent of the population of Stockton, California.[16]

Equivalency issues occur when Asian Americans are combined with Latinos and African Americans into a monolithic class of minority voters. The theory supporting the combination of groups looks at the common histories of racial discrimination and the convergence of political interests that arise because of racial subordination. The theory opposing the combination of groups looks at the dissimilarities among groups: racial and ethnic differences, immigration history, antagonisms between groups. On some issues, such as immigration, the interests of Asian Americans and Latinos may converge because of similar histories, while white and African American voters may align in opposition because of perceptions that immigrants take jobs from U.S.-born workers. On other issues, such as school desegregation or property taxation, Asian Americans and whites may align in one direction because of their higher suburban concentrations, while blacks and Latinos may align in the opposite direction. The realities are always situational. Coalitions may gel, or antagonisms may flare, depending on the issues, the candidates, and the local politics.[17]

In *Growe v. Emison*,[18] the United States Supreme Court assumed for the sake of argument that minorities could be combined as a single voting bloc, but the Court struck down a federal district court's remedial plan that combined racial minorities. The lower court had created a majority-minority district in Minneapolis, Minnesota, composed of blacks, Latinos, and Asian Americans, by presuming political cohesiveness among the groups. The Supreme Court struck down the plan because the lower court had not reviewed any statistical or anecdotal evidence before producing its plan. Interminority coalition building is consistent with Asian American bloc voting, but the Supreme Court correctly noted the dangers of combining minority groups without satisfying one of the basic requirements under the law—evidence of prior political cohesiveness.

The obverse of minority group equivalency is the presumptive linkage of Asian American populations with white populations. In the 1991 New York City Council redistricting process, Lower Manhattan's Chinatown population—the city's largest concentration of Asian Americans—was combined with the predominantly white populations of Battery Park, Tribeca, and Soho, despite arguments presented by the Asian American advocacy groups that the Chinatown population shared more common political and economic interests with Latinos in the Lower East Side. Asian American candidates were soundly defeated in subsequent elections.[19]

Redistricting also poses the difficult problem of intergroup conflict. When minority groups propose different electoral district lines, tensions inevitably arise because lines that benefit one minority group may come at the expense of one or more other minority groups. When the Coalition of Asian Pacific Americans for Fair Reapportionment (CAPAFR) proposed state assembly district lines in Central Los Angeles, it attempted to combine population concentrations of Koreans, Filipinos, Japanese, and Chinese. The NAACP and the Mexican American Legal Defense and Educational Fund (MALDEF) had also drawn up plans in Central Los Angeles to benefit African Americans and Latinos. All three of the plans compromised the other groups' plans: The CAPAFR plan divided the African American community and prevented the Latino community from creating a district with enough voting age citizens. The MALDEF plan cut the Koreatown and the Filipino concentration in half. The NAACP plan also divided Koreatown in half. There was no clear legal remedy for the situation, since the Voting Rights Act was supposed to protect all of the groups. The advocates simply agreed to disagree.[20]

But conflict was not inevitable. When CAPAFR prepared its district lines

for the San Gabriel Valley—the region with the most geographically compact Asian American populations and the best track record of pan-Asian voting behavior—it was able to work cooperatively with Latino advocates in
crafting mutually beneficial district lines. The commitment to preserve voting rights for both Asian Americans and Latinos enabled the two groups to
present district lines that maintained communities of interest which were later
incorporated into the California Supreme Court's final set of plans.[21]

Asian Americans and Affirmative Action

The nonrecognition of Asian Americans has become less of a problem in the
area of race-conscious affirmative action. Rather, special recognition and re-
jection pose the real problems; Asian Americans are more often used as the
example of a racial minority group that does not need affirmative action and
that should be intentionally excluded from affirmative action programs.
Neoconservatives, who often couch their rhetoric in the language of color-
blindness, become quite color-conscious when portraying Asian Americans
as victims of affirmative action and using Asian Americans to justify the abolition of affirmative action.[22]

The inclusion or exclusion of Asian Americans from any affirmative action program rests on fulfilling the underlying goals of affirmative action. One
goal of affirmative action is remedying the present effects of past discrimination; another is preventing ongoing and future discrimination; a third goal
may be encouraging inclusiveness and diversity within an institution such as
a college or a corporation.[23] Depending on context, the argument can be made
that Asian Americans should be included in programs to promote any or all
of the general goals of affirmative action.

In the corporate sector, there is a "glass ceiling" that prevents many Asian
Americans from progressing to the upper levels of management. The 1995 report of the bipartisan Federal Glass Ceiling Commission found major barriers
to the advancement of Asian Americans, including widespread acceptance of
the popular (and paradoxical) stereotype that Asian Americans are not affected by the glass ceiling; widespread acceptance of the stereotype that Asian
Americans make superior professionals and technicians but are not suited for
management leadership; and benign neglect and ignorance of the complexity, needs, and differences among Asian Americans.[24] According to a survey
of senior-level managers in Fortune 1000 industrial and Fortune 500 service
industries, only 0.3 percent of the nation's senior executives were Asian American, even though Asian American representation in the national population
is ten times that figure. Disparities for Asian American women were even more

severe: Asian American men held less than 0.2 percent of board of directors' seats in publicly held Fortune 1500 firms; Asian American women held less than 0.01 percent of the board seats.[25]

Wage disparities involving Asian Americans demonstrate the need for affirmative action to remedy employment discrimination. Despite high levels of education, Asian Americans earn less than whites with comparable educations: college-educated whites earn almost 11 percent more than college-educated Asians; white high school graduates earn 26 percent more than their Asian American counterparts.[26] Even controlling for immigration status, Asian American incomes fall below white incomes. In the field of engineering, where Asian Americans as a group are well-represented, native-born Asian Americans are more likely than foreign-born immigrants of European origin to be relegated to the lower echelons of their profession.[27]

Disparities in public sector employment and contracting also point to institutional discrimination requiring remedial affirmative action. A 1994 survey of Southern California police and fire departments found extensive underrepresentation of Asian Americans in the sworn personnel of many departments.[28] For example, even though Asian Americans constituted over 10 percent of the population in both Los Angeles County and Orange County, only 2.6 percent of the Los Angeles County firefighters and 2.1 percent of the Orange County firefighters were Asian American. Percentages were even lower among county sheriffs: 2.5 percent of the Los Angeles County sheriff's officers and 1.2 percent of the Orange County sheriff's officers were Asian American. Several departments in the region had no Asian American officers or firefighters at all.

During the 1980s, Asian American construction firms in San Francisco received less than 1 percent of the city's construction contracts, and only about 5 percent of the total dollars for the school district's construction contracts. Yet Asian American firms made up 20 percent of the available pool.[29] An independent review of the San Francisco Unified School District found that the school district staff employed inconsistent bidding and contract procedures and also withheld information from minority contractors; moreover, the staff conducted no significant outreach, and actual contracts were substantially smaller for minority and women contractors. Only after an affirmative action plan was instituted did Asian American participation increase.

When implemented, affirmative action programs have been able to correct serious workplace disparities involving Asian Americans. During the 1970s there were only a handful of Asian American officers on the San Francisco Police Department. Because of affirmative action there were nearly three hundred officers in 1996, the same year in which Fred Lau became San Francisco's first Asian American chief of police. Similarly, under a 1988 court-ordered consent decree, the San Francisco Fire Department agreed to a race-conscious and gender-conscious hiring and promotion policy, with goals designed to remedy past discrimination against racial minorities and women.[30] Because of affirmative action, the number of Asian American firefighters increased fivefold in the span of ten years.

The question of whether some or all Asian Americans should be *excluded* from a particular affirmative action program is situational. If the objective of an affirmative action program is population parity, Asian Americans may be excluded from programs where their institutional numbers exceed their proportionate numbers in the local population. But because of the ethnic and economic heterogeneity of the Asian American population, remedies should vary depending on the circumstances. In California, where one out of every ten people is Asian American—with even higher proportions in some of the largest cities—ethnic considerations may be more appropriate because of the large size of Asian immigrant populations. In areas of the country in which Asian Americans form a much smaller percentage of the population, aggregated pan-Asian considerations may be more fitting. In addressing a "glass ceiling" problem in which there are no Asian Americans at all in the upper-level management of a large corporation, race-based affirmative action may be the proper remedy. But in higher education, where Asian Americans often form large percentages of college student bodies, ethnic-based and class-based recruitment and admissions policies action may be more appropriate to address the underrepresentation of seriously disadvantaged Asian ethnic groups such as Vietnamese, Cambodians, Laotians, and Hmong.

Racialization and Affirmative Action

The racialization of Asian Americans—as immigrants and, more importantly, as the "model minority"—generates a host of issues in the area of race-conscious affirmative action. Racialization has led to intergroup conflicts in which Asian Americans are used as a wedge by opponents of affirmative action. As Frank Wu notes, the attention placed on Asian Americans "pits Asian Americans against African Americans, as if one group can succeed only by the failure of the other. Asian Americans are encouraged to view African Americans, and programs for them, as threats to their own upward mobility. African Americans are led to see Asian Americans, many of whom are immigrants, as another group that has usurped what was meant for them."[31]

IMMIGRATION AND AFFIRMATIVE ACTION

Opponents of immigration and affirmative action have linked the two issues by proposing public policies to limit or dismantle both. Conservatives writers have generated several arguments employing both anti-immigrant rhetoric and anti-affirmative-action rhetoric: (1) immigrants are not entitled to affirmative action and should be denied access to it; (2) affirmative action is a failure and should be ended because it benefits immigrants rather than blacks; and (3) immigration should be limited because it undermines the basic goals of affirmative action.[32]

The first argument—immigrants are not entitled to affirmative action—parallels arguments that have been used to support laws such as Proposition 187 and federal welfare reform legislation. Immigrants as a class should be denied government benefits and services to ensure that an already scarce resource is available to citizens. Affirmative action is just like any other form of government entitlement; therefore, it should be limited to American citizens.

The other two arguments are more insidious. One says that because immigrants—assumed to be undeserving because they are recent arrivals—are now the primary beneficiaries of affirmative action instead of African Americans, affirmative action programs should be dismantled as fundamentally flawed. The other says that immigration has shifted the demographics of the United States so much that blacks are being pushed further down the social ladder; therefore, immigration itself should be limited or halted to prevent any further slippage of blacks, who are the most worthy recipients of affirmative action.

Besides having a divisive theme of pitting people of color against each other, these arguments rest on the same faulty assumptions: affirmative action should be limited only to African Americans, discrimination against immigrants is not a significant problem, and dismantling either immigration or affirmative action will solve the problem of providing African Americans with equal opportunities.

The racialization of Asian Americans as foreign outsiders suggests that the goals of affirmative action are actually too narrow if they only remedy past discrimination against African Americans. With the growth of contemporary nativism, the subordination of immigrants has become pervasive, and the racialization of Asian Americans as immigrants has caused discrimination against both citizens and noncitizens. The solution is not to eliminate affirmative action programs or to limit immigration, but to try to combine remediation for African Americans with programs that address anti-immigrant discrimination. The goals of affirmative action do not have to be mutually exclusive.

"MODEL MINORITY" RACIALIZATION

The racialization of Asian Americans as the "model minority" causes the greatest problems of intergroup conflict in the area of affirmative action. As a racialized stereotype, the model minority image prevents the betterment of many Asian Americans facing social or economic disadvantages by omitting them as a matter of course from affirmative action programs. In higher education, for example, where Asian Americans as a racial group form large percentages of many student bodies, ethnic groups such as Southeast Asians and Pacific Islanders are not well represented and are often excluded from recruitment programs designed to increase the representation of racial minorities.

More importantly, the model minority stereotype places Asian Americans in a falsely elevated position relative to blacks and Latinos, and sometimes even relative to whites. The stereotype creates the perception that Asian Americans are actually victims of affirmative action in higher education admissions, because places that might be available to Asian Americans through "merit" are made available to African Americans or Latinos through affirmative action. The policy adopted by the Regents of the University of California in 1995 to repeal affirmative action in admissions was portrayed as a boon for Asian American students, who were expected to increase their numbers on several campuses.[33]

The ideology of the model minority myth operates in two directions. First, model minority racialization subordinates blacks and Latinos by linking to Asian Americans a set of "positive" ethnic characteristics—family values, hard work, quiet persistence—that are meant to serve as a "model" for other minorities. In other words, blacks and Latinos should try to act more like Asians. The invidiousness of this type of subordination lies in its failure to recognize racism's power in creating stereotypical ethnic characteristics. The treatment of Asian Americans as a superior racial minority group serves little purpose other than sharpening negative stereotypes of other groups and pushing those groups further down in the racial hierarchy.

Second, model minority racialization gives Asian Americans themselves a false sense of security, as if the model minority stereotype could protect them from racial discrimination. By couching achievement in higher education in "merit"—which is illusory since "merit" can be defined in any number of ways, not just by grades or test scores—some Asian Americans come to believe that success can always be achieved through adherence to the model minority stereotype. But racial discrimination is still widespread, and outside of the academic setting, the representation of Asian Americans in employment, business, and contracting remains well below parity.

Admissions Ceilings

Opponents of affirmative action have often pointed to the Lowell High School litigation to illustrate one of the reputed perils of race-consciousness—the undue burdens placed on Asian Americans through the admission of other racial minorities with lesser academic credentials. After Chinese parents initiated litigation in *Ho v. San Francisco Unified School District* to challenge the Lowell admissions policy, the policy was changed voluntarily in 1996 to eliminate differential test scores broken down by race or ethnicity. Instead, like many university admissions programs, Lowell High School began using a two-track system of admissions, with one track based on index scores, and another track based on scores, income, and underrepresentation.[34] Nevertheless, the *Ho* lawsuit was not dropped in 1996; the Chinese parents still sought the removal of the racial ceilings under the desegregation consent decree.

Lowell High School's admissions program is much like a university's admission program, but it differs in one important respect. Lowell High School is part of a school district that is bound by a desegregation order. Race-consciousness is inevitable when the underlying goal of a remedial policy is to prevent the resegregation of a public school system. But the facts of the *Ho* case raise basic questions about the bearing of burdens under any race-conscious remedial system, including university affirmative action programs. Can Asian Americans be required to bear a heavier burden than other racial groups, including whites?

Placing the onus on Asian Americans relative to whites in order to promote a race-conscious policy—a concept that Jerry Kang calls "negative action"[35]—clearly existed when the Lowell High School litigation was first filed. Chinese American students had been required to score higher than all other racial and ethnic groups, including white students, on an admissions index score. Kang suggests that negative action is illegal because it singles out a racial minority group to bear a greater burden than the white population. Setting a ceiling on Asian American admissions is different from establishing goals to address the discrimination suffered by traditionally underrepresented groups. The former burdens a specific racial minority group, the latter spreads burdens among nonbeneficiaries of affirmative action programs. Thus, if both Asian Americans and whites are not included in an affirmative action program, they bear the incidental burdens of the program equally.

The problem of negative action arises out of the trend developing on many college campuses where Asian American are pluralities—even majorities—of the student bodies. For example, at the University of California, Irvine, over one-half of the student body is Asian American. Asian Americans may thus appear to be "overrepresented" on many college campuses. It becomes possible, therefore, for white students to argue that they are "underrepresented" at college campuses relative to their population in the community. Even whites might seek to be included in affirmative action programs in order to enter a university populated by disproportionately large numbers of Asians.

When "diversity" is the goal of an admissions program, it makes sense to ensure that a college student body is representative of the general population; a college campus is not racially diverse if 95 percent of its student body is Asian American and white, and only 5 percent is African American, Latino, and Native American. But if the goal of a program is to address the past and present effects of racial discrimination, it does not make sense to treat whites as an underrepresented group when whites as a class do not suffer from the racial subordination endured by people of color. The specter of "too many Asians" displacing other racial minority groups should not be used as a pretext to ensure that universities remain largely white.

Race- and Class-Based Affirmative Action

During the 1980s, several leading universities and colleges—including Harvard, Brown, Princeton, Stanford, and several campuses at the University of California—were alleged to have discriminated against Asian American applicants by limiting their admissions. Applications from Asian Americans increased during the decade, but admissions numbers often stayed constant at many campuses. After internal reviews and investigations by the Department of Education, only one graduate program at UCLA was found to be in violation of the law. As Dana Takagi notes, however, the admissions controversy involving Asian Americans in higher education took on a larger role when it helped produce a shift in the rhetoric of affirmative action. A "retreat from race" occurred when opponents of affirmative action used the Asian American admissions controversy to advocate for class-based rather than race-based admissions policies.[36]

Many neoconservatives have supported the use of economic class over race and ethnicity in affirmative action programs. A class-based affirmative action system has some appeal because it appears to accommodate many low-income racial and ethnic minorities without having to look directly at race. Because of the heterogeneity of the Asian American population, it is appropriate to consider economic class when attempting to remedy social disadvantages suffered by sectors of the Asian American population that may be overlooked in purely race-conscious programs. Thus students from Southeast Asian refugee families who continue to endure severe social and economic disadvantage would not be submerged among other Asian ethnic populations who are well represented at colleges or in other institutions.

But substituting class for race ignores the basic problem of racial discrimination in American society. Class-based affirmative action is an anti-poverty policy, not an anti-racism policy. Color-blind advocates envision a world where race and ethnicity can somehow be ignored. We do not yet live in such a world, and it seems doubtful that we will soon attain that ideal, given what psychologists and other social scientists tell us about the nature of discrimination and how unconscious racism pervades our social realities. An affirmative action regime that looks at race, ethnicity, and class—along with other factors that define individual identity—and that attempts to remedy disadvantage caused by those characteristics is preferable to a rigid system that looks simply at race or class but nothing else.

Intergroup Conflict and Racial Violence

People of color are not immune from racial and ethnic stereotyping. A national survey conducted by the National Conference of Christians and Jews in 1994 found that racial minorities are more likely than whites to agree with negative stereotypes about other minority groups. Asked if they agreed that Asian Americans are "wary, suspicious, and unfriendly toward non-Asians," 46 percent of Latinos agreed, 42 percent of African Americans agreed, while 30 percent of white respondents agreed. Responding to the statement that Latinos "tend to have bigger families than they are able to support, 68 percent of Asian Americans agreed, 49 percent of African Americans agreed, and 50 percent of whites agreed. In response to the statement that African Americans "even if given a chance, aren't capable of getting ahead," 33 percent of Latinos, 22 percent of Asian Americans, and 12 percent of whites agreed.[37]

Stereotyping, prejudice, and intergroup tensions often rise to the level of violence. When Asian Americans are racialized as outsiders, violence becomes more tolerable. The nameless "foreign enemy" or "foreign competitor" takes on a dehumanized role, regardless of the identity of the victim or the victimizer. When Asian Americans are racialized as the model minority, another dynamic occurs. The model minority role places Asian Americans in the middle of the racial hierarchy, between black and white. Resentment and anger arise when Asian Americans become the standards by which other people of color are judged, or when Asian Americans take on the role of economic "middleman"—such as the store owner who services a racial minority community but becomes socially detached from that community because of differences based on race and class.[38]

The most prominent interracial conflicts involving Asian Americans have arisen in areas such as New York City and Los Angeles between Asian American store owners and African American residents. Paul Ong, Edna Bonacich, and Lucie Cheng have suggested that racial discrimination in traditional labor markets and changes in the global economy are operating to push Asian immigrants out of the labor market and into entrepreneurship.[39] Entrepreneurship in turn leads to racial conflict because many Asian immigrants open businesses in poor, predominantly black and Latino neighborhoods and may engage in exploitative employment practices, such as employing undocumented Latino laborers in garment factories, or in exploitative retail trade practices, such as selling liquor.

A combination of crime, language and cultural differences, and strained consumer versus merchant relationships have exacerbated racial tensions between store owners and residents. Korean entrepreneurs are the best-known players, but they are not unique; parallels can be found among other Asian ethnic entrepreneurs who provide goods and service in predominantly black or Latino neighborhoods. (Historically, Jewish merchants played a role similar to Korean merchants in the Los Angeles area during the 1960s and 1970s, and were among those targeted during the 1965 Watts riots.)[40]

Even before the civil unrest in April and May of 1992, tensions between Korean merchants and blacks in Los Angeles ran high. The shooting death of black teenager Latasha Harlins by Korean store owner Soon Ja Du was a key incident that pre-dated the rioting against Korean stores. After Mrs. Du received a light sentence for the shooting, tensions ran even higher. The rioting in Los Angeles during 1992 was seen not only as a response to the verdict in the Rodney King beating case, but as an expression of the pent-up anger and resentment against Korean merchants, who suffered discrimination both as immigrants and as a model minority.

Racial tensions continued during the rebuilding process in Southern California. City ordinances designed to limit the reopening of liquor stores in predominantly black neighborhoods illuminated significant differences among racial communities. Many African American activists sought to rid the neighborhoods of easy access to liquor, which was considered a bane to community development. Korean store owners, on the other hand, simply sought to rebuild their businesses, which had sold liquor as one of many retail items. Although the laws allowed store owners to make transitions to other businesses, most of the store owners simply abandoned their efforts because of the maze of administrative requirements.[41]

The limits of the legal system become clear in attempting to resolve the major divides between racial communities. A 1996 study by the MultiCultural

Collaborative, a community-based coalition created after the civil unrest, found that the human relations infrastructure in Los Angeles is fundamentally inadequate in addressing interracial and interethnic tensions.[42] Government resources devoted to resolving interracial conflict have been minimal, and media and educational institutions have provided limited support to foster tolerance and racial harmony. Civil rights laws by themselves have not had a significant effect on improving human relations. The solutions require creating and sustaining social and economic institutions that minimize intergroup conflicts and help people get along with each other through the promotion of common goals and agendas.

Conflict and Cooperation in Public Housing

A less publicized interracial dynamic has developed in San Francisco's public housing projects during the 1990s. Because housing costs in San Francisco are among the highest in the nation, federally subsidized public housing is the only option for many of the city's poorest families. With the growth of Southeast Asian refugee populations in San Francisco, over one-half of the families on the waiting list for public housing have been of Asian ancestry, although only about 15 percent of the actual residents in public housing projects have been Asian American.

In 1988, the federal Department of Housing and Urban Development (HUD) prepared a study of San Francisco's public housing and found what was deemed to be a pattern of racial segregation: ten of the twenty-four projects were over 70 percent black, and two were over 90 percent Asian. Based on these findings, HUD required the San Francisco Housing Authority in 1992 to implement a policy that steered families toward projects based on race. Unfortunately, the racial integration strategy did nothing to address language and cultural barriers, tenant conflicts, or the lack of social services for tenants in the public housing projects.

The result was a sharp increase in racial violence against Asian American families. The integration policy had actually created a perception that Southeast Asian families were receiving preferential treatment when moving into predominantly African American projects. One consequence was a backlash against the families. By the end of 1993, the number of Asian American households in the ten largely African American projects, far from increasing, had declined by 35 percent under the integration plan. Many of the families left the public housing projects in fear. Other families became so terrified that they literally became prisoners in their own homes.

A series of lawsuits was initiated to challenge the Housing Authority's

policies. The Asian Law Caucus, which represented the Southeast Asian families, also began efforts to improve safety conditions and to organize the tenants so they could cope with the maze of bureaucratic procedures needed to
gain improvements in housing conditions. As a result of the settlement of one
lawsuit, the Housing Authority implemented a telephone translation system,
hired an Asian American staff person to improve access for tenants, and
adopted a new policy to transfer families who were the targets of violence.
The violence did not end, but tenant organizing proved to be useful in empowering the tenants and in improving interethnic relations. In addition, the
Asian Law Caucus represented both Asian American and African American
tenants in administrative proceedings with the San Francisco Housing Authority to improve safety conditions in the housing projects.

The experiences in San Francisco's public housing are instructive on several levels. First, housing desegregation is an important social goal, but without attention to racial differences and deeper institutional problems, it can
lead to intergroup conflict and violence that defeat desegregation's underlying purposes. Second, successful civil rights strategies do not necessarily have
to focus solely on gaining redress for victims of racial conflicts; the Asian Law
Caucus's litigation strategy addressed institutional reform rather than simple
finger pointing among the tenants. Third, civil rights litigation works best as
part of a broader set of strategies designed to empower clients. As Gen Fujioka,
an attorney with the Asian Law Caucus, has noted:

> None of these initiatives alone will eliminate the interethnic conflict
> and violence which continues to divide San Francisco's public
> housing. But through providing direct assistance to the victims of
> violence and bringing together those victims to realize their common
> experiences and interests we can see the possibilities for positive
> change. Integration in this context cannot be imposed as in Little
> Rock, Arkansas in the '50s, with bayonets and federal marshals.
> Integration in multiethnic public housing systems will come when
> common interests are promoted and when residents can meaningfully
> participate in the development of their own projects.[43]

Transracial Rights and Remedies

The work of the Asian Law Caucus in San Francisco's public housing projects
shows the potential of addressing multiracial and multiethnic conflict through
both institutional reform and the promotion of cooperative strategies, rather
than the placement of racial conflict at the center of disputes and litigation.
It would have been very easy to characterize the assaults on Vietnamese ten-

ants in public housing simply as anti-Asian violence and to seek hate crimes prosecutions. But the attempt would have only exacerbated the underlying problems. The use of civil rights litigation to reform the basic institution of public housing proved to be a more effective means of addressing interracial violence.

The limits of the civil rights laws become apparent when looking at multiracial and multiethnic interaction. Civil rights frameworks constructed from black-white racial paradigms are barely able to address the needs of predominantly immigrant communities such as Asian Americans and Latinos. The many questions that exist in multiracial and multiethnic settings are far more nuanced and convoluted, and often escape even the most perceptive legislators and policy makers. The differentiated subordination experienced by various communities of color and the intergroup conflicts that arise in multiethnic settings pose problems that often inspire more pessimism than creativity.

One potential approach is to place civil rights and remedies in a *transracial* framework, to develop remedies that accommodate racial differences without instituting zero-sum solutions that are bound to pit one group against another. The Asian Law Caucus's litigation strategy—addressing basic safety conditions in San Francisco public housing projects—reflected a transracial approach to racial conflict. Deborah Ramirez has labeled such an approach "multicultural empowerment," to stress both the multiethnic nature of racial problems and the importance of empowering subordinated groups through transracial remedies.[44]

Another example of a transracial civil rights remedy can be found in the area of voting rights, where election systems such as cumulative voting or preference voting can serve as alternatives to explicitly race-conscious districting.[45] Although often shunned as too radical a departure from at-large or district elections, alternative systems are commonplace in corporate voting and in many democratic systems outside the United States. By allowing voters to cast multiple votes for individual candidates (cumulative voting) or to rank candidates to indicate stronger preferences for candidates of choice (preference voting), these systems permit minority voters to express meaningful support for minority candidates without having to reside in a majority-minority district. The election system itself is race-neutral, but the system can remedy the racial bloc voting that often submerges minority voters in at-large election systems.

In situations such as higher education admissions, which are competitive by design, it may be impossible to prevent contests for scarce resources such as seats in a medical school or law school class. The number of rejected applicants will usually exceed the number of accepted applicants, regardless of

race. A regime of "negative action" against Asian Americans is not acceptable, because it imposes specific racial burdens that only perpetuate racial hierarchies. Nor is a "color-blind" regime a transracial remedy, since it can
maintain the subordination of blacks and Latinos to accommodate the interests of some Asian Americans and whites in a "merit"-driven system. Merit
can just as easily be defined to include the benefits that someone from a particular racial or ethnic background brings to an academic setting that has traditionally lacked people of those backgrounds.

From a transracial perspective, the better approach is to review the fundamental goals of an admissions system, to look creatively, beyond zero-sum
solutions, at how resources are structured and allocated. The underlying problem in the San Francisco Unified School District is that there is only one
Lowell High School. While prestige and exclusivity add to its allure, Lowell
High School need not be the only school that offers a rigorous academic curriculum that prepares students for college. The solution to the problems surrounding affirmative action policies as applied to Lowell High School is not
a lawsuit to abolish desegregation efforts—the solution is to build better
schools.

Conclusion

Derrick Bell has offered the disquieting but apt observation that "racism is an integral, permanent, and indestructible component of this society."[1] Contemporary discourse and public policy making regarding race suggest that racial subordination will continue to be an intractable problem, shaping the lives of all Americans, including Asian Americans. But the proposition that racism is a permanent fixture in American life should not imply that racial justice is an impossibility, nor should it imply that the law cannot promote racial equality. Law can make a difference, but the problem of racism is much wider and much deeper than many of us are willing to acknowledge, and the legal system can only address those problems that we as a society are willing to solve. Indeed, law itself is often at the root of the problem.

Throughout this book, I have stressed the importance of differences. A racial paradigm based on unidimensional differences—differences between black and white—is wholly inadequate in addressing the racial problems facing Asian Americans. Differences set Asian Americans apart from whites; differences set Asian Americans apart from blacks; and differences frequently set Asian Americans apart from each other. The racialization of Asian Americans as immigrants, as foreigners, or as model minorities demonstrates that the failure to recognize racial differences only promotes racial injustice.

The interplay of multiple racial and ethnic experiences in the United States makes the task of achieving racial equality far more complex and challenging than a black-white paradigm allows. The recognition of basic racial differences has to be the starting point of any vision for a multiracial and multiethnic society, especially one that is being transformed by global migration.

A "color-blind" vision of U.S. race relations is not premature; it is fundamentally flawed. Racial justice and racial equality can only be achieved through color-consciousness.

Asian American experiences illuminate the limits of the antidiscrimination laws, but what can Asian American experiences tell us about the trajectory of race relations in the United States? How can Asian American experiences help us move in the right direction to achieve racial justice?

First, the basic vocabulary of race must be expanded to accommodate the racial realities and varied forms of subordination that confront Asian Americans and "Other non-Whites." Racism comes in many forms—nativist racism, patriotic racism, even idealistic "model minority" racism—that do not fall within the four corners of a black-white framework. Unless we are better able to articulate the racial subordination that affects broad segments of the population, which are growing larger through immigration, our discourse on race and racism will always be incomplete.

Second, the realities of global migration and the role of immigrants within American society must be expounded in race relations discourse—and not through reactionary and nativist legislation such as California's Proposition 187. Immigration, whether it is undocumented, family-based, employment-based, or humanitarian, poses major challenges for American race relations. The incorporation of ethnic and linguistic minorities into American society is a daunting task, but it will not be accomplished through citizens-only or English-only legislation. The more basic questions of political membership and participation must be resolved to prevent the subordination of immigrant populations, who by their very status lack the power to shift political discourse.

Third, questions about the recognition of language and cultural differences, already a component of debates over the education of Asian immigrant children, have growing applicability to U.S.-born minority populations. The furor that arose over the decision in 1996 by the school board in Oakland, California, to recognize "Ebonics," or "Black English," in teaching black children shows how civil rights issues facing Asian Americans can converge with civil rights issues facing African Americans. Whether Ebonics is a language, a dialect of English, or just slang is not the real issue. The recognition of difference—the fact that many African American children enter the school system without a knowledge of standard English—and the responses to difference raise the more fundamental issues.

Fourth, the differences within the Asian American population serve as a microcosm for the racial differences that exist within the American population as a whole. Ethnic, class, and generational variations point to differential racialization within Asian America. All Asians are not the same. Nor are all people of color the same. The "model minority" stereotype subordinates blacks and Latinos by first recognizing differences, highlighting those areas where Asian Americans achieve more as a group than blacks and Latinos as groups, and then discounting differences with the question "Why can't blacks and Latinos be more like Asians?" In many circumstances blacks, Latinos, and Asian Americans are not the same, and they should not be treated the same.

Recognizing that race and racism differ among groups does not, however, imply that long-standing problems of racial subordination should be ignored. Expanding the civil rights agenda to include Asian Americans cannot come at the expense of African Americans. Anti-black racism is not the only form of racism in the United States, but it may in fact be the most pervasive and virulent form of racism. Acknowledging that anti-black racism remains a deep-seated problem is just as important as acknowledging that nativistic racism is a serious problem for Asian Americans. The growing recognition of immigrant rights should never be accomplished at the expense of African American racial rights, for as William R. Tamayo notes:

> [I]mmigrants, especially non-white immigrants, must remember that they owe their success and opportunities in part to the vision, sacrifices, and commitment of the Civil Rights Movement. If immigrants are to share in these civil rights gains, they must also play a role in this Movement and help address the plight of the African American community. They must develop the compassion to understand historical conditions which have shaped the present.[2]

As American society moves into the next century, our discourse on race must expand dramatically to include both racial and transracial thinking. What is needed is not a homogeneous, color-blind system of racial values, but a set of core values that recognizes and appreciates differences, both racial and non-racial. We must, as Bill Ong Hing writes, "explore new ways of being American, and recognize the variety of racial and ethnic issues that face our society."[3] As a society—a national community—we cannot afford to do anything less.

Notes

Introduction

1. Andrew Hacker, *Two Nations: Black and White, Separate, Hostile, Unequal,* rev. ed. (New York: Ballantine Books, 1995). Hacker even suggests that Asian Americans and Latinos particularly second- and later-generation individuals, are "merging" into the white race, through intermarriage and assimilation (18–19).
2. Ishmael Reed. "O.J. Bias—Black and White," *San Francisco Chronicle,* 10 February 1997, p. A23.
3. *Report of the National Advisory Commission on Civil Disorders* (New York: Bantam, 1968), 1.
4. Gary Y. Okihiro, *Margins and Mainstreams: Asians in American History and Culture* (Seattle and London: University of Washington Press, 1994), 34.
5. Frank H. Wu, "Neither Black nor White: Asian Americans and Affirmative Action," *Boston College Third World Law Journal* 15 (Summer 1995): 225, 249–251.
6. 4 Cal. 399, 404 (1854).
7. 275 U.S. 78, 87 (1927).
8. James W. Loewen, *The Mississippi Chinese: Between Black and White* (Cambridge, Mass.: Harvard University Press, 1971).
9. *Gong Lum v Rice,* 275 U.S. 78, 79 (1927).
10. Ian F. Haney López, *White by Law: The Legal Construction of Race* (New York and London: New York University Press, 1996).
11. Ibid., appendix A. As Haney López notes, a legal strategy arguing for whiteness rather than blackness may have had some tactical advantage at the time, because the 1870 naturalization statute employed a geographic test rather than a racial test of eligibility for blacks: the law referred to persons of "African nativity, or African descent," rather than to "black persons." More likely, though, Asian American plaintiffs sought to distinguish themselves from blacks because of the stigmas attached to being black, and sought the only available alternative—to be classified as white.
12. 260 U.S. 178 (1922); 261 U.S. 204 (1923).
13. Note, "Racial Violence against Asian Americans," *Harvard Law Review* 106 (June 1993): 1926.

14. United States Commission on Civil Rights, *Recent Activities against Citizens and Residents of Asian Descent*, Clearinghouse Publication No. 88 (Washington. D.C., 1986), 5.

15. National Asian Pacific American Legal Consortium, *1996 Audit of Violence against Asian Pacific Americans* (Washington. D.C.: National Asian Pacific American Legal Consortium, 1997).

16. Nelson Kempsky, *A Report to Attorney General John K. Van de Kamp on Patrick Purdy and the Cleveland School Killings* (Sacramento: California Department of Justice, Office of the Attorney General, 1989).

17. *Vietnamese Fishermen's Association v. Knights of the Ku Klux Klan*. S43 F. Supp. 198 (S.D. Tex. 1982) (permanent injunction); *Vietnamese Fishermen's Association v. Knights of the Ku Klux Klan*, 518 F. Supp. 993 (S.D. Tex. 1981) (preliminary injunction).

18. "Grisly Account of Ly Killing Believed Penned by Suspect." *Los Angeles Times* (Orange County Edition) 7 March 1996.

19. Davan Maharaj, "Ex-UC Student Indicted in Cyberspace Hate Crime Case." *Los Angeles Times*, 14 November 1996. p. A1.

20. Gen Fujioka, "Turning the Tide of Terror and Indifference," *The Reporter* (Asian Law Caucus newsletter), vol. 16, no. 3 (October 1994): 1.

21. National Asian Pacific American Legal Consortium, *1994 Audit of Violence against Asian Pacific Americans* (Washington. D.C.: National Asian Pacific American Legal Consortium, 1995), 4.

22. National Asian Pacific American Legal Consortium, *1995 Audit*, 26–27.

23. Aurelio Rojas, "Turning a Blind Eye to Hate Crimes: Most Attacks in California Go Unprosecuted," *San Francisco Chronicle*, 22 October 1996. p. A1.

24. The Asian American Legal Defense and Education Fund found that one-half of the incidents of anti-Asian violence in New York City during 1994 could be traced to police misconduct. National Asian Pacific American Legal Consortium, *1994 Audit*, 12.

25. John Higham. *Strangers in the Land: Patterns of American Nativism, 1860–1925* (New York: Atheneum, 1970), 4.

26. Robert S. Chang, "Toward an Asian American Legal Scholarship Critical Race Theory, Post-Structuralism, and Narrative Space," *California Law Review* 81 (October 1993): 1241, 1255.

Chapter 1 Legacies of Discrimination

1. U.S. Bureau of the Census, Population Division, Release PPL–57, *United States Population Estimates, by Age, Sex, Race, and Hispanic Origin, 1990 to 1996* (Washington, D.C., 1997).

2. Marina E. Espina, *Filipinos in Louisiana* (New Orleans: A. F. Laborde & Sons, 1988), 1.

3. Ronald Takaki, *Strangers from a Different Shore: A History of Asian Americans* (Boston: Little, Brown and Company, 1989).

4. Assembly Committee on Mines and Mining Interests, *Report*, Cal. Assembly, 3d Sess., Appendix to the Journal of the Assembly (1852), 830.

5. "Governor's Special Message," *Daily Alta California*, 25 April 1852, p. 2, col. 2.

6. Quoted in Takaki, *Strangers from a Different Shore*, 201.

7. Ibid., 296.

8. Ibid., 327–328.

9. Ibid., 325.

10. Gary Y. Okihiro, *Margins and Mainstreams: Asians in American History and Culture* (Seattle and London: University of Washington Press, 1994), 77–78.

11. *Statutes at Large* 1 (1790): 103 (emphasis added).

12. *Statutes at Large* 16 (1870): 254. The United States Supreme Court ruled fourteen years later in *Elk v. Wilkins* that an American Indian born in the United States but under tribal authority did not acquire citizenship at birth. 112 U.S. 94 (1884).

13. The Senate defeated an amendment that would have read: "That the naturalization laws are hereby extended to aliens of African nativity, and to persons of African descent, and to persons born in the Chinese empire." E. P. Hutchinson, *Legislative History of American Immigration Policy* (Philadelphia: University of Pennsylvania, 1981), 5–6.

14. 1 F. Cas. 223 (C.C.D. Cal. 1878).

15. 169 U.S. 649 (1898).

16. Ibid., 693.

17. Ibid., 702 (quoting *Fong Yue Ting v. United States*, 149 U.S. 698, 716 (1893)).

18. 260 U.S. 178 (1922).

19. Ibid., 197.

20. Ibid. Ironically, the Court concluded its opinion with the following: "Of course, there is not implied either in the legislation or in our interpretation of it, any suggestion of individual unworthiness or racial inferiority." Ibid.

21. 261 U.S. 204 (1923).

22. Ibid., 215.

23. Ibid., 214.

24. *Statutes at Large* 42 (1922): 1021.

25. *Statutes at Large* 66 (1952): 163.

26. *Statutes at Large* 18 (1875): 477.

27. *Statutes at Large* 22 (1882): 58.

28. Bill Ong Hing, *Making and Remaking Asian America through Immigration Policy, 1850–1990* (Stanford: Stanford University Press, 1993), 47.

29. 130 U.S. 581 (1889).

30. Ibid., 606.

31. 149 U.S. 698 (1893).

32. *Statutes at Large* 39 (1917): 874.

33. Hing, *Making and Remaking Asian America*, 32.

34. *Statutes at Large* 43 (1924): 153.

35. *Statutes at Large* 48 (1934): 456.

36. *Toyota v. United States*, 268 U.S. 402, 410 (1925).

37. *Statutes at Large* 66 (1952): 163.

38. Takaki, *Strangers from a Different Shore*, 82.

39. 4 Cal. 399 (1854).

40. United States Commission on Civil Rights, *Civil Rights Issues Facing Asian Americans in the 1990s* (Washington, D.C., February 1992), 7–8.

41. 118 U.S. 356 (1886).

42. Ibid., 374.

43. *Wong Him v. Callahan*, 119 F. 381 (1903).

44. 275 U.S. 78 (1927).

45. 349 U.S. 483 (1954).

46. *Terrace v. Thompson*, 263 U.S. 197 (1923); *Porterfield v. Webb*, 263 U.S. 225 (1923).

47. 263 U.S. 197, 220–221.

48. *Oyama v. California*, 332 U.S. 633 (1948).

49. Takaki, *Strangers from a Different Shore*, 330.

50. *Loving v. Virginia*, 388 U.S. 1 (1967).
51. Peter Irons, *Justice at War: The Story of the Japanese American Internment Cases* (New York: Oxford University Press, 1983), 46.
52. 320 U.S. 81 (1943).
53. Ibid., 98.
54. 320 U.S. 115 (1943).
55. 323 U.S. 214 (1944).
56. Ibid., 216.
57. Ibid.
58. 323 U.S. 283 (1944).
59. *Korematsu v. United States*, 584 F. Supp. 1406 (N.D. Cal. 1984); *Hirabayashi v. United States*, 828 F.2d 591 (9th Cir. 1987).
60. *Statutes at Large* 102 (1988): 903.
61. Mary L. Dudziak, "Desegregation as a Cold War Imperative," *Stanford Law Review* 41 (November 1988): 61.
62. 332 U.S. 633 (1948).
63. Ibid., 647.
64. 334 U.S. 410 (1948).
65. *Namba v. McCourt*, 185 Ore. 579 (1949).
66. *Fujii v. California*, 38 Cal. 2d 718 (1952).
67. 1967 Wash. Laws, ch. 163, sec. 7.
68. 32 Cal. 2d 711, 198 P.2d 17 (1948).
69. *Shelley v. Kraemer*, 334 U.S. 1 (1948).
70. *Statutes at Large* 79 (1965): 911.
71. 414 U.S. 563 (1974).
72. Sharon M. Lee and Barry Edmonston, "The Socioeconomic Status and Integration of Asian Immigrants," in *Immigration and Ethnicity: The Integration of America's Newest Arrivals*, ed. Barry Edmonston and Jeffrey S. Passel (Washington, D.C.: The Urban Institute Press, 1994).
73. Statement by Attorney General Robert F. Kennedy before Subcommittee No. 1 of the House Judiciary Committee, H.R. Doc. 7700, 88th Cong., 2d Sess., *Congressional Record* (22 July 1964), 16590–16592.
74. United States Immigration and Naturalization Service, *1989 Statistical Yearbook*, (Washington, D.C., 1990); United States Immigration and Naturalization Service, *1995 Statistical Yearbook* (Washington, D.C., 1996).
75. Hing, *Making and Remaking Asian America*, 126.
76. Under the Refugee Act of 1980, which created rules by which the United States would employ international standards to determine refugee status, any person with a "well-founded fear of persecution" can enter as a refugee. *Statutes at Large* 94 (1980): 102.
77. *Statutes at Large* 101 (1987): 1329–1342.
78. Robert Warren, *Estimates of the Unauthorized Immigrant Population Residing in the United States, By Country of Origin and State of Residence: October 1992* (U.S. Immigration and Naturalization Service, Washington, D.C., April 29, 1994, photocopy), table 2.
79. Charles B. Keely, "The Immigration Act of 1965," in *Asian Americans and Congress: A Documentary History*, ed. Hyung-Chan Kim (Westport, Conn.: Greenwood Press, 1996), 529, 531–532. Estimates from the Immigration and Naturalization Service put the undocumented Asian population in 1992 at close to 300,000.
80. United States Department of Commerce, Bureau of the Census, *Statistical Brief: The Nation's Asian and Pacific Islander Population—1994* (Washington, D.C., 1995), 1.

81. Douglas S. Massey and Nancy A. Denton, *American Apartheid: Segregation in the Making of the Underclass* (Cambridge, Mass. and London: Harvard University Press, 1993), 86–88.

82. *Statutes at Large* 100 (1986): 3359.

83. United States General Accounting Office, *Immigration Reform: Employer Sanctions and the Question of Discrimination* (Washington, D.C., 1990).

84. *Statutes at Large* 104 (1990): 4978.

85. Paul Feldman and Patrick J. McDonnell, "Prop. 187 Backers Elated—Challenges Imminent," *Los Angeles Times*, 9 November 1994, p. A1.

86. *League of United Latin American Citizens v. Wilson*, 908 F. Supp. 755 (C.D. Cal. 1995).

87. Lee Romney and Julie Marquis, "Youth Dies as Medical Treatment Is Delayed," *Los Angeles Times*, 23 November 1994, p. A1.

88. Coalition for Humane Immigrant Rights of Los Angeles, *Hate Unleashed: Los Angeles in the Aftermath of 187* (Los Angeles: Coalition for Humane Immigrant Rights of Los Angeles, 1995); National Asian Pacific American Legal Consortium, *1994 Audit of Violence against Asian Pacific Americans* (Washington, D.C.: National Asian Pacific American Legal Consortium, 1995).

89. *Statutes at Large* 110 (1996): 2105.

90. Janet Hook, "Accord Includes Clinton's Promise to Fix Welfare Law," *Los Angeles Times*, 4 May 1997.

91. *Statutes at Large* 110 (1996): 3009.

92. Charles J. McClain, *In Search of Equality: The Chinese Struggle against Discrimination in Nineteenth-Century America* (Berkeley and Los Angeles: University of California Press, 1994).

93. *Fiallo v. Bell*, 430 U.S. 787, 792 (1977) (citing *The Chinese Exclusion Case* and *Fong Yue Ting v. United States*); *Adarand Constructors, Inc. v. Peña*, 115 S. Ct. 2097, 2106–2107 (1995) (citing *Korematsu v. United States*).

Chapter 2   Discrimination and Antidiscrimination Law

1. Nolan W. S. Zane, David T. Takeuchi, and Kathleen N. J. Young, eds., *Confronting Critical Health Issues of Asian and Pacific Islander Americans* (Thousand Oaks, London, and New Delhi: Sage Publications, 1994).

2. Ian F. Haney López, *White by Law: The Legal Construction of Race* (New York: New York University Press, 1996).

3. 481 U.S. 604, 611 n. 4 (1987).

4. The Latino category—"Hispanic"—is considered an ethnic grouping that cuts across racial categories. Some groups, such as Arab Americans, have not been recognized under the system as either an ethnic or a racial category. Efforts to include "multiracial" in census and other tabulation systems reflect both the imprecision of biologically based categories and evolving notions of racial identity.

5. Jean Stefancic, "Funding the Nativist Agenda," in *Immigrants Out! The New Nativism and the Anti-Immigrant Impulse in the United States*, ed. Juan F. Perea (New York and London: New York University Press, 1997), 119, 129–130.

6. Michael Omi and Howard Winant, *Racial Formation in the United States: From the 1960s to the 1990s*, 2d ed., (New York and London: Routledge, 1994).

7. Ibid., 55.

8. Charles R. Lawrence III, "The Id, the Ego, and Equal Protection: Reckoning with Unconscious Racism," *Stanford Law Review* 39 (January 1987): 317, 322.

9. Ibid.; Linda Hamilton Krieger, "The Content of Our Categories: A Cognitive Bias Approach to Discrimination and Equal Employment Opportunity." *Stanford Law Review* 47 (July 1995): 1161.

10. Milton Kleg, *Hate Prejudice and Racism* (Albany: State University of New York Press, 1993), 174–183.

11. "Sen. D'Amato Apologizes for Faking Japanese Accent / Remarks on Radio Were Aimed at Judge Ito," *San Francisco Chronicle*, 6 April 1995, p. A2.

12. Seth Mydans, "New Unease for Japanese-Americans," *New York Times*, 4 March 1992, p. A8.

13. Michael Omi, "Out of the Melting Pot and Into the Fire: Race Relations Policy," in *The State of Asian Pacific America: Policy Issues to the Year 2020* (Los Angeles: LEAP Asian Pacific American Public Policy Institute and UCLA Asian American Studies Center, 1993), 199, 207.

14. 438 U.S. 265, 407 (1978).

15. "State Propositions: A Snapshot of Voters," *Los Angeles Times*, 7 November 1996.

16. *Washington v. Davis*, 426 U.S. 229 (1976).

17. For instance, under Title VII of the Civil Rights Act of 1964, a workplace policy that has an adverse effect on a protected group may be illegal. In *Griggs v. Duke Power Co.*, the Supreme Court ruled that Title VII "proscribes not only overt discrimination but also practices that are fair in form, but discriminatory in operation." 401 U.S. 424, 431 (1971). The Voting Rights Act was amended in 1982 to ensure that discriminatory intent would not be required to prove a violation of section 2. The amendment reversed a decision of the Supreme Court, *City of Mobile v. Bolden*, 446 U.S. 55 (1980), that established an intent requirement under the Voting Rights Act.

18. Lawrence, "The Id, the Ego, and Equal Protection"; Laurence H. Tribe, *American Constitutional Law*, 2d ed. (Mineola, N.Y.: Foundation Press, 1988), 1515–1521.

19. Kimberlé Williams Crenshaw, "Race, Reform, and Retrenchment: Transformation and Legitimation in Antidiscrimination Law," in *Critical Race Theory: The Key Writings that Formed the Movement*, ed. Kimberlé Williams Crenshaw et al. (New York: The New Press, 1995), 103, 118.

20. My analysis of three traditions—liberalism, constitutionalism, and federalism—is drawn largely from an analysis by Christopher Edley. Christopher Edley, Jr., *Not All Black and White: Affirmative Action and American Values* (New York: Hill and Wang, 1996), 52–63.

21. Ibid.

22. Ibid.

23. *San Antonio Independent School District v. Rodriguez*, 411 U.S. 1 (1973).

24. Tribe, *American Constitutional Law*, 1688–1720.

25. 505 U.S. 377 (1992).

26. The Supreme Court has upheld the constitutionality of hate crimes laws that enhance the punishment for violent crime based on discriminatory intent. *Wisconsin v. Mitchell*, 508 U.S. 476 (1993).

27. 5 U.S. 137 (1803).

28. Tribe, *American Constitutional Law*, ch. 16, 1436–1672.

29. Gerald Gunther, "The Supreme Court, 1971 Term—Foreword: In Search of Evolving Doctrine on a Changing Court: A Model for a Newer Equal Protection," *Harvard Law Review* 86 (1972): 1, 8.

30. 323 U.S. 214 (1994)

31. Laws that affect "fundamental rights"—limited to the right to vote, the right to

have access to the courts, and the right to travel between states—are also subject to strict scrutiny.

32. John Hart Ely, *Democracy and Distrust: A Theory of Judicial Review* (Cambridge, Mass. and London: Harvard University Press, 1980).
33. 163 U.S. 537 (1896); 347 U.S. 483 (1954).
34. 115 S. Ct. 2097 (1995). The Court overruled *Fullilove v. Klutznick*, 448 U.S. 448 (1980), and *Metro Broadcasting v. Federal Communications Commission*, 497 U.S. 547 (1990). The *Adarand* decision put the federal standard of review in line with the strict scrutiny standard for state and local affirmative action laws that the Court had established six years earlier in the case of *City of Richmond v. J. A. Croson Co.*, 488 U.S. 469 (1989).
35. *League of United Latin American Citizens v. Wilson*, 908 F. Supp. 755 (C.D. Cal. 1995).
36. *Serrano v. Priest*, 18 Cal. 3d 728, 557 P.2d 929, 135 Cal. Rptr. 345 (1976).
37. *Statutes at Large* 89 (1975): 400, 403.
38. United States Commission on Civil Rights, *Federal Title VI Enforcement to Ensure Nondiscrimination in Federally Assisted Programs* (Washington, D.C., June 1996).
39. *International Brotherhood of Teamsters v. United States*, 431 U.S. 324 (1977).
40. *Statutes at Large* 105 (1991): 1071. The act overturned, in whole or in part, the following cases: *Wards Cove Packing Co. v. Atonio*, 490 U.S. 642 (1989); *Patterson v. McLean Credit Union*, 491 U.S. 164 (1989); *Martin v. Wilks*, 490 U.S. 755 (1989); *Price Waterhouse v. Hopkins*, 490 U.S. 228 (1989); *Lorance v. AT&T Technologies, Inc.*, 490 U.S. 990 (1989); *Equal Employment Opportunity Commission v. Arabian American Oil Co.*, 499 U.S. 244 (1991); *West Virginia University Hospitals v. Casey*, 499 U.S. 83 (1991).
41. Assembly Member Grace Napolitano introduced two pieces of legislation, Assembly Bills 2521 and 81. In 1994, I testified before the California Assembly Committee on the Judiciary in support of Assembly Bill 2521, which would have added immigration status as a protected category under California's hate crimes law. The bill was passed by the legislature in August 1994, then vetoed by the governor in September 1996. Assembly Bill 81, which stated that all persons in California have the right to be free from intimidation on the basis of citizenship or legal residency, was passed by the legislature in August 1996 and vetoed by the governor in September 1996.
42. Ronald Brownstein, "Key Civil Rights Post Left Empty as Search Falters," *Los Angeles Times* 22 May 1994, p. A1.
43. *City of Richmond v. J.A. Croson Company*, 488 U.S. 469, 499 (1989).
44. 490 U.S. 642 (1989).
45. Ibid., 664 n. 4.
46. *Statutes at Large* 105 (1991): 1071, 1099.
47. *Atonio v. Wards Cove Packing Co.*, 10 F.3d 1485 (9th Cir. 1993).

Chapter 3 *Looking Like the Enemy*

1. *Korematsu v. United States*, 584 F. Supp. 1406 (N.D. Cal. 1984).
2. Transcript of Arguments on Coram Nobis Petition, U.S. District Court for the Northern District of California, *Korematsu v. United States* (10 November 1983), reprinted in *Justice Delayed: The Record of the Japanese American Internment Cases*, ed. Peter Irons (Middletown, Conn.: Wesleyan University Press, 1989) 213, 220–221.
3. Neil Gotanda, "'Other Non-Whites' in American Legal History: A Review of

Justice at War," *Columbia Law Review* 85 (June 1985): 1186; Neil Gotanda, "Asian American Rights and the 'Miss Saigon Syndrome,'" in *Asian Americans and the Supreme Court: A Documentary History,* ed. Hyung-Chan Kim (Westport, Conn.: Greenwood Press, 1992), 1087. Gotanda has also proposed that Asian Americans are defined more specifically as foreigners in an Occidental-Oriental dichotomy. Drawing parallels between European Orientalism and American race relations regarding Asian Americans, he suggests that Asian Americans have been constructed oppositionally, like Asian societies, as non-Western "others," allowing white Americans, like European societies, to dominate the "Oriental" and to define their own positive characteristics. Neil Gotanda, "Towards Repeal of Asian Exclusion: The Magnuson Act of 1943, the Act of July 2, 1946, the Presidential Proclamation of July 4, 1946, the Act of August 9, 1946, and the Act of August 1, 1950," in *Asian Americans and Congress: A Documentary History,* ed. Hyung-Chan Kim (Westport, Conn.: Greenwood Press, 1996), 309.

4. Kevin R. Johnson, "An Essay on Immigration Politics, Popular Democracy, and California's Proposition 187: The Political Relevance and Legal Irrelevance of Race," *Washington Law Review* 70 (July 1995): 629.

5. Larry B. Stammer and Carla Hall, "U.S. Muslims Feel Sting of Accusations; Harassment: Talk of a Middle East Link Led to Epithets against Ethnic Community," *Los Angeles Times,* 22 April 1995, p. A22.

6. Evelyn Iritani, "Foreign Donation Furor Dampens Fund-Raising," *Los Angeles Times,* 21 October 1996, p. A1.

7. United States General Accounting Office, *Immigration Reform: Employer Sanctions and the Question of Discrimination* (Washington, D.C., 1990).

8. Jonathan Peterson, "Clinton Calls for 'Soft Money' Ban," *Los Angeles Times,* 22 January 1997, p. A11.

9. Editorial, "Thanked with an Insult: Asian Americans are Right to be Offended by Democrats' Inquiries," *Los Angeles Times,* 3 March 1997.

10. 4 Cal. 399, 404 (1854).

11. 149 U.S. 698, 717 (1893).

12. Annual Report of the Commissioner General of Immigration, 1919–1920, quoted in Arthur W. Helweg, "The Immigration Act of 1917: The Asian Indian Exclusion Act," in *Asian Americans and Congress: A Documentary History,* ed. Hyung-Chan Kim (Westport, Conn.: Greenwood Press, 1996), 153, 167.

13. 263 U.S. 197, 220 (1923).

14. Ibid., 220.

15. Ibid., 220–221.

16. 261 U.S. 204, 215 (1923).

17. Commission on Wartime Relocation and Internment of Civilians, *Personal Justice Denied* (Washington, D.C., 1982), 71–72.

18. Testimony of Lt. General John L. DeWitt before House Naval Affairs Subcommittee to Investigate Congested Areas, Part 3, pp. 739–740 (78th Cong., 1st Sess.), quoted in *Korematsu v. United States,* 323 U.S. 214, 236 & n. 2 (Murphy, J., dissenting).

19. 169 U.S. 649 (1898).

20. 49 F. Supp. 222 (1942).

21. Brief for Appellant, *Regan v. King,* quoted in Jacobus tenBroek et al., *Prejudice, War and the Constitution* (Berkeley: University of California Press, 1954), 315.

22. 320 U.S. 81 (1943); 320 U.S. 115 (1943).

23. 320 U.S. 81, 96 (1943).

24. 323 U.S. 214, 218–219 (1944).

25. Ibid., 223 (emphasis in original).

26. 323 U.S. 214, 233 (1944).
27. Ibid., 239.
28. 584 F. Supp. 1406, 1420 (N.D. Cal. 1984).
29. United States Commission on Civil Rights, *Civil Rights Issues Facing Asian Americans in the 1990s* (Washington, D.C., February 1992), 40–41.
30. Dennis Hayashi, "The Case Against the U.S. Coast Guard," *The Reporter* (Asian Law Caucus newsletter), vol. 12, no. 1 (Jan. 1991): 2.
31. *Statutes at Large* 104 (1990): 2979.
32. United States Commission on Civil Rights, *Recent Activities against Citizens and Residents of Asian Descent,* Clearinghouse Publication no. 88 (Washington, D.C., 1986), 40.
33. Michael McCabe, "Climate of Fear for Asian Americans: Japan-Bashing over Trade Seems to Encourage Hate Crimes," *San Francisco Chronicle,* 3 February 1992.
34. United States Commission on Civil Rights, *Civil Rights Issues Facing Asian Americans in the 1990s,* 26.
35. National Asian Pacific American Legal Consortium, *1994 Audit of Violence Against Asian Pacific Americans* (Washington, D.C.: National Asian Pacific American Legal Consortium, 1995), 9.
36. Dick Mountjoy et al., *Argument in Favor of Proposition 187, California Ballot Pamphlet: General Election November 8, 1994,* 54.
37. *Wilson v. United States,* 97 Daily Journal D.A.R. 308 (9th Cir. Jan. 7, 1997); *New Jersey v. United States,* 91 F.3d 463 (3rd Cir. 1996); *Padavan v. United States,* 82 F.3d 23 (2d Cir. 1996); *Chiles v. United States,* 69 F.3d 1094 (11th Cir. 1995), *cert. denied,* 116 S. Ct. 1674 (1996).
38. *Statutes at Large* 110 (1996): 3009.
39. Patrick J. McDonnell, "Reinforcement of Border Control Measure Begins," *Los Angeles Times,* 18 January 1996, p. A3.
40. Lee Romney, "Over the Line? Citing Questioning of Mayor, Activists Say Border Patrol Targets All Latinos," *Los Angeles Times* (San Gabriel Valley Section), 2 September 1993.
41. *U.S. Code,* vol. 8, sec. 287 (1994).
42. *Statutes at Large* 110 (1996): 1214.
43. *U.S. Code,* vol. 8, sec. 1324a (1994).
44. United States General Accounting Office, *Immigration Reform.*
45. Lina M. Avidan, *Employment and Hiring Practices under the Immigration Reform and Control Act of 1986: A Survey of San Francisco Businesses* (San Francisco: Public Research Institute, San Francisco State University, and Coalition for Immigrant and Refugee Rights and Services, January 1990), iii.
46. United States Commission on Civil Rights, *Civil Rights Issues Facing Asian Americans in the 1990s,* 149 (emphasis in original).
47. *U.S. Code,* vol. 8, sec. 1324b (1994).
48. *U.S. Code,* vol. 8, sec. 1324b(a)(6) (1994).
49. *League of United Latin American Citizens v. Wilson,* 908 F. Supp. 755 (C.D. Cal. 1995).
50. *Statutes at Large* 110 (1996): 2105.
51. *Espinoza v. Farah Manufacturing Company,* 414 U.S. 86 (1973).

Chapter 4   Race, Immigration, and Citizenship

1. Angelo N. Ancheta, "Our Immigrant Heritage: A Struggle for Justice," *UCLA Asian Pacific American Law Journal* 2 (1994): 101–102.

2. Thomas Muller, "Nativism in the Mid-1990s: Why Now?" in *Immigrants Out! The New Nativism and the Anti-Immigrant Impulse in the United States*, ed. Juan F. Perea (New York and London: New York University Press, 1997), 105.

3. *Oyama v. California*, 332 U.S. 633, 658–659 (1948).

4. Daniel B. Wood, "Ballot Vote on Illegal Immigrants Set for Fall in California," *Christian Science Monitor*, 1 June 1994, p. 1.

5. Sara Catania, "County Report: A Message Hits Home," *Los Angeles Times*, 20 November 1994, p. B1.

6. Gebe Martinez and Patrick J. McDonnell, "Prop. 187 Backers Counting on Message, Not Strategy," *Los Angeles Times*, 30 October 1994, p. A1.

7. Peter Brimelow, *Alien Nation: Common Sense about America's Immigration Disaster*, rev. ed. (New York: HarperCollins, 1996) 215.

8. Ibid., 264.

9. Ibid., 10.

10. Frank H. Wu, "The Limits of Borders: A Moderate Proposal for Immigration Reform," *Stanford Law and Policy Review* 7, no. 2 (1996): 35.

11. U.S. Constitution, art. I, sec. 8, cl. 4.

12. 130 U.S. 581 (1889).

13. Ibid., 603.

14. Ibid., 606.

15. Ibid., 595.

16. Ibid., 606.

17. 142 U.S. 651, 659 (1892).

18. Ibid.

19. Ibid.

20. 149 U.S. 698 (1893).

21. Ibid., 713.

22. Ibid., 707.

23. 189 U.S. 86 (1903).

24. Ibid., 97.

25. *United States* ex rel. *Knauff v. Shaughnessy*, 338 U.S. 537, 544 (1950).

26. 408 U.S. 753, 766 (1972).

27. Ibid. (citations omitted).

28. 430 U.S. 787 (1977).

29. Hiroshi Motomura, "Immigration after a Century of Plenary Power: Phantom Constitutional Norms and Statutory Interpretation," *Yale Law Journal* 100 (1990): 545.

30. *Statutes at Large* 104 (1990): 4978.

31. In March 1997, the most seriously backlogged category contained the brothers and sisters of United States citizens entering from the Philippines, who had a waiting period of nearly twenty years. Only visa holders with visas approved before December 1, 1977, were able to immigrate to the United States. United States Department of State, Bureau of Consular Affairs, *Visa Bulletin*, no. 72 (February 1997).

32. 426 U.S. 67 (1976).

33. Ibid., 79–80.

34. 426 U.S. 88 (1976).

35. Ibid., 116.

36. *Mow Sun Wong v. Campbell*, 626 F.2d 739 (9th Cir. 1980), *cert. denied*, 450 U.S. 959 (1981); *Vergara v. Hampton*, 581 F.2d 1281 (7th Cir. 1978), *cert. denied*, 441 U.S. 905 (1979).

37. 334 U.S. 410 (1948).

38. 403 U.S. 365 (1971).

39. *Nyquist v. Mauclet*, 432 U.S. 1 (1977).
40. 413 U.S. 634 (1973).
41. Ibid., 647.
42. In re *Griffiths*, 413 U.S. 717 (1973) (law); *Examining Board v. Flores de Otero*, 426 U.S. 572 (1976) (civil engineering); *Bernal v. Fainter*, 467 U.S. 216 (1984) (notaries public).
43. *Foley v. Connelie*, 435 U.S. 291 (1978) (state troopers); *Ambach v. Norwick*, 441 U.S. 68 (1979) (public school teachers); *Cabell v. Chavez-Salido*, 454 U.S. 432 (1982) (probation officers).
44. 441 U.S. 68, 87 (1979) (Blackmun, J., dissenting (joined by Brennan, Marshall, Stevens)).
45. 457 U.S. 202 (1982).
46. Ibid., 213.
47. Ibid., 230.
48. 116 S. Ct. 1620, 1628 (1996).
49. Kevin R. Johnson, "An Essay on Immigration Politics, Popular Democracy, and California's Proposition 187: The Political Relevance and Legal Irrelevance of Race," *Washington Law Review* 70 (July 1995): 629.
50. "Times Poll/A Look at Electorate," *Los Angeles Times*, 10 November 1994, p. B2.
51. *Cabell v. Chavez-Salido*, 454 U.S. 432, 439–440 (1982).
52. Thomas Alexander Aleinikoff, "Citizens, Aliens, Membership and the Constitution," *Constitutional Commentary* 7 (Winter 1990): 9; Susan K. Lee, "Racial Construction through Citizenship in the U.S.," *Asian American Policy Review* 6 (Spring 1996): 89.
53. Kenneth L. Karst, *Belonging to America: Equal Citizenship and the Constitution* (New Haven and London: Yale University Press, 1989), 3.
54. Jamin B. Raskin, "Legal Aliens, Local Citizens: The Historical, Constitutional and Theoretical Meanings of Alien Suffrage," *University of Pennsylvania Law Review* 141 (April 1993): 1391; Gerald M. Rosberg, "Aliens and Equal Protection: Why Not the Right to Vote?" *Michigan Law Review* 75 (April–May 1977): 1092.
55. Raskin, "Legal Aliens, Local Citizens."
56. *U.S. Code*, vol. 8, secs. 1421–1458 (1994).
57. *Dred Scott v. Sandford*, 60 U.S. 393 (1856).
58. 169 U.S. 649 (1898).
59. Ibid., 693.
60. 169 U.S. 649, 702 (1898) (quoting *Fong Yue Ting v. United States*, 149 U.S. 698, 716 (1893)).
61. Ibid., 698–699.

Chapter 5 **Language and Legal Conformity**

1. 483 F.2d 791 (9th Cir. 1973).
2. 414 U.S. 563 (1974).
3. Ibid., 566.
4. Ibid.
5. *U.S. Code*, vol. 20, sec. 1703 (1994).
6. L. Ling-Chi Wang, "*Lau v. Nichols*: History of a Struggle for Equal and Quality Education," in *Counterpoint*, ed. Emma Gee (Los Angeles: Asian American Studies Center, University of California, 1976), 240.
7. *Revisiting the Lau Decision: Twenty Years After, Symposium Proceedings*, (Oakland, Calif.: ARC Associates, 1996), 16.

8. U.S. Department of Commerce, Bureau of the Census, *We the American Asians* (Washington, D.C. 1993) table 3; U.S. Department of Commerce, Bureau of the Census, *We the American Pacific Islanders* (Washington, D.C., 1993), table 3.

9. "Insurance Company Language Discrimination Suit Settled," *ACLU News* (Newspaper of the American Civil Liberties Union of Northern California) vol. 60, no. 4 (Summer 1996): 5.

10. James Crawford, *Hold Your Tongue: Bilingualism and the Politics of "English Only"* (Reading, Mass.: Addison-Wesley Publishing Company, 1992) 17–18.

11. United States Commission on Civil Rights, *Civil Rights Issues Facing Asian Americans in the 1990s* (Washington, D.C., 1992), 76–80.

12. Christopher Newfield and Avery F. Gordon, "Multiculturalism's Unfinished Business," in *Mapping Multiculturalism*, ed. Avery F. Gordon and Christopher Newfield, (Minneapolis and London: University of Minnesota Press, 1996), 76.

13. Ibid., 84–85.

14. Neil Gotanda, "Towards Repeal of Asian Exclusion: The Magnuson Act of 1943, the Act of July 2, 1946, the Presidential Proclamation of July 4, 1946, the Act of August 9, 1946, and the Act of August 1, 1950," in *Asian Americans and Congress: A Documentary History*, ed. Hyung-Chan Kim (Westport, Conn.: Greenwood Press, 1996), 309.

15. 115 S. Ct. 2097, 2119 (1995) (Scalia, J., concurring).

16. 434 F.2d 386 (2d Cir. 1970).

17. *U.S. Code*, vol. 28, sec. 1827 (1994).

18. *Jara v. Municipal Court*, 21 Cal. 3d 181, 578 P.2d 94, 145 Cal. Rptr. 847 (1978), *cert. denied*, 439 U.S. 1067 (1979).

19. *Guadalupe Organization, Inc. v. Tempe Elementary School District*, 587 F.2d 1022 (9th Cir. 1978). The federal Bilingual Education Act, first enacted in 1968, creates no entitlement to federal services; the law only creates a discretionary grant program that relies on congressional appropriations. The federal contribution to bilingual education programs has never amounted to more than 5 to 10 percent of total revenues for local bilingual education programs.

20. *Carmona v. Sheffield*, 475 F.2d 738 (9th Cir. 1973) (no right to unemployment notices in Spanish); *Toure v. United States*, 24 F.3d 444 (2d Cir. 1994) (no rights to notice of administrative seizure in French); *Soberal-Perez v. Heckler*, 717 F.2d 36 (2d Cir. 1983) (no right to Social Security notices in Spanish), *cert. denied*, 466 U.S. 929 (1984).

21. *Frontera v. Sindell*, 522 F.2d 1215 (6th Cir. 1975).

22. California Government Code sec. 7290.

23. American Civil Liberties Union of Northern California, "Bilingual Public Services in California," in *Language Loyalties: A Source Book on the Official English Controversy*, ed. James Crawford (Chicago: University of Chicago Press, 1992), 303–311.

24. Reynaldo F. Macías, "LEP Enrollment Increase Almost 5 Percent in 1996," *LMRI Newsletter* (University of California Linguistic Minority Research Institute), vol. 6, no. 1 (1996).

25. *U.S. Code*, vol. 20, sec. 1703 (1994).

26. United States Commission on Civil Rights, *Civil Rights Issues Facing Asian Americans in the 1990s* (Washington, D.C., February 1992), 82–83.

27. Mae Chu-Chang, ed., *Asian- and Pacific-American Perspectives in Bilingual Education: Comparative Research* (New York and London: Teachers College Press, 1983).

28. William J. Bennett, "The Bilingual Education Act: A Failed Path," in *Language Loyalties: A Source Book on the Official English Controversy*, ed. James Crawford (Chicago: University of Chicago Press, 1992), 358–363.

29. Lily Wong Fillmore, "Against Our Best Interest: The Attempt to Sabotage Bilingual Education," in *Language Loyalties: A Source Book on the Official English Controversy*, ed. James Crawford (Chicago: University of Chicago Press, 1992), 367.

30. United States Commission on Civil Rights, *Civil Rights Issues*, 77.

31. Ibid., 87–88

32. In *Castañeda v. Pickard*, the United States Court of Appeals for the Fifth Circuit ruled in 1981 that to comply with the Equal Educational Opportunity Act, school districts must meet two basic concerns of LEP students: (1) acquiring English-language skills to compete academically with their English-speaking peers, and (2) not suffering educational deficiencies because of their lack of English proficiency. 648 F.2d 989 (5th Cir. 1981). The court also established a three-part test to determine whether a school district has met these goals. The three parts, based on theory, implementation, and results, are as follows: Is the district "pursuing a program informed by an educational theory recognized as sound by some experts in the field"? Is the program "reasonably calculated to implement effectively the educational theory adopted by the school"? Does the program "produce results indicating that the language barriers confronting students are actually being overcome"? *Id.* at 1009–1010. The *Castañeda* test has become the national standard by which LEP programs are judged to be in compliance with *Lau* and the EEOA. However, bilingual education was neither required nor dismissed as a sound theory by the *Castañeda* court.

33. *U.S. Code*, vol. 42, sec. 1973aa (1994).

34. Ibid.

35. Ibid., sec. 203.

36. *Statutes at Large* 106 (1992): 921.

37. The other counties providing voting assistance in Asian languages are Alameda, San Francisco (Chinese), and Orange (Vietnamese) in California; Honolulu (Filipino, Japanese), Kauai, and Maui (Filipino) in Hawaii; and Kings, New York, and Queens (Chinese) in New York.

38. One problem affecting Asian Americans in the implementation of section 203 is the use of decennial census data to calculate the benchmark for jurisdictional coverage. Because of the fast-paced growth of Asian ethnic populations through immigration, many groups whose citizen populations now exceed the ten thousand benchmark in a jurisdiction are not covered because they were below ten thousand in 1990. Recognizing this problem, voluntary efforts such as the one in California's Santa Clara County to provide bilingual ballots in Vietnamese have been adopted. These efforts are laudatory, particularly since they are not compelled by federal law. The problem exists in other parts of the country, and without federal mandates recognizing the population changes between decennial censuses, many language groups will continue to lack equal access to the ballot.

39. National Asian Pacific American Legal Consortium, *Bilingual Assistance: How to Use the Voting Rights Act* (Washington, D.C.: National Asian Pacific American Legal Consortium, 1995).

40. Bill Tamayo, "Major Voting Rights Victory for Alameda County Chinese Voters," *The Reporter* (Asian Law Caucus newsletter), vol. 17, no. 1 (June 1995): 1.

41. National Asian Pacific American Legal Consortium, *Bilingual Voting Assistance*, 7–13.

42. Benjamin Franklin, "Observations Concerning the Increase of Mankind," reprinted in *The Papers of Benjamin Franklin*, vol. 4, ed. Leonard W. Larabee et al. (New Haven: Yale University Press, 1961), 227, 234.

43. Crawford, *Hold Your Tongue*, 182–185.

44. *Statutes at Large* 39 (1917): 874, 877.
45. Commission on Naturalization, Report to the President (November 8, 1905), reprinted in H.R. Doc. 46, 59th Cong., 1st Sess. (1905), 11.
46. *U.S. Code*, vol. 8, sec. 1423 (1994).
47. The states are Alabama (1990), Arizona (1988), Arkansas (1987), California (1986), Colorado (1988), Florida (1988), Georgia (1986), Illinois (1969), Indiana (1984), Kentucky (1984), Louisiana (1811), Mississippi (1987), Montana (1995), Nebraska (1920), New Hampshire (1995), North Carolina (1987), North Dakota (1987), South Carolina (1987), South Dakota (1987), Tennessee (1984), Virginia (1986), and Wyoming (1996). In addition, Hawaii has adopted both English and Hawaiian as official languages.
48. Crawford, *Hold Your Tongue*, 16, 91.
49. 69 F.3d 920 (9th Cir. 1995), *vacated and remanded*, 117 S. Ct. 1055 (1997).
50. Ibid., 942.
51. The Court ruled that the litigation was moot because the plaintiff had left her government job to enter the private sector. *Arizonans for Official English v. Arizona*, 117 S. Ct. 1055 (1997).
52. 262 U.S. 390 (1923).
53. Ibid., 401.
54. 271 U.S. 500 (1926).
55. Ibid., 528.
56. 273 U.S. 284 (1927).
57. 500 U.S. 352 (1991).
58. Ibid., 371–372.
59. United States Department of Commerce, Bureau of the Census, *We the American Asians* (Washington, D.C., 1993).
60. 716 F. Supp. 1328 (C.D. Cal. 1989).
61. Ibid., 1330.
62. Ibid.
63. Ibid., 1332.
64. 750 F.2d 815 (10th Cir. 1984).
65. 717 F.2d 36 (2d Cir. 1983), *cert. denied*, 466 U.S. 929 (1984).
66. 618 F.2d 264 (5th Cir. 1980).
67. 998 F.2d 1480, 1487 (9th Cir. 1993).
68. *Gutierrez v. Municipal Court*, 838 F.2d 1031, 1039 (9th Cir. 1988), *vacated as moot*, 490 U.S. 1016 (1989).
69. *U.S. Code*, vol. 42, sec. 1973b(f)(1) (1994).
70. 618 F.2d 264, 270 (5th Cir. 1980).
71. Mari J. Matsuda, "Voices of America: Accent, Antidiscrimination Law, and a Jurisprudence for the Last Reconstruction," *Yale Law Journal* 100 (March 1991): 1352.
72. "For Santa Clara County," *San Jose Mercury News*, 18 October 1988, p. 6B; "Mercury News Editorial Article Stirs Protest: Asians Call Remark on Accent Unfair to Candidate," *San Jose Mercury News*, 27 October 1988, p. 1B.
73. United States General Accounting Office, *Immigration Reform: Employer Sanctions and the Question of Discrimination* (Washington, D.C., 1990) 50–52.
74. Richard Lu, "Filipino Security Guards Win Settlement," *The Reporter* (Asian Law Caucus Newsletter), vol. 16, no. 2 (July 1994): 1.
75. 888 F.2d 591 (9th Cir. 1989), *cert. denied*, 494 U.S. 1081 (1990).
76. Ibid., 596.
77. 699 F. Supp. 1429 (D. Hawaii 1987).
78. 775 F. Supp. 338 (C.D. Cal. 1991).

79. Ibid., 344.
80. 587 F.2d 1022, 1027 (9th Cir. 1978).
81. Ibid.
82. 13 F.3d 296, 298 (9th Cir. 1993) (Reinhardt, J., dissenting from denial of rehearing en banc) (citations omitted).
83. John Horton and José Calderón, "Language Struggles in a Changing California Community," in *Language Loyalties: A Sourcebook on the Official English Controversy*, ed. James Crawford (Chicago: University of Chicago Press, 1992), 186.

Chapter 6   Race and Identity

1. Bill Ong Hing, *Making and Remaking Asian America through Immigration Policy, 1850–1990* (Stanford: Stanford University Press, 1993), 180.
2. William Wei, *The Asian American Movement* (Philadelphia: Temple University Press, 1993).
3. Michael Omi, "Out of the Melting Pot and Into the Fire: Race Relations Policy," in *The State of Asian Pacific America. A Public Policy Report: Policy Issues to the Year 2020* (Los Angeles: LEAP Asian Pacific American Public Policy Institute and UCLA Asian American Studies Center, 1993), 199.
4. Asian Americans / Pacific Islanders in Philanthropy, *He Alo A He Alo: Face to Face with the Real Hawai'i* (New York: Asian Americans/Pacific Islanders in Philanthropy, 1996).
5. Yen Le Espiritu, *Asian American Panethnicity: Bridging Institutions and Identities* (Philadelphia: Temple University Press, 1992), 14.
6. Ethnic groups can also transcend existing nation-states in Asia. Tibetan immigrants, for instance, are stateless because of the annexation of their homeland by China; many emigrate from Nepal or India. Similarly, Hmong immigrants do not have an existing country of origin; most Hmong immigrants originally resided in Laos, but many also lived in nearby areas geographically located in China. Someone who is Chinese may be from China, Taiwan, or Hong Kong—or from any number of countries in Asia that have sizable Chinese populations.
7. Espiritu, *Asian American Panethnicity*, 15.
8. Ibid., 19–52.
9. United States Department of Commerce, Bureau of the Census, *1992 Survey of Minority-Owned Business Enterprises—Asians and Pacific Islanders, American Indians, and Alaska Natives* (MB92–3) (Washington, D.C., 1996).
10. Leadership Education for Asian Pacifics, *Beyond Asian American Poverty: Community Economic Development Policies and Strategies* (Los Angeles: LEAP Asian Pacific American Public Policy Institute, 1993), 53.
11. Ngoan Le, "The Case of the Southeast Asian Refugees: Policy for a Community 'At-Risk,'" in *The State of Asian Pacific America. A Public Policy Report: Policy Issues to the Year 2020* (Los Angeles: LEAP Asian Pacific American Public Policy Institute and UCLA Asian American Studies Center, 1993), 167.
12. Ian F. Haney López, *White by Law: The Legal Construction of Race* (New York: New York University Press, 1996).
13. Prior to the issuance of Directive 15, there were only three categories: "Negro," "White," and "Other Races."
14. California Government Code sec. 11092.
15. Espiritu, *Asian American Panethnicity*, 121.
16. Ibid.
17. None of the categories is necessarily fixed, however; for example, for the year 2000

census, Native Hawaiian advocates seek to be moved from the Asian and Pacific Islander category to the category that includes members of Native American tribes.

18. Statement of Secretary Robert A. Mosbacher on Adjustment of the 1990 Census, *Federal Register* 56 (22 July 1991): 33582.

19. *Wisconsin v. City of New York*, 116 S. Ct. 1091 (1996).

20. Bijan Gilanshah, "Multiracial Minorities: Erasing the Color Line," *Law and Inequality: A Journal of Theory and Practice* 12 (December 1993): 183.

21. Larry Hajime Shinagawa and Gin Yong Pang, "Asian American Panethnicity and Intermarriage," *Amerasia Journal* 22, no. 2 (1996): 127–152.

22. Intraethnic marriages constituted 18.4 percent of marriages with Asian men and 16.4 percent of marriages with Asian women. Interracial marriages constituted 10.5 percent of marriages with Asian men, and 19.6 percent of marriages with Asian women. Ibid.

23. Office of Management and Budget, "Recommendations from the Interagency Committee for the Review of the Racial and Ethnic Standards to the Office of Management and Budget Concerning Changes to the Standards for the Classification of Federal Data on Race and Ethnicity; Notice," *Federal Register* 62, no. 131 (9 July 1997): 36873.

24. Ruth Colker, *Hybrid: Bisexuals, Multiracials, and Other Misfits under American Law* (New York and London: New York University Press, 1996), 245.

25. Elizabeth Bartholet, "Where Do Black Children Belong? The Politics of Race Matching in Adoption." *University of Pennsylvania Law Review* 139, no. 5 (May 1991): 1163.

26. Crystal Chappell, "American, Korean, or Both? Politics of Identity Reach Personal Levels" (statement of Brooke Chappell) (accessed 31 January 1997; http://www.medill.nwu.edu/people/chappell/identity.issues.html).

27. Institute for Justice Web site (accessed 29 April 1997; http://www.institutefor justice.org).

28. *U.S. Code*, vol. 25, secs. 1901 et seq. (1994).

29. *U.S. Code*, vol. 42, sec. 5115a (1994).

30. The closest case is *Palmore v. Sidoti* (422 U.S. 429 [1984]), in which the Court unanimously ruled that the custody of a white child, awarded to the mother when the child's parents divorced, could not be taken from the mother because she had cohabited with and eventually married a black man. The Court stated:

> It would ignore reality to suggest that racial and ethnic prejudices do not exist or that all manifestations of those prejudices have been eliminated. There is a risk that a child living with a stepparent of a different race may be subject to a variety of pressures and stresses not present if the child were living with parents of the same racial or ethnic origin.
>
> The question, however, is whether the reality of private biases and the possible injury they might inflict are permissible consideration for removal of an infant child from the custody of its natural mother. We have little difficulty concluding that they are not. The Constitution cannot control such prejudices but neither can it tolerate them. Private biases may be outside the reach of the law, but the law cannot, directly or indirectly, give them effect. (433)

31. Lani Guinier, "[E]racing Democracy: The Voting Rights Cases," *Harvard Law Review* 108 (1994): 109.

32. 478 U.S. 30, 50–51 (1986).

33. 509 U.S. 630 (1993); 115 S. Ct. 2475 (1995).
34. Steven P. Erie et al., *Paths to Political Incorporation for Latinos and Asian Pacifics in California*, California Policy Seminar Research Report (Berkeley: University of California, 1993).
35. Don Nakanishi, "The Next Swing Vote? Asian Pacific Americans and California Politics," in *Racial and Ethnic Politics in California*, ed. Byran O. Jackson and Michael B. Preston (Berkeley: Institute of Governmental Studies, University of California, 1991), 25; Paul Ong and Don Nakanishi, "Becoming Citizens, Becoming Voters: The Naturalization and Political Participation of Asian Pacific Immigrants," in *The State of Asian Pacific America: Reframing the Immigration Debate*, ed. Bill Ong Hing and Ronald Lee (Los Angeles: LEAP Asian Pacific American Public Policy Institute and UCLA Asian American Studies Center, 1996), 275.
36. National Asian Pacific American Legal Consortium, *Conducting Exit Polls: A Guide to Using Exit Polls to Safeguard Asian Pacific American Voter Participation* (Washington, D.C., National Asian Pacific American Legal Consortium, 1995), 4.
37. Ibid.
38. National Asian Pacific American Legal Consortium, *Asian Pacific American Electoral Participation: Three Region Study* (Washington, D.C.: National Asian Pacific American Legal Consortium, 1995).
39. Ibid.; Asian Law Caucus, *1996 San Francisco Bay Area Exit Poll Report: An Analysis of Asian Pacific American Demographics, Behavior, and Political Participation* (San Francisco: Asian Law Caucus, 1997); Asian Pacific American Legal Center of Southern California, *1996 Southern California Asian Pacific American Exit Poll Report: An Analysis of APA Voter Behavior and Opinions* (Los Angeles: Asian Pacific American Legal Center of Southern California, 1997).
40. Stewart Kwoh and Mindy Hui, "Empowering Our Communities: Political Policy," in *The State of Asian Pacific America. A Public Policy Report: Policy Issues to the Year 2020* (Los Angeles: LEAP Asian Pacific American Public Policy Institute and UCLA Asian American Studies Center, 1993), 189; Leland T. Saito, "Asian Americans and Latinos in San Gabriel Valley, California: Interethnic Political Cooperation and Redistricting 1990–1992," in *Los Angeles—Struggles toward Multiethnic Community: Asian American, African American, and Latino Perspectives*, ed. Edward T. Chang and Russell C. Leong (Seattle and London: University of Washington Press, 1994), 55.
41. Brief of the Coalition of Asian Pacific Americans for Fair Reapportionment (CAPAFR) as Amicus Curiae, *Wilson v. Eu*, 1 Cal. 4th 707, 823 P.2d 545, 4 Cal. Rptr. 2d 379 (1992).
42. *Wilson v. Eu*, 1 Cal. 4th 707, 823 P.2d 545, 4 Cal. Rptr. 2d 379 (1992).
43. Annie Nakao, "Asian Vote a New Force," *San Francisco Examiner*, 20 October 1996, p. C1.
44. Aurelio Rojas, "A Rising Power in Northwest: Locke First Asian American Governor in Mainland U.S.," *San Francisco Chronicle*, 18 January 1997, p. A1.
45. National Asian Pacific American Legal Consortium, *Conducting Exit Polls*, 4.
46. Angela P. Harris, "Race and Essentialism in Feminist Legal Theory," *Stanford Law Review* 42 (1990): 581; Leti Volpp, "(Mis)identifying Culture: Asian Women and the 'Cultural Defense,'" *Harvard Women's Law Journal* 17 (1994): 57.
47. Volpp, "(Mis)identifying Culture."
48. Lora Jo Foo, "The Vulnerable and Exploitable Immigrant Workforce and the Need for Strengthening Worker Protective Legislation," *Yale Law Journal* 103 (June 1994): 2179.
49. EEOC v. *Tortilleria La Mejor*, 758 F. Supp. 585 (E.D. Cal. 1991).

50. 40 F.3d 1551, 1560 (9th Cir. 1994).
51. Ibid., 1562 (citations omitted).

Chapter 7 Law and Racial Hierarchy

1. *San Francisco NAACP v. San Francisco Unified School District*, 576 F. Supp. 34 (N.D. Cal. 1983).
2. Ibid., 53.
3. Selena Dong, "'Too Many Asians': The Challenge of Fighting Discrimination against Asian-Americans and Preserving Affirmative Action," *Stanford Law Review* 47 (May 1995): 1027, 1032.
4. Ibid., 1033 (quoting press statement of the Chinese American Democratic Club, 3 March 1993).
5. Joan Walsh, "Can This Man Fix Our Schools," *San Francisco Focus*, (October 1993): 60, 134 (quoting Lulann McGriff).
6. Nanette Asimov, "Mixed Reaction to Lowell Decision: New Admissions Rule Doesn't Thwart Suit," *San Francisco Chronicle*, 29 February 1996, p. A13; Nanette Asimov, "S.F. Schools Diversity Plan Under Attack: Chinese Parents Renew Fight Over Consent Decree," *San Francisco Chronicle*, 15 November 1996, p. A21.
7. United States Department of Commerce, Bureau of the Census, *County and City Data Book* (Washington, D.C., 1994), table 3.
8. Gordon Dillow and Emily Adams, "Communities Struggle to Rebuild after Riots," *Los Angeles Times* (Long Beach section), 8 November 1992, p. J1.
9. Paul Ong and Tania Azores, "Asian Immigrants in Los Angeles: Diversity and Divisions," in *The New Asian Immigration in Los Angeles and Global Restructuring*, ed. Paul Ong et al. (Philadelphia: Temple University Press, 1994), 100.
10. Leland T. Saito and John Horton, "The New Chinese Immigration and the Rise of Asian American Politics in Monterey Park, California," in *The New Asian Immigration in Los Angeles and Global Restructuring*, ed. Paul Ong et al. (Philadelphia: Temple University Press, 1994), 234.
11. United States Commission on Civil Rights, *Civil Rights Issues Facing Asian Americans in the 1990s* (Washington, D.C., 1992), 28–29.
12. Davan Maharaj, "Rights Suit Involving Police Photos is Settled," *Los Angeles Times* (Orange County edition), 12 December 1995, p. A1.
13. K. Connie Kang, "Police Department Begins Recruiting Asian Americans," *Los Angeles Times*, 11 May 1995, p. B1.
14. Angelo N. Ancheta and Kathryn K. Imahara, "Multi-Ethnic Voting Rights: Redefining Vote Dilution in Communities of Color." *University of San Francisco Law Review* 27 (Summer 1993): 815.
15. *U.S. Code*, vol. 42, sec. 1973(c)(3) (1994).
16. 956 F.2d 884 (9th Cir. 1992); see also *Romero v. City of Pomona*, 883 F.2d 1418 (9th Cir. 1989). In both *Badillo* and *Romero* the courts ruled that the combined Latino and African American plaintiff classes lacked political cohesiveness to show a violation of the Voting Rights Act. Asian American voters were omitted altogether, even though they constituted nearly 7 percent of the population in Pomona and nearly 23 percent of the population in Stockton.
17. Whether the Voting Rights Act actually allows the combination of different classes of minority voters has been disputed in the federal courts. In *Campos v. City of Baytown*, 849 F.2d 943 (5th Cir. 1988), a federal court of appeals upheld a multiethnic minority lawsuit, indicating that the proper standard is to look at the voting behavior of a combined group of minority voters, not as separate racial

groups who need to show evidence that they have voted for each other's candidates. On the other hand, a court of appeals ruled in *Nixon v. Kent County*, 76 F.3d 1381 (6th Cir. 1996), that multiple minority groups—as a matter of law—could not be combined into a single class, pointing to the absence of language on coalitions in the act and drawing distinctions between black voters and language-minority voters.

The Voting Rights Act is completely silent on the viability of multiethnic minority lawsuits, so one could just as easily argue that they are permitted, as long as the basic requirements under *Thornburg v. Gingles* are being met. Moreover, a distinction between racial minorities and language minorities is specious, since Latino plaintiffs, like African American plaintiffs, have routinely won litigation challenging discriminatory at-large election systems. The *Campos* court employed the proper reading: if an election system harms all racial minority voters, there is no reason why a common right and remedy should not be available through the Voting Rights Act.

18. 507 U.S. 25 (1993).
19. Margaret Fung, "Voters and Voting Rights," in *The Asian American Almanac: A Reference Work on Asians in the United States*, ed. Susan Gall and Irene Natividad (Detroit: Gale Research, Inc., 1995), 351, 353.
20. Stewart Kwoh, "Asian American Involvement in the Political Process: Case Study," in *The Asian American Almanac: A Reference Work on Asians in the United States*, ed. Susan Gall and Irene Natividad (Detroit: Gale Research, Inc., 1995), 343–344.
21. Leland T. Saito, "Asian Americans and Latinos in San Gabriel Valley, California: Interethnic Political Cooperation and Redistricting 1990–1992," in *Los Angeles—Struggles toward Multiethnic Community: Asian American, African American, and Latino Perspectives*, ed. Edward T. Chang and Russell C. Leong (Seattle and London: University of Washington Press, 1994), 55.
22. Benjamin Pimentel, "Asian Americans' Awkward Status: Some Feel Whites Use Them as a 'Racial Wedge' with Others," *San Francisco Chronicle*, 22 August 1995, p. A1.
23. It is an open question whether promoting racial diversity is a compelling governmental interest that could satisfy a strict scrutiny standard. In *Regents of the University of California v. Bakke*, 438 U.S. 265 (1978), Justice Lewis Powell articulated the view that creating a diverse student body could justify a public university admissions program that took race into account as one of several factors. In *Metro Broadcasting, Inc. v. Federal Communications Commission*, 497 U.S. 547 (1990), the case whose use of an intermediate standard of review was overruled in 1995 by the *Adarand* decision, the Supreme Court held that racial diversity in broadcasting was an *important* governmental interest. The Court did not have to decide whether it was a *compelling* interest, however, because the Court used a lower standard of review. In *Hopwood v. Texas*, 78 F.3d 932 (5th Cir. 1996), a federal appeals court ruled that racial diversity in higher education is *not* a compelling governmental interest, striking down a race-conscious admissions program at the University of Texas law school and explicitly rejecting the reasoning of Justice Powell in *Bakke*. The Supreme Court chose not to hear the appeal in *Hopwood* on procedural grounds—the law school had already abandoned its challenged admissions policy—leaving for another day the question of whether promoting racial diversity is a compelling governmental interest.
24. Federal Glass Ceiling Commission, *Good for Business: Making Full Use of the Nation's Human Capital* (Washington, D.C., March 1995), 9.

25. Ibid., 115.
26. "Asian/Pacific Islanders Trail Whites in Earnings; Comparable Education Fails to Close the Gap," *Washington Post*, 18 September 1992.
27. Federal Glass Ceiling Commission, *Good for Business*, 111.
28. American Civil Liberties Union of Southern California, *Of the Community and For the Community: Racial and Gender Integration in Southern California Police and Fire Departments* (Los Angeles: American Civil Liberties Union of Southern California, 1994).
29. City and County of San Francisco, *Progress Report: Minority/Women/Local Business Enterprise Ordinance II* (San Francisco: City and County of San Francisco, 1990), 14.
30. *United States v. City and County of San Francisco*, 696 F. Supp. 1287 (N.D. Cal. 1988).
31. Frank H. Wu, "Neither Black nor White: Asian Americans and Affirmative Action," *Boston College Third World Law Journal* 15 (Summer 1995): 225–226.
32. Terry Eastland, *Ending Affirmative Action: The Case for Colorblind Justice* (New York: Basic Books, 1996) 143–158; Mark Krikorian, "Affirmative Action and Immigration," in *Debating Affirmative Action: Race, Gender, Ethnicity, and the Politics of Inclusion*, ed. Nicolaus Mills (New York: Delta, 1994), 300.
33. Popular media often omitted the fact that the University of California admissions policy guarantees places in its first-year classes for all students who graduate in the top 12.5 percent of their high school classes; only certain campuses such as Berkeley and UCLA have adopted competitive admissions procedures because of the large number of applications. At UCLA, for instance, there were 28,400 applications filed for the 1996–97 freshman class. Of these applicants, 10,900 were offered admission and about 3,825 (13 percent of those who had applied) attended UCLA. David Greenwald, "Humanists at the Gate: The Process of Selecting Students for UCLA Demands Sensitivity and Stamina," *UCLA Magazine* 8, no. 3 (February 1997): 12.
34. Nanette Asimov, "Single Standard for Admissions at Lowell High," *San Francisco Chronicle*, 28 February 1996, p. A1.
35. Jerry Kang, "Negative Action against Asian Americans: The Internal Instability of Dworkin's Defense of Affirmative Action," *Harvard Civil Rights-Civil Liberties Law Review* 31 (Winter 1996): 1.
36. Dana Y. Takagi, *The Retreat from Race: Asian-American Admissions and Racial Politics*. New Brunswick, N.J.: Rutgers University Press, 1992.
37. National Conference, *Taking America's Pulse: A Summary Report of the National Survey on Inter-Group Relations* (New York: National Conference, 1994), 5.
38. Pyong Gap Min, *Caught in the Middle: Korean Communities in New York and Los Angeles* (Berkeley and Los Angeles: University of California Press, 1996).
39. Paul Ong, Edna Bonacich, and Lucie Cheng, "The Political Economy of Capitalist Restructuring and the New Asian Immigrant," in *The New Asian Immigration in Los Angeles and Global Restructuring*, ed. Paul Ong et al. (Philadelphia: Temple University Press, 1994), 3.
40. Edward T. Chang, "Jewish and Korean Merchants in African American Neighborhoods: A Comparative Perspective," in *Los Angeles—Struggles toward Multiethnic Community: Asian American, African American and Latino Perspectives*, ed. Edward T. Chang and Russell C. Leong (Seattle: University of Washington Press, 1994), 5.
41. Greg Krikorian, "The Bottleneck: Squeezed by Tough Restrictions, Only a Few of the Hundreds of Liquor Stores Damaged during the Riots Have Reopened," *Los Angeles Times*, 29 August 1993.

42. MultiCultural Collaborative, *Race, Power, and Promise in Los Angeles: An Assessment of Responses to Human Relations Conflict* (Los Angeles: MultiCultural Collaborative, 1996).

43. Gen Fujioka, "Turning the Tide of Terror and Indifference," *The Reporter* (Asian Law Caucus Newsletter) vol. 16, no. 3 (October 1994): 2–3.

44. Deborah Ramirez, "Multicultural Empowerment: It's Not Just Black and White Anymore," *Stanford Law Review* 47 (May 1995): 957.

45. Lani Guinier, *The Tyranny of the Majority: Fundamental Fairness in Representative Democracy* (New York: The Free Press, 1994).

Conclusion

1. Derrick Bell. *Faces at the Bottom of the Well: The Permanence of Racism* (New York: Basic Books, 1992), ix.

2. William R. Tamayo, "When the 'Coloreds' Are neither Black nor Citizens: The United States Civil Rights Movement and Global Migration," *Asian Law Journal* 2 (May 1995): 1, 25.

3. Bill Ong Hing. *To Be an American: Cultural Pluralism and the Rhetoric of Assimilation* (New York: New York University Press, 1997), 178.

Selected Bibliography

Aguilar-San Juan, Karin, ed. *The State of Asian America: Activism and Resistance in the 1990s.* Boston: South End Press, 1994.

Aleinikoff, Thomas Alexander. "Citizens, Aliens, Membership and the Constitution." *Constitutional Commentary* 7 (Winter 1990): 9–34.

Aleinikoff, Thomas Alexander, and David A. Martin. *Immigration Process and Policy.* 2d ed. St. Paul, Minn.: West Publishing Company, 1991.

Ancheta, Angelo N. "Community Lawyering." *California Law Review* 81 (October 1993): 1363–1399.

———. "Fighting Hate Violence." *Trial* 29, no. 7 (July 1993): 16–21.

———. "Our Immigrant Heritage: A Struggle for Justice." *UCLA Asian Pacific American Law Journal* 2 (1994): 101–106.

———. "Protecting Immigrants against Discrimination." *Trial* 32, no. 2 (February 1996): 46–50.

Ancheta, Angelo N., and Kathryn K. Imahara. "Multi-Ethnic Voting Rights: Redefining Vote Dilution in Communities of Color." *University of San Francisco Law Review* 27 (Summer 1993): 815–872.

Avidan, Lina M. *Employment and Hiring Practices under the Immigration Reform and Control Act of 1986: A Survey of San Francisco Businesses.* San Francisco: Public Research Institute, San Francisco State University, and Coalition for Immigrant and Refugee Rights and Services, January 1990.

Bell, Derrick. *Faces at the Bottom of the Well: The Permanence of Racism.* New York: Basic Books, 1992.

California Attorney General's Asian and Pacific Islander Advisory Committee. *Final Report.* Sacramento, December 1988.

Chang, Edward T., and Russell C. Leong, eds. *Los Angeles—Struggles toward Multiethnic Community: Asian American, African American, and Latino Perspectives.* Seattle and London: University of Washington Press, 1994.

Chang, Robert S. "Toward an Asian American Legal Scholarship: Critical Race Theory, Post-Structuralism, and Narrative Space," *California Law Review* 81 (October 1993): 1241–1323.

Chew, Pat K. "Asian Americans: The 'Reticent' Minority and Their Paradoxes," *William and Mary Law Review* 36 (October 1994): 1–94.

Chu-Chang, Mae, ed. *Asian- and Pacific-American Perspectives in Bilingual Education: Comparative Research*. New York and London: Teachers College Press, 1983.

Coalition for Humane Immigrant Rights of Los Angeles. *Hate Unleashed: Los Angeles in the Aftermath of 187*. Los Angeles: Coalition for Humane Immigrant Rights of Los Angeles, 1995.

Colker, Ruth. "Anti-Subordination Above All: Sex, Race, and Equal Protection." *New York University Law Review* 61 (December 1986): 1003–1066.

———. *Hybrid: Bisexuals, Multiracials, and Other Misfits under American Law*. New York and London: New York University Press, 1996.

Commission on Wartime Relocation and Internment of Civilians. *Personal Justice Denied*. Washington, D.C., 1982.

Crawford, James. *Hold Your Tongue: Bilingualism and the Politics of "English Only."* Reading, Mass.: Addison-Wesley Publishing Company, 1992.

———, ed. *Language Loyalties: A Source Book on the Official English Controversy*. Chicago: University of Chicago Press, 1992.

Crenshaw, Kimberlé Williams, Neil Gotanda, Gary Peller, and Kendall Thomas, eds. *Critical Race Theory: The Key Writings that Formed the Movement*. New York: The New Press, 1995.

Delgado, Richard, ed. *Critical Race Theory: The Cutting Edge*. Philadelphia: Temple University Press, 1995.

Dong, Selena. "'Too Many Asians': The Challenge of Fighting Discrimination against Asian-Americans and Preserving Affirmative Action." *Stanford Law Review* 47 (May 1995): 1027–1057.

Edley, Christopher, Jr. *Not All Black and White: Affirmative Action and American Values*. New York: Hill and Wang, 1996.

Edmonston, Barry, and Jeffrey S. Passel, eds. *Immigration and Ethnicity: The Integration of America's Newest Arrivals*. Washington, D.C.: The Urban Institute, 1994.

Erie, Steven P., Harold Brackman, and James Warren Ingram III. *Paths to Political Incorporation for Latinos and Asian Pacifics in California*. California Policy Seminar Research Report. Berkeley: Regents of the University of California, 1993.

Espiritu, Yen Le. *Asian American Panethnicity: Bridging Institutions and Identities*. Philadelphia: Temple University Press, 1992.

Federal Glass Ceiling Commission. *Good for Business: Making Full Use of the Nation's Human Capital*. Washington, D.C., March 1995.

Fix, Michael, and Jeffrey S. Passel. *Immigration and Immigrants: Setting the Record Straight*. Washington, D.C.: The Urban Institute, 1994.

Gall, Susan, and Irene Natividad, eds. *The Asian American Almanac: A Reference Work on Asians in the United States*. Detroit: Gale Research Inc., 1995.

Gee, Emma, ed. *Counterpoint*. Los Angeles: Asian American Studies Center, University of California, 1976.

Gordon, Avery F., and Christopher Newfield, eds. *Mapping Multiculturalism*. Minneapolis and London: University of Minnesota Press, 1996.

Gotanda, Neil. "A Critique of 'Our Constitution is Color-Blind.'" *Stanford Law Review* 44 (November 1991): 1–68.

Guinier, Lani. *The Tyranny of the Majority: Fundamental Fairness in Representative Democracy*. New York: The Free Press, 1994.

Hacker, Andrew. *Two Nations: Black and White, Separate, Hostile, Unequal*. Rev. ed. New York: Ballantine Books, 1995.

Haney López, Ian F. *White by Law: The Legal Construction of Race*. New York: New York University Press, 1996.

Higham, John. *Strangers in the Land: Patterns of American Nativism, 1860–1925*. New York: Atheneum, 1970.

Hing, Bill Ong. "In the Interest of Racial Harmony: Revisiting the Lawyer's Duty to Work for the Common Good." *Stanford Law Review* 47 (May 1995): 901–956.

———. *Making and Remaking Asian America through Immigration Policy, 1850–1990.* Stanford: Stanford University Press, 1993.

———. *To Be an American: Cultural Pluralism and the Rhetoric of Assimilation.* New York: New York University Press, 1997.

Hing, Bill Ong, and Ronald Lee, eds. *The State of Asian Pacific America: Reframing the Immigration Debate.* Los Angeles: LEAP Asian Pacific American Public Policy Institute and UCLA Asian American Studies Center, 1996.

Human Rights Watch and American Civil Liberties Union. *Human Rights Violations in the United States: A Report of U.S. Compliance with the International Covenant on Civil and Political Rights.* New York: Human Rights Watch and American Civil Liberties Union, 1993.

Hutchinson, E. P. *Legislative History of American Immigration Policy.* Philadelphia: University of Pennsylvania, 1981.

Irons, Peter. *Justice at War: The Story of the Japanese American Internment Cases.* New York: Oxford University Press, 1983.

———, ed. *Justice Delayed: The Record of the Japanese American Internment Cases.* Middletown, Conn.: Wesleyan University Press, 1989.

Jackson, Bryan O., and Michael B. Preston, eds. *Racial and Ethnic Politics in California.* Berkeley: Institute of Governmental Studies, University of California, 1991.

Jennings, James, ed. *Blacks, Latinos, and Asians in Urban America: Status and Prospects for Politics and Activism.* Westport, Conn.: Praeger Publishers, 1994.

Johnson, Kevin R. "An Essay on Immigration Politics, Popular Democracy, and California's Proposition 187: The Political Relevance and Legal Irrelevance of Race." *Washington Law Review* 70 (July 1995): 629–673.

Kang, Jerry. "Negative Action against Asian Americans: The Internal Instability of Dworkin's Defense of Affirmative Action." *Harvard Civil Rights-Civil Liberties Law Review* 31 (Winter 1996): 1–47.

Karst, Kenneth L. *Belonging to America: Equal Citizenship and the Constitution.* New Haven and London: Yale University Press, 1989.

———. "Myths of Identity: Individual and Group Portraits of Race and Sexual Orientation." *UCLA Law Review* 43 (December 1995): 263–369.

Kim, Hyung-Chan. *A Legal History of Asian Americans, 1790–1990.* Westport, Conn.: Greenwood Press, 1994.

———, ed. *Asian Americans and Congress: A Documentary History.* Westport, Conn.: Greenwood Press, 1996.

———, ed. *Asian Americans and the Supreme Court: A Documentary History.* Westport, Conn.: Greenwood Press, 1992.

Kleg, Milton. *Hate Prejudice and Racism.* Albany: State University of New York Press, 1993.

Kluger, Richard. *Simple Justice: The History of* Brown v. Board of Education *and Black America's Struggle for Equality.* New York: Alfred A. Knopf, Inc., 1976.

Krieger, Linda Hamilton. "The Content of Our Categories: A Cognitive Bias Approach to Discrimination and Equal Employment Opportunity." *Stanford Law Review* 47 (July 1995): 1161–1248.

Lawrence, Charles R., III. "The Id, the Ego, and Equal Protection: Reckoning with Unconscious Racism." *Stanford Law Review* 39 (January 1987): 317–388.

Leadership Education for Asian Pacifics. *Beyond Asian American Poverty: Community Economic Development Policies and Strategies.* Los Angeles: LEAP Asian Pacific American Public Policy Institute, 1993.

Leadership Education for Asian Pacifics and UCLA Asian American Studies Center.

The State of Asian Pacific America. A Public Policy Report: Policy Issues to the Year 2020. Los Angeles: LEAP Asian Pacific American Public Policy Institute and UCLA Asian American Studies Center, 1993.

Lee, Susan K. "Racial Construction through Citizenship in the U.S." *Asian American Policy Review* 6 (Spring 1996): 89–116.

Legomsky, Stephen H. *Immigration Law and Policy.* University Casebook Series. Westbury, N.Y.: The Foundation Press, 1992.

López, Gerald P. *Rebellious Lawyering: One Chicano's Vision of Progressive Law Practice.* Boulder: Westview Press, 1992.

Lowe, Lisa. *Immigrant Acts: On Asian American Cultural Politics.* Durham and London: Duke University Press, 1996.

Massey, Douglas S., and Nancy A. Denton. *American Apartheid: Segregation in the Making of the Underclass.* Cambridge, Mass. and London: Harvard University Press, 1993.

Matsuda, Mari J. "Voices of America: Accent, Antidiscrimination Law, and a Jurisprudence for the Last Reconstruction," *Yale Law Journal* 100 (March 1991): 1329–1407.

McClain, Charles J. *In Search of Equality: The Chinese Struggle against Discrimination in Nineteenth-Century America.* Berkeley and Los Angeles: University of California Press, 1994.

Min, Pyong Gap. *Caught in the Middle: Korean Communities in New York and Los Angeles.* Berkeley and Los Angeles: University of California Press, 1996.

MultiCultural Collaborative. *Race, Power, and Promise in Los Angeles: An Assessment of Responses to Human Relations Conflict.* Los Angeles: MultiCultural Collaborative, 1996.

Nakanishi, Don T., and Tina Yamano Nishida, eds. *The Asian American Educational Experience: A Source Book for Teachers and Students.* New York and London: Routledge, 1995.

National Asian Pacific American Legal Consortium. *Asian Pacific American Electoral Participation: Three Region Study.* Washington, D.C.: National Asian Pacific American Legal Consortium, 1995.

———. *Bilingual Assistance: How to Use the Voting Rights Act.* Washington, D.C.: National Asian Pacific American Legal Consortium, 1995.

———. *1995 Audit of Violence against Asian Pacific Americans.* Washington, D.C.: National Asian Pacific American Legal Consortium, 1996.

———. *1996 Audit of Violence against Asian Pacific Americans.* Washington, D.C.: National Asian Pacific American Legal Consortium, 1997.

National Conference. *Taking America's Pulse: The National Survey on Inter-Group Relations.* New York: National Conference, 1994.

Okihiro, Gary Y. *Margins and Mainstreams: Asians in American History and Culture.* Seattle and London: University of Washington Press, 1994.

Omi, Michael, and Howard Winant. *Racial Formation in the United States: From the 1960s to the 1990s.* 2d ed. New York and London: Routledge, 1994.

Ong, Paul, ed. *The State of Asian Pacific America: Economic Diversity, Issues, and Policies.* Los Angeles: LEAP Asian Pacific American Public Policy Institute and UCLA Asian American Studies Center, 1994.

Ong, Paul, Edna Bonacich, and Lucie Cheng, eds. *The New Asian Immigration in Los Angeles and Global Restructuring.* Philadelphia: Temple University Press, 1994.

Orfield, Gary, and Diane Glass. *Asian Students and Multiethnic Desegregation.* Cambridge, Mass.: The Harvard Project on School Desegregation, October 1994.

Perea, Juan F. "Demography and Distrust: An Essay on American Languages, Cultural Pluralism, and Official English." *Minnesota Law Review* 77 (December 1992): 271–373.

————, ed. *Immigrants Out! The New Nativism and the Anti-Immigrant Impulse in the United States.* New York and London: New York University Press, 1997.

Pincus, Fred L., and Howard J. Ehrlich, eds. *Race and Ethnic Conflict: Contending Views on Prejudice, Discrimination, and Ethnoviolence.* Boulder: Westview Press, 1994.

Ramirez, Deborah. "Multicultural Empowerment: It's Not Just Black and White Anymore." *Stanford Law Review* 47 (May 1995): 957–992.

Raskin, Jamin B. "Legal Aliens, Local Citizens: The Historical, Constitutional and Theoretical Meanings of Alien Suffrage." *University of Pennsylvania Law Review* 141 (April 1993): 1391–1470.

Shinagawa, Larry Hajime, and Gin Yong Pang. "Asian American Panethnicity and Intermarriage." *Amerasia Journal* 22, no. 2 (1996): 127–152.

Sonenshein, Raphael J. *Politics in Black and White: Race and Power in Los Angeles.* Princeton: Princeton University Press, 1993.

Takagi, Dana Y. *The Retreat from Race: Asian-American Admissions and Racial Politics.* New Brunswick, N.J.: Rutgers University Press, 1992.

Takaki, Ronald. *Strangers from a Different Shore: A History of Asian Americans.* Boston: Little, Brown & Company, 1989.

Tamayo, William R. "When the 'Coloreds' Are neither Black nor Citizens: The United States Civil Rights Movement and Global Migration," *Asian Law Journal* 2 (May 1995): 1–32.

tenBroek, Jacobus, Edward N. Barnhart, and Floyd W. Matson. *Prejudice, War and the Constitution.* Berkeley: University of California Press, 1954.

Tribe, Laurence H., *American Constitutional Law.* 2d ed. Mineola, N.Y.: Foundation Press, 1988.

United States Commission on Civil Rights. *Civil Rights Issues Facing Asian Americans in the 1990s.* Washington, D.C., February 1992.

————. *Federal Title VI Enforcement to Ensure Nondiscrimination in Federally Assisted Programs.* Washington, D.C., June 1996.

————. *Recent Activities against Citizens and Residents of Asian Descent.* Clearinghouse Publication no. 88. Washington, D.C., 1986.

United States Department of Commerce, Bureau of the Census. *1992 Survey of Minority-Owned Business Enterprises—Asians and Pacific Islanders, American Indians, and Alaska Natives* (MB92–3). Washington, D.C., 1996.

————. *Statistical Brief: The Nation's Asian and Pacific Islander Population—1994.* Washington, D.C., 1995.

————. *We the American Asians.* Washington, D.C., 1993.

————. *We the American Pacific Islanders.* Washington, D.C., 1993.

United States General Accounting Office. *Immigration Reform: Employer Sanctions and the Question of Discrimination.* Washington, D.C., 1990.

Volpp, Leti. "(Mis)identifying Culture: Asian Women and the 'Cultural Defense.'" *Harvard Women's Law Journal* 17 (1994): 57–101.

Wei, William. *The Asian American Movement.* Philadelphia: Temple University Press, 1993.

Williams, Juan. *Eyes on the Prize: America's Civil Rights Years 1954–1965.* New York: Penguin Group, 1987.

Wu, Frank H. "The Limits of Borders: A Moderate Proposal for Immigration Reform." *Stanford Law and Policy Review* 7, no. 2 (1996): 35–74.

————. "Neither Black nor White: Asian Americans and Affirmative Action." *Boston College Third World Law Journal* 15 (Summer 1995): 225–284.

Zane, Nolan W. S., David T. Takeuchi, and Kathleen N. J. Young, eds. *Confronting Critical Health Issues of Asian and Pacific Islander Americans.* Thousand Oaks, Calif.: Sage Publications, 1994.

Table of Cases Cited in the Text

Marbury v. Madison, 5 U.S. 137 (1803)
Mathews v. Diaz, 426 U.S. 67 (1976)
Meyer v. Nebraska, 262 U.S. 390 (1923)
Miller v. Johnson, 115 S. Ct. 2475 (1995)
Nishimura Ekiu v. United States, 142 U.S. 651 (1892)
Oyama v. California, 332 U.S. 633 (1948)
Ozawa v. United States, 260 U.S. 178 (1922)
People v. Hall, 4 Cal. 399 (1854)
Perez v. Sharp, 32 Cal. 2d 711, P. 2d 17 (1948)
Plessy v. Ferguson, 163 U.S. 537 (1896)
Plyler v. Doe, 457 U.S. 202 (1982)
R.A.V. v. City of St. Paul, 505 U.S. 377 (1992)
Regan v. King, 49 F. Supp. 222 (1942)
Regents of the University of California v. Bakke, 438 U.S. 265 (1978)
Romer v. Evans, 116 S. Ct. 1620 (1996)
Saint Francis College v. Al-Khazraji, 481 U.S. 604 (1987)
Shaw v. Reno, 509 U.S. 630 (1993)
Soberal-Perez v. Heckler, 717 F.2d 36 (2d Cir. 1983)
Sugarman v. Dougall, 413 U.S. 634 (1973)
Takahashi v. Fish and Game Commission, 334 U.S. 410 (1948)
Terrace v. Thompson, 263 U.S. 197 (1923)
Thornburg v. Gingles, 478 U.S. 30 (1986)
United States ex rel. Negrón v. New York, 434 F.2d 386 (2d Cir. 1970)
United States v. Thind, 261 U.S. 204 (1923)
United States v. Wong Kim Ark, 169 U.S. 649 (1898)
Wards Cove Packing Co. v. Atonio, 490 U.S. 642 (1989)
Yasui v. United States, 320 U.S. 115 (1943)
Yick Wo v. Hopkins, 118 U.S. 356 (1886)
Yniguez v. Arizonans for Official English, 69 F.3d 920 (9th Cir. 1995), *vacated*, 117 S. Ct. 1055 (1997)
Yu Cong Eng v. Trinidad, 271 U.S. 500 (1926)

Index

About the Author

Angelo N. Ancheta is a civil rights lawyer based in San Francisco. He has practiced law and worked with community-based organizations serving the Asian American population in both Northern and Southern California. He has also been on the faculty of the UCLA School of Law, where he received his law degree in 1986.